PRAISE FOR
Unshakeable

"We wholeheartedly appreciate Jo-ann Rosen's dedicated work, loving service, and steadfast practice with our community for so many years. Her love for the Plum Village teachings and tradition has manifested as her dedication to help us become more informed about the language and delivery of the practices so that we can be more inclusive and sensitive to the collective trauma of our times related to the social issues of race, gender identity, history, and also the neuropsychology and biology of what makes this embodied spirit tick. Jo-ann Rosen's presentations during our retreats have not only been educational, inspiring, and effective, but they are imbued with a high quality of presence and ease that is, for sure, a result of her own personal practice and transformation. And of course, just as important, her presentations are also a lot of fun. Smiling to the ripening!"

—**BROTHER CHAN PHAP DUNG**, senior Dharma teacher and former abbot of Deer Park Monastery, a mindfulness practice center in Thich Nhat Hanh's Plum Village tradition, Escondido, California

"I think there is a great need to understand the human nervous system and how this knowledge integrates with Buddhist teachings. Jo-ann Rosen has combined the teachings and concept of the Community Resiliency Model with her depth of understanding as a Dharma teacher to inspire the possibility of greater mind and body healing for all."

—**ELAINE MILLER-KARAS, LCSW**, cofounder of the Trauma Resource Institute in Claremont, California and author of *Building Resilience to Trauma*

"In *Unshakeable*, Jo-ann Rosen masterfully integrates neuroscience, psychology, and mindfulness practice. From this synthesis flow the practical tools that people who want to heal the world need to sustain themselves and the communities that nurture them in their struggle. Activism is stressful and takes place in a world of unrelenting stress. This is a must-read for anybody who wants to make the world a better place—she translates wisdom into practical tools that activists can use to regulate themselves in the face of ongoing trauma so that they can sustain their work and their communities as happy, resilient people."

—**ROD FUJITA, PhD**, senior scientist and director of research and development at the oceans program of the Environmental Defense Fund and author of *Making Shift Happen*

"Please read this book! Both practical and profound, it offers unique and compelling wisdom on how we can take good care of suffering, heal trauma, and deeply enjoy life, both as individuals and as a community. Jo-ann Rosen details the way the Dharma, particularly of Thich Nhat Hanh's Plum Village tradition, shines light on and can deepen the application of neuroscientific findings, and she brings the insights of somatic psychology and nervous system regulation into wildly fruitful dialogue with Buddhist mind-training practices, pushing the Dharma further to become more neurosensitive. She lifts up the essential role of community in both spiritual and scientific wisdom for personal and collective healing so that we can see clearly enough for a future to be possible."

—**KAIRA JEWEL LINGO**, author of *We Were Made for These Times: Ten Lessons on Moving through Change, Loss, and Disruption*

"Jo-ann Rosen has done all of us an enormous favor by writing this book. In *Unshakeable*, she bridges the gap between mindfulness and the needs of the many individuals for whom mindfulness must be practiced in ways that feel both safe and accessible. As a professor and researcher, I apply her tools both with my students and the community youth with whom I partner, many of whom have experienced trauma and marginalization. As a physician, I am grateful for the concrete links Rosen draws between the mindfulness practices offered by the Buddha ("a brilliant neuroscientist") and the insights of contemporary neuroscience. Rosen's approach, rooted in a deep understanding of Thich Nhat Hanh's teachings and her decades of experience helping to heal individuals and communities, is practical, matter of fact, personal, and a great read. *Unshakeable* is a book that I look forward to consulting and sharing frequently. Thank you, Jo-ann Rosen!"

—**COLETTE AUERSWALD, MD**, professor of Community Health Sciences at the University of California, Berkeley, and director of the UC Berkeley–UC San Francisco joint medical program; cofounder and codirector of i4Y (Innovations for Youth); and founder and faculty lead of Ending Youth Homelessness Catalyst Group

"*This* is the book we've all been waiting for in the mindfulness field. Jo-ann Rosen is a seasoned mindfulness teacher and respected leader in the field of trauma-informed care. Rosen's unwavering commitment to moving modern mindfulness beyond the realm of self-care and toward the shift in collective consciousness is the approach we so desperately need now."

—**MEENA SRINIVASAN**, executive director of Transformative Educational Leadership (TEL) and author of *SEL Every Day* and *Teach, Breathe, Learn*

"Buddhism's interchange with psychotherapy has been one of its most, if not the most, robust realms of fruitful interchange in our time. Jo-ann Rosen holds a space where these streams are balanced in a potent, practice-based, dynamic equipoise, accessible to everyone. I have personally witnessed her deep commitment to healing and transformation in a number of ways—from one-on-one counseling and group workshops to Palestinian-Israeli dialogues for peace. Innovative, no-nonsense wisdom and boundless, joyful compassion."

—**GARY GACH,** University of San Francisco faculty in theology and religious studies and the author of *The Complete Idiot's Guide to Buddhism* and *Pause, Breathe, Smile*

Unshakeable

Unshakeable

Trauma-Informed Mindfulness for Collective Awakening

JO-ANN ROSEN

PARALLAX PRESS
Berkeley, California

CONTENTS

ILLUSTRATIONS

INTRODUCTION

We're all moving
on a journey to nowhere
taking it easy
taking it slow

So goes an endearing song commonly heard in the Plum Village Buddhist community, the Zen tradition in which I practice. Are you kidding? Looking around me, I don't see very many folks taking it easy *or* taking it slow! For most of us, the following Zen story might sound more familiar:

> A horse came running swiftly down a road, carrying a rider on its back. A passer-by hailed the rider, shouting, "Hey, where are you going?" As they whizzed past, the rider retorted, "I don't know, ask the horse!"

Where *are* we going in this whirlwind of a life? Sometimes it seems like we forget to ask this fundamental question before we find ourselves already embarked toward our next destination, at breakneck speed, only to find out that our path is being chosen for us. For a more satisfying ride, wouldn't it be better to make friends with the horse, to get to know its nature, and to do what we can to provide guidance? Along the way, things may spook the horse, uneven ground may cause it to stumble, or it might get frustratingly stuck in muddy patches. Instead of simply hanging onto the reins obliviously, we need to learn to anticipate obstacles, to adjust the way we ride to avoid ditches, and to hang on for dear life when we need to.

That's the individual picture. Pulling back a bit, we can see that the path we're riding down is part of a complex network of roads, all of them affected by common issues: if it rains, we all have to navigate mud puddles; if nobody maintains the roads, we all get stuck in ruts. There is no need to enumerate the collective problems facing every world citizen today; this book is meant to inspire, and a litany of downers won't do that. But if we as a species are to survive, we need to be able to work collaboratively. We need to find both individual and collective balance in order to become calm enough to hear a variety of views, to broaden our perspectives, and to find the creativity needed to solve problems—big ones.

Today, our inner lives are chaotic. We're letting the horses we're riding get out of control, and we're not making good decisions—individually, in our communities, in our governments, and in our collective psyche. To find our way down the road more effectively, we need to learn how to create an inner life of wisdom and compassion, to stay regulated in difficult situations, and to function collaboratively without our individual nervous systems derailing us. We need to learn how to find inner stability amid the outer chaos; in short, we need to become *unshakeable*.

As a tree standing in the forest may encounter strong winds that blow its branches around wildly, to survive, it must have a strong trunk and be held in the ground by formidable roots. It knows how to take in nourishment from above and below. This tree is also supported by the root systems of all the other trees in the forest. Together they produce the oxygen that supports all of life; that is their calling. So, too, may our journey to wholeness lead us to participate in the collective awakening that is needed for a future of complex life to be possible.

Some 2,600 years ago, the Buddha, troubled by our human predicament, set out to find a way to transform the immense human suffering that he saw around him. This was also the situation that led the Vietnamese Buddhist monk Thich Nhat Hanh to explore this path for himself in the 1940s and 50s, vowing to renew a Buddhism that had lost track of its mission in a century—and in a country—that urgently needed its teachings and practices. In this new millennium, this is again where we are, needing to readapt this journey to our own times and incorporate the knowledge that science and spirit have been gathering together for many years.

This book is about how Buddhist practice, understood through the lineage of Thich Nhat Hanh and the Plum Village tradition, offers us a firm foundation to meet the challenges of our times—individually, in our communities, and in the world. (After all, Buddhists have spent more than 2,600 years crafting very skillful means of encountering and overcoming adversity!) It is about understanding our inner life and learning how to take good care of it so that it can bring us into the only destination there is, this very moment, clear and bright and wondrous. This journey along the Way of Understanding and Love—another title for the Buddhist path—offers many doors into the goodness of life.

There is the door of mind training, of actually sculpting the physiology of the brain that shapes our experience. Through diligent practice, mind training can alter our default demeanors, balance the dark and light in our lives, and help us endure the inevitable slings and arrows of life whizzing by and through us. Developing a clear mind affects the way we see, feel, hear, and taste our lives.

There is the door of community, discovering a sense of belonging in a world that appears lonely. We learn how to truly connect to the outside world when we are deeply connected to our inner selves. Our individual relationships become more satisfying. Belonging to a diverse community gives us entry into a larger sense of belonging—where we fit into the web of life, and where the web faithfully lives inside us.

There is the door of purpose. In Zen, the highest purpose of life is called the Bodhisattva Vow: to live our lives for the benefit of all sentient beings, to help others live lives of safety, happiness, and liberation. It is about cultivating altruism and maintaining the intention to make our lives about something much larger than self-improvement and self-satisfaction. Having such purpose in life can buoy us through fear and darkness, helping us get it together to be unshakeable in our vision.

Sounds good, doesn't it? But let's get real right from the start so you can relax and know that you're not alone if you have doubts about your ability to follow this path.

I, myself, have felt like an impostor as a Buddhist practitioner because the chattering monkey mind is incessantly alive in the jungle of my head. When I first began to explore Buddhism, I was deeply unfamiliar with Eastern culture, and at times I felt like I had an allergy to anything spiritual! In fact, it was only after I had finished college, in the late 1960s, that I discovered that I had an inner life at all. This strikes me, now, as almost unthinkable—how could someone live over twenty years without ever noticing something going on inside that could come into conscious awareness, something that could be an object of curiosity and deep satisfaction? Why had I not run into this concept before?

Perhaps it was because I was born when the chill of World War II was still fresh in the air. In our anxiety-driven Jewish home, there was never any talk of inner territory. My father was busy running collections for my uncle the bookie, and later, selling used cars on commission. He was too proud to "let" my mother work, and the end of each month was tension-packed to see if we could make ends meet.

The story I was told, which I unquestioningly adopted as my own, was that the war "didn't affect our family." Perhaps that was because my grandparents had emigrated to the US at the turn of the twentieth century, escaping the pogroms of Bessarabia in Eastern Europe; most of their relatives who remained there had already perished before the Holocaust began. In any case, my family—like the families of most of my peers—insisted on not looking back and thought that bringing up the past was uncomfortable and unnecessary. But later, I understood how the past lived on in our nervous systems, even if we didn't talk about it. The past emerged in my father's angry outbursts, in my mother's fearful distance. I can understand now that my mother had no skills to keep the overwhelm of our family history at bay, so it was simply buried. Likewise, my father had no skills to deal with the volcano of emotions that came up when he felt abandoned. As a child, I learned from my mother how to protect myself from overwhelm through creating distance, and from my father, how to unload the pain when I perceived others disconnecting from me. This was my inheritance.

As a result of never talking about the past, I lost my history, my sense of connection, the stories that would help me make sense of my life. I sensed somehow that the world was unsafe and if I explored deeper, I'd have to go it alone. This would stunt my curiosity for many formative years to come.

It wasn't until 1995 that I began to reconnect with my ancestral inheritance, while attending a retreat with Thich Nhat Hanh in northern California. Knowing virtually nothing at the time about Buddhist practice or the Plum Village tradition, I didn't understand what a revolutionary form of Buddhism I had run into. Like me, this practice seemed very practical. I had no idea of just how relentless and horrific the conditions were that had birthed this path, nor how it had evolved to be so helpful to my daily life. All I could see was the golden rolling hills and all the beautiful people stretched out on blankets—it was like Buddhist Woodstock.

As I came into the Plum Village community, while the forms were unfamiliar, it didn't take long for me to find comfort in the practices of bowing, sitting, silence, and being in community. Slowly, I began to realize that many of the practices were curiously similar to those of my own heritage. Gatha practices were like the mitzvot; a day of mindfulness, Shabbat; the wearing of the robes like yarmulkas and tallit; meditation, davening; mindful eating, kashrut; entering and leaving spaces with a bow like touching a mezuzah. Recognizing these similarities piqued my curiosity about other ways I'd rejected my roots. I began to feel more connected, not only to those roots, but to life in general. Beyond insight and appreciation, this was a healing step for me: healing my childhood, healing the traumas of my ancestors, and hopefully, aiding in healing for future generations.

I began to find great understanding and compassion for myself and my family, yet my quick, judgmental reactivity didn't seem to change much. *Thay*, as his students called him ("teacher," in Vietnamese), talked about Right Effort and how to deal with difficult emotions by holding them like a baby. I didn't get it. By the time I knew what difficult emotions were even hitting me, I'd already mouthed off in some way that I often regretted. Bewildered by this hijacking, not only was I a bit of an emotional wreck, my body was often in a state of shock: tense, overheated, shaky, like I was carbonated too much of the time.

You would think that my training as a psychotherapist and my experiences as a client would have given me some clue as to what was happening in my body. After all, I'd trained in various counseling methods that were aimed at trauma healing. But our physiology wasn't a point of inquiry during the 1990s; at that time, psychotherapy was all about *story*, about providing clients with an empathetic listener. Yet as a client, telling my story seemed to do very little to my reactivity. What seemed most effective for me were quirky tricks that focused on my *body*. I began to study the nervous system and learn about the new field of *somatic psychology*. The field is expanding quickly, but for our purposes, somatic psychology teaches that unless we can change our bodily reaction to trauma-related stimuli, we will remain under the spell of trauma. Somatic modalities impact bodily reactions to being *triggered*—the sudden limbic response to a perceived threat. When we can stop this reaction, the real story is more available to us, and healing of both body and mind occurs.[1]

Connecting the dots, I could see that what traumas I'd inherited still resided in my body, and that practicing with my body had begun to make an impact on that reactive self that Buddhism had revealed to me.

Over the next several years, as the neuroscience-based protocols that I had found calmed my body, I became impressed at how much they mirrored what I was learning about Buddhist psychology. Developing an engaged Buddhist practice felt like a way to offer much-needed support on a larger scale, and in a way I had not been able to achieve as a counselor, which I was doing with individuals and small groups. Although many people find support in counseling settings, many others do not. Some think that going to a counselor means there is something wrong or broken or sick about themselves. Others may not be able to find someone they can trust, or identify with, or afford. And others dislike having their problems seen as an individual matter, rather than as the result of institutional or cultural illness. I began to work with larger numbers of people, offering instruction in how to regulate their nervous systems (both as individuals and in groups).

At the same time, I was becoming more involved in the Plum Village community and realizing that many Buddhist practitioners lack the support they need to understand and deal with their overburdened nervous systems. As a therapist, I recognized that the degree of suffering in my community, as well as communities I was working with in Israel and the West Bank, was so much more widespread than any army of therapists could possibly support. Offering these body-based practices seemed like an answer—a way to scale up. Yet I also felt that vital elements were missing that really could only be addressed within an ethical/spiritual framework, and in a community that was oriented toward understanding the mind, working in community, and offering service. Not only was Buddhism poised to address these issues, it had already developed a body-based psychology of healing that was extremely compatible with what I was learning and teaching.

It was when I could see the Dharma through the lens of neuroscience, to feel this scientific accompaniment to the search for goodness, that I could drop the notion that I was "faking it" as a Buddhist, and have a deeper compassion, not just for my own situation, but for the whole of the present human catastrophe.

Writing this book became a mission to help others avoid some of the pitfalls and obstacles I've encountered on this path.

This book is meant to support you, to help you realize we're all in the same boat of human predicament, and to make this path more accessible and useful to other self-proclaimed imposters.

In this book I focus on establishing stability or unshakeability, understanding how to identify and navigate the difficulties we might encounter with both formal and informal practice, and opening into interbeing—all of which leads to getting out of the pickle we're in. It offers what I call a *neuro-informed approach* to Buddhist practice, using basic principles of neuroscience to enhance stability so that the wondrous and healing elements of the practice are more widely accessible and effective in relieving suffering.

This book is not a deep dive into the subtleties of Buddhist practice. Although *Unshakeable* is rooted in the Buddhist tradition, we can see that this path does not have to be a religious one—though if you go deep, it can be wondrous, even miraculous. Likewise, it is not a deep dive into neuroscience. It is not meant to reduce the path to a linear, scientific view. It is meant to be a set of awarenesses to help us greet the difficulties we encounter—inside and out—with a bit more understanding, compassion, and skill. Although we will explore the nature of trauma and how diligent practice may produce healing, the aim of the book is not overcoming trauma or other psychological obstacles. It is how to benefit from the practice without being shaken by the challenges we find along the way.

This book calls us all to come to terms with what it means to be in a human body with a human nervous system, what it means to have inherited a legacy of unbroken trauma, and what it will take to begin to slow that legacy down to a standstill. Although trauma has strong roots in biology, it takes its toll not only on the body but on the underlying social structure that human life depends on for our very survival. And although some trauma is a response to purely physical phenomena like earthquakes, floods, and drought, there is often a social component as well: racism, sexism, ageism, ableism, xenophobia. To heal as individuals and as a planet, these ills and their roots—greed, hatred, and delusion—must be addressed as well. Unless we allow for a very personal experience with the dynamics of trauma and its healing, we won't be able to heal ourselves or contribute to the collective healing of the world.

Unshakeable takes us beyond the legacy of trauma because it also incorporates our human legacy of resilience, helping us recognize, celebrate, and resource ourselves as part of the healing process that brings us into the miraculous wholeness of our potential.

The Buddha was a brilliant neuroscientist. In a relatively short time, using his surroundings as a laboratory and with a sample size of one, he discovered basically all the processes of how our body and mind work together, and how to transcend the traumatic experiences of this life. Yet the Buddha was not content with keeping these healing discoveries to himself; he was on a mission to bring them to as many suffering souls as he could. In order to do that, he developed a large community that could reach out further than any one person could and that would last beyond one person's individual lifespan.

So, too, did Thich Nhat Hanh find the need to develop a community of practice that now has thousands of members in small groups all over the world. This community, the Plum Village lineage, is an applied Buddhism that weaves together four pillars of daily life: study, practice, work, and play. It makes this journey workable for masses of people living a modern life, people who are not able or inclined to sit hours each day in meditation. Instead, one is expected to be "practicing" in every aspect of daily life. We are invited to walk the Buddhist Eightfold Path while leading an ordinary lay life.

The Plum Village tradition offers a trip planner for the journey of a lifetime. It may not be the only travel agent around, to further the analogy, but it offers a blend of the contemplative practices that are specifically adapted to lay life. This is quite different from traditional monastic Buddhist practice, which follows an apprenticeship model: novices are trained by the fully ordained, who are in turn guided by seasoned teachers. Additionally, through living together, they learn what might be called skillful means of living in harmony. For us lay people, practicing with other lay people, that kind of guidance, and that kind of intensive learning, is rare. This book is meant to be a guide to how we, too, can benefit from a spiritual journey and ease our suffering—to find a path we can follow in daily life, and to make a contribution to resolving the mess we're in. It is not meant to be a substitute for careful guidance of an elder.

This lineage is also a conscious acknowledgment of the need for renewal and change, having emerged out of extremely tumultuous times. As we will see in Chapter 1, Thich Nhat Hanh, much like the Buddha, developed both his practices and his community out of his own needs, driven by his compassion and love for the people. These emerged from the hardships he experienced to become lifelines to wholeness, healing, and thriving during unrelenting traumatic circumstances.

Chapter 2 begins a very simple exploration of the human nervous system, linking up our miraculous biology with our Buddhist practice. This chapter presents the science behind our neuro-informed approach to mindfulness. We will take a look at just what is happening in our bodies when we are faced with challenges above and beyond what we're equipped to encounter—and how to rebalance our system when we become dysregulated. Along the way, we take a broad look at the experience of trauma to help make sense of what might be happening in and around us.

Chapter 3 begins our journey of seeing Buddhism through a neuroscience lens while it makes the basic teachings easy to understand. We can see the Buddhist psychological concepts have clear albeit not exact parallels in today's neuroscientific terminology that can ease the mind into deeper experience of those concepts: The Four Noble Truths, The Eightfold Path, and the Buddhist "anatomy" of the mind with its consciousness, seeds and planting grounds and nourishments.

Chapter 4 goes deeper into this crucial skill of regulating and stabilizing when things get rough, both in your Buddhist practice and in daily life. We'll learn how to rebalance a dysregulated nervous system and prepare for what might come up as we begin formal practice. Building on these key principles, in Chapter 5 we get into specifics: here you will find lots of useful tools and exercises to try out, including how to find and shape the anchors of your personal practice and how to adapt things along the way if they become too difficult. With any effective medicine, there can be side effects—so, too, with a contemplative path. These two chapters also act as a primer on the various forms of ruts and potholes one may find on the contemplative journey. Recognizing the signs of trouble can help us avoid or recover from any adverse effect that may come up in practice.

In Chapter 6, we get down to what we most often think of when we talk about Buddhist mindfulness practice. (But don't be fooled—everything we've been doing up until now is practice, too!) This chapter digs deeper into the essential teachings while blending them with the neuroscience we've learned so far to give a more accessible understanding of what might, at times, seem esoteric.

In most lineages this would be the end of the book, but the centering of community of practice brings us a whole added dimension of the Plum Village tradition. In Chapter 7 we learn about the interbeing nature of the sangha—the interconnectedness of well-being of the individual and community—and the miracle of coregulation that we can consciously take advantage of as we journey into communal practices.

Chapter 8 explores the full potential of a harmoniously functioning sangha and the collective healing it can offer. To reach its full potential, however, we need to apply the same principles to the sangha that we do to ourselves. In this chapter, we will investigate the nervous system of our community: how to keep it healthy and what to do when it becomes dysregulated. You'll find concrete guidelines for how to lead and nurture neuro-informed mindfulness in any group situation—not just spiritual communities, but even among friends and families—and learn principles of good facilitation.

The Plum Village tradition is a path of engaged Buddhism, and so in Chapter 9 we broaden our view even further. This chapter urges us to see that we all can contribute to healing the world, one personal purpose at a time, and provides a simple framework for getting started and keeping on going.

The teachings contained in every one of these chapters is worthy of a lifetime of study. For those of you who are already quite familiar with Buddhist teachings, this is a reminder of what's really at play here. For those of you for whom the material is new, these teachings are an invitation to look deeper. In either case, and all those in between, reading this book forms just one stop along the journey.

Throughout the chapters you will find opportunities to have a direct experience of the ideas put forth in the form of suggested exercises. These exercises are all processes that invite you to refine your ability to be present to what is. In these, you will be encouraged to begin tailoring your practices to fit your unique self. You are free to adapt the exercises to what supports you while you stretch—just a bit. Not too much, and not too little! It might be helpful to use a small notebook to keep track of your findings and insights.

Is the journey easy? No. Is it guaranteed to fix your life? No. Is it fun? Depends on your definition of fun! Is it worth it? Try some of it out and see for yourself how it might support you on your path. It's no overstatement for me to say that this lineage of learning has been a lifeline for me. I offer you this book as a guide, a shelter in the storm of our everyday lives, and a call to find the roots of our collective strength.

1 The Map Maker

A Brief History of the Plum Village Tradition

I was spending the winter at Deer Park Monastery in Southern California when the announcement came, on January 21, 2022, that Thich Nhat Hanh had passed away peacefully at Từ Hiếu Temple in Huế, Vietnam. It was a strange moment. A long-awaited shoe had dropped, and the impact it had on me was quite unexpected.

We, in the monastery, lived in two worlds simultaneously. In one, plans meticulously prepared for his passing fell into place with precision: a banner reading "A Cloud Never Dies" was hoisted up over the entry to the Ocean of Peace Meditation Hall; an ancestor altar was swiftly constructed, with candles, incense, orchids, and a portrait of Thay holding his lighted lamp of wisdom. When we weren't busy arranging our own rituals, our eyes were glued on the enormous television screen in the hall, livestreaming the ceremonies taking place in Vietnam and the seemingly endless stream of followers passing through the Từ Hiếu Temple to pay their respects. In the other world, people were walking around in a haze—one which had, in truth, been suspended over the sangha for the previous eight years, since a massive stroke had taken our teacher into a world of seemingly wordless mystery.

It is only when someone or something passes from this world that we see the space they had occupied for us. Thay's place, or rather its absence, inside me took me quite by surprise. In the months just before his death, I'd been tearing through books, journals, and personal interviews trying to understand what Thay's formative years were like: his childhood, his life as a young monk, the stages of his evolution into his twenty-first-century self. You know how people who have had near-death experiences sometimes talk about seeing their entire life flashing before their eyes? This felt like that—only with someone else's life. Spending such a condensed time learning about Thay's life, the circumstances and events of nine decades, produced a vivid history swirling around in my head. It transformed my understanding of who this man was, and with it, my own personal relationship with him.

During that time of memorial ceremonies, right after Thay's passing, I took the opportunity to pay my respects to the ancestor altar just after breakfast, when no one else was around. I suddenly remembered the ceremony that had taken place when I became a Dharma teacher. Usually, in this ceremony, I would have stood in front of Thay with an unlit lamp, which he would have lit with the flame from his own, signifying the transmission of wisdom. But at the time of my ceremony, travel to Plum Village was not possible, and I'd had to do it remotely and by proxy. But now, standing there in front of his nearly life-sized portrait, I felt that I was finally receiving the lamp directly from him. With his life's history emblazoned so recently in my mind, my heart began to fill with gratitude and inspiration. I felt flooded with his energy, his vision of bringing relief to those who were suffering, his faith that Buddhism held effective medicine for masses of people, his determination not to let anything stop him, and his willingness to speak truth to power, even to challenge Buddhist doctrine. Above all, I felt the humility, integrity, resilience, and courage he needed to forge an unconventional path through his own traumatic past.

Originally, my mission for this book was to infuse the Plum Village lineage with what has become known as a "trauma-sensitive" perspective: to offer the practice in a way that helps heal our own past trauma. As I researched the topic, I quickly began to see that the very underpinnings of our lineage, born out of centuries of occupation, violence, and war in Vietnam, was itself a trauma-sensitive renewal of a Buddhism that had lost touch with its ancient aspiration.

Reading about his early years as a monk, I could see that Thich Nhat Hanh was using his own experience of encountering trauma and developing resilience to craft a practice made for extremely difficult times. Although he was a voracious scholar, and surely he had some foundation in Buddhist psychology from his monastic studies, much of the practice he developed was rooted in his own personal experiences and his need to manage the seemingly unbearable stresses surrounding his life. In the midst of devastation and destruction, he began to develop a path that could help to heal and, to some extent, prevent the psychological and spiritual wounds in the sea of fire that was Vietnam throughout his life. The circumstances, although potentially devastating, were a living laboratory in which to renew and update a Buddhism that could speak to and meet the needs of the population he so dearly loved. Thich Nhat Hanh was convinced that a renewed Buddhism could be of infinite benefit to the people. With an uncanny intuition of how to keep a nervous system balanced; how to rebalance it when dysregulated; and most importantly, how to maintain hope, joyful determination, and purpose, Thay developed an approach to practice that could keep people afloat and help them find those delights that made life worth living.

If we look through a more modern psychological and scientific lens, we might say Thich Nhat Hanh was a master of nervous system self-regulation. As we will see in Chapter 2, self-regulation occurs when we are overwhelmed by the nervous system but find a way to relax into knowing that it's okay, we can handle it. Self-regulation is finding a place of calm clarity inside that can somehow find the strength to manage. Thay calls this *our true home.*

I have arrived
I am HOME
in the here
and in the now

I am solid,
I am free,
in the ultimate
I dwell.[1]

Home is a place where we are not carried away by circumstance, where the nervous system acts as an integrated whole, where our body is calm, where we are able to direct our attention over a sustained period and see things as they are. This is the miracle of what is termed *mindfulness*. From this insight comes the knowledge of how to proceed, felt deeply in every cell. Finding home is the first step: a place of calm and safety, unshakeable.

Although he did not use scientific language to describe his approach to Buddhism, Thich Nhat Hanh had an openness to experiment and see how practices actually worked. In addition to developing a personal healing practice, he ingeniously constructed a path that also incorporated, at its core, the healing elements of belonging to a community—a notion that is just now being recognized as essential to healing in the world of trauma research. His vision for a renewed Buddhism transcended individual self-regulation to strive for *collective* regulation: he saw the *sangha*, or community of practice, as a living organism itself, an organism that has its own potential for awakening.

Studying how Thich Nhat Hanh began to renew the efforts for a truly engaged Buddhist practice, one accessible by ordinary people in ordinary—and extraordinary—circumstances, can help inspire and point the way for us to continue in this process for the years to come. First, let's look at the circumstances surrounding his beginnings, to understand the scope of devastation that was the birthplace of this lineage. Along the way, we can see, step by step, how the Plum Village practice emerged and evolved into what it is today: a practice that preserves and heals the individual, a practice that develops community, and a practice that offers the wisdom of community to the world.

Early Experiences of Home

Thich Nhat Hanh, born Nguyen Xuan Bao in 1926, lived in the home of his paternal grandmother, with a rich extended family of his five siblings, aunts, uncles, and cousins. The setting was idyllic: a large home with a traditional courtyard and garden, a lotus pond, and bamboo groves, located just inside the walled imperial capital of Hue. From Thay's writings, we know that his childhood was peaceful and safe, and that he enjoyed an especially loving and supportive relationship with his mother. Beginning life well-loved, he grew up with a heart that was able to be compassionate by way of his own received experience and the modeling from his extended family.

Within this nest of safety, he was free to develop curiosity for and delight in each new encounter. Later, he would share the story in his Dharma talks of, how, after receiving a cookie as a youngster, he could spend expansive amounts of time languishing over each tiny bit of cookie. This was because his little nervous system had a chance to develop a deep sense of safety, caring, belonging, and protection; he lived with enough ease to be able to simply relax into another world, whether with a cookie, with nature, or with his troupe of buddies and protective elders. In short, his early experiences taught him what *home* felt like.

This often-told story has become a benchmark for his lifelong career: At age nine, young Xuan Bao saw a picture on the cover of his elder brother's Buddhist magazine. The Buddha was sitting serenely on the grass, naturally at ease and smiling, and Xuan Bao was captivated by the image. This image was a stark contrast to the injustice and suffering he saw around him under French colonial rule. The impression of the Buddha, so peaceful and at ease, stuck with his young self.

One day, a conversation ensued with his brothers and friends about what they wanted to be when they grew up. Nho, the elder brother, was the first to declare his aspiration to be a monk. Many years later, Thich Nhat Hanh would recall, "During that discussion, it was clear that some decision or some aspiration was there, very strong in me already. Inside, I knew that I wanted to be a monk."[2] By the end of the conversation, Xuan

Bao and his friends had made a pact: they, too, would all become monks.

Conditions were just right for Xuan Bao to recognize his calling. The seed of *home* was growing, watered by the deep love and belonging he felt in his home life and in the natural world that surrounded him. He was supported socially by his peers, whose aspirations were also to become monks. And he knew a feeling of safety and serenity in his body, something he would be able to draw on in the trying years to come.

Beginning Monastic Life

In 1942, at the age of sixteen, Xuan Bao entered monastic life. In keeping with the Zen way of instruction, he was given little verbal guidance and was mainly told to observe carefully how everything was done and do it accordingly. Buddhism in Vietnam has historically followed a Mahayana Zen tradition, a lineage in which the path to individual enlightenment is walked by helping relieve the suffering of all sentient beings. But for Xuan Bao, the Buddhism being practiced around him was far removed from this ideal: for the most part, it was limited to prayers, ancestor worship, chants, and offerings. The one guide he had was a small book of poems to memorize and recite while doing his daily tasks. These small poems, or *gathas*, were a set of intentions to guide the heart so that each mundane task became a metaphor for developing the love and caring needed to realize his aspiration to serve all living beings. In this way, he spent his days blending the mundane and the spiritual, fortifying his determination to be as serene as the Buddha. However, although he recounts that these early monastic years were supportive and nurturing, it was hardly the whole picture.

As a kindness to the reader, I want to caution that the following few paragraphs contain descriptions of suffering that may be disturbing. In 1944–45, Vietnam was in complete turmoil. The rise of communism in the north caused rivers of fear and migration from north to south. An embargo on coal forced the populace to burn rice for needed fuel, which contributed to a famine in which some two million people starved to death. The monastery where Xuan Bao lived was raided more than once for its meager supplies, and the streets around him were littered with emaciated bodies. Xuan Bao was in the thick of it: the traumas he experienced during this time were both individual and collective, one feeding the other.

Ultimately, however, this only reinforced his determination to create a renewed Buddhism—one that went beyond chanting and prayers to include real physical, emotional, and spiritual support. It was then that Xuan Bao left his root temple with two of his fellow monks to further his studies and determination to be a bodhisattva of action. They each took a new name that ended in the word *Hạnh*, meaning *action*. To this Xuan Bao added the traditional Vietnamese word *Thích*, indicating monasticism, and the word *Nhất*, meaning *one*. Hence he became Thich Nhat Hanh, meaning Monk of One Action. The one action he would come to focus on would be renewal.

The Buddhist renewal movement had roots in the late 1800s but it had seen new efforts put forward in the 1920s and 1940s. In fact, the magazines Thich Nhat Hanh had found so influential were part of this movement, called *Chấn hưng Phật giáo*. He dreamed of a renewed Buddhism that would directly speak to the youth, speak to families, transcend factions, and unite the populace. In addition to his own studies, he worked incessantly on this passion of renewing Buddhism by writing and publishing books, magazine articles, and pamphlets; training young monks;

and making himself known as a people's poet, a lyrical and powerful witness to the death and destruction surrounding him.

With the rise of the Diem regime came a suppression of everything Buddhist, and many of Thay's friends and colleagues were murdered in the ensuing chaos. At least fifty-seven monastics carried out public self-immolations in protest of the regime and its oppression of Buddhists. Thich Nhat Hanh later talked about the significance these self-immolations had to him. While horrific, the stark realities of suffering they expressed increased his immense caring and compassion and powered his vision ever more.

Finding Refuge at Phuong Boi

By 1957, Thay was on the verge of overload. His journals from this time recount that he didn't think his friends' practice was strong enough to endure the violence surrounding them. They needed a hermitage where they could devote themselves to practice: to heal their wounds, nourish themselves, and prepare for new initiatives that were needed for the people who were suffering so deeply. He was able to find sixty acres of rural countryside to establish his first practice center, which he called Phuong Boi (Fragrant Palm Leaves). Here, away from the unrelenting realities of daily life, Thay could recover some balance. While continuing to work on his dream of a new Buddhism, he also had time to play; to walk in the forest; and to nourish himself with edible food, sense impressions, and the company of kindred spirits.

This balance of work and retreat was itself the renewal of Buddhism that he had been seeking; to paraphrase one of his mottos, "there is no way to renewal; renewal is the way." Phuong Boi added an important element to the new lineage Thay was creating: the essential role of sanctuary, a retreat community, a place where practitioners could recover the ability to rebalance their depleted nervous systems and spirits during difficult times. This was Thay's response to recognizing he was about to go beyond his own limits of what he could manage under extreme stress. This awareness of one's limits, and the skillful response to return to a place of refuge, is known in neuroscience as staying within the *window of tolerance*—a crucial concept we will explore in detail in Chapter 2.

But even at Phuong Boi, the stresses didn't come to a stop. When funding was cut for the key publication that Thay depended on for a more public voice, it was a severe blow. To Thay, this was not just a matter of economics, but rather an undercutting by the conservative Buddhist hierarchy, dashing his hopes for their support of his vision. This was followed by another severe blow: his mother's death, the loss of a fundamental component of his core sense of home. Thay became very ill and was hospitalized, and along with it, he experienced a deep depression that no doctor was able to treat. He experimented with ways of counting steps and breath to counter his hopelessness and severe insomnia. We might conclude that these practices must have been somewhat successful, as Thay left the hospital after three weeks, returning to Phuong Boi and to his call for a Buddhist renewal. Thay continued to deepen his practice with walking and breathing, using his intense suffering as an opportunity to refine these essential skills.

Thay's success in keeping his depression from completely debilitating him came from finding a way to give his body and mind a break. It took time and skillfulness to reregulate his nervous system, fueled by his unrelenting caring and commitment to the people. The principal at play here—as we will explore in this book—is to stop or distract the mind from hyperfocusing on *threat*, and to substitute an activity that instead signals *safety* to the nervous system. For Thay, this safety, this sense of home, was breath, walking, and his unwavering compassion for his countrypeople. At every turn, Thay was making good use of the grist in his mill to grind out a neuro-informed Buddhist practice, one traumatic stressor at a time.

Small glimmers of hope began to emerge that kept him going:

> For eight years, we tried to speak about the need for a humanistic Buddhism and a unified Buddhist Church in Vietnam that could respond to the needs of the people. We sowed those seeds against steep odds, and while waiting for them to take root, we endured false accusations, hatred, deception, and intolerance. Still we refused to give up hope . . . Now some of those seeds have begun to grow. As discontent with the political regime is growing, the idea of a Buddhism for the people is taking shape. One evening while . . . on a visit to a poor hamlet, I heard a mother singing one of our protest songs to lullaby her child to sleep! I wanted to weep.[3]

Following his discovery of how to rebalance his own nervous system, Thay began to learn how to hold the experience of dysregulation to see it more deeply and with compassion: compassion for the suffering he witnessed, compassion for himself for the witnessing, and compassion spreading to the entire country. In the ensuing years, Thay began to focus on this skill of holding difficulties, using mindfulness to gently light the path.

Walking mindfully on the earth,
a grassy path,
my feet make the promise

to embrace the early morning
and touch the peace of the present moment.

Autumn leaves fall and cover the path,
unrolling a carpet of walking meditation.
A shy squirrel, hiding behind the oak tree,
looks at me, surprised,
then dashes to the top of the tree
and disappears behind a cluster of leaves[4]

Growing the Sphere of Engaged Buddhism

In the year following his first hospitalization, Thich Nhat Hanh's reputation grew significantly through his writings. Thay was launched into the international arena in 1959, when he was invited to attend a worldwide gathering of Buddhists in Japan. This experience woke something in Thay, catapulted him into a larger arena of influence, and introduced him into a network of Buddhist thought. On top of all he was doing, he set himself to the task of learning English, which opened a door to bringing his idea of a renewed Buddhism to the Western world.

Perhaps it was serendipity that, soon after returning from Japan, Thay held a lecture series where he met a group of young university students who took interest in his ideas. Together, they would form the School for Youth in Social Services (SYSS), a group that would bring Thay's vision of a Buddhist renewal into reality: education and relief services blended with spiritual practice that would also buoy hope. They referred to themselves as the "thirteen cedars," a grove of trees that would eventually grow into a forest of ten thousand social workers bringing this engaged Buddhist practice out into the countryside and, eventually, the world. Among them was Cao Ngoc Phuong, a young biologist already doing relief work in the slums. Phuong was a good match for Thay, with her strong intention and limitless energy; she would later become among the first ordained monastics in this lineage and was given the name Sister Chan Khong, True Emptiness. Together, they created a beehive of industry, each of them teaching, writing, and doing social service organizing. They worked together for the next six decades, combining their skills and bringing their gifts to the world.

When you read about their early work, you can see that many of the seeds of present-day practices of the Plum Village tradition were present from the beginning. They had begun to put Buddhist principles into practice during the stressful situations they found themselves in, like being apprehended by authorities; working in the villages while under siege; warding off depression and despair while losing many of their closest colleagues to the violence around them; spending years working abroad; and, finally, resigning themselves to live in exile.

At the base of their strength was the breath, something that they could carry with them into all circumstances that would help them to feel grounded. They clung to the rejuvenating power of mindfulness practice, constantly making sure to set aside days, or at least part-days, to practice together, diligently strengthening their sense of faith in the practice, their togetherness and well-being. Their involvement in villages and poor areas of the city also kept them deeply connected with the suffering of the people. This is what kept them going in their tireless efforts to bring peace to their beloved country: the love of the people kept them energized, and the practice kept them nourished.

In doing my research I wanted so much to be able to travel back in time and see just how those practices were being embodied on the ground. We get glimpses into Chan Khong's daily practice in the midst of harrowing daily escapades:

> One night we stopped in Son Khuong, a remote village where the fighting was especially fierce. As we were about to go to sleep in our boat, we suddenly heard shooting, then screaming, then shooting again. The young people in our group were seized with panic, and a few young men jumped into the river to avoid the bullets. I sat quietly in the boat with two nuns and breathed consciously to calm myself. Seeing us so calm, everyone stopped panicking, and we quietly chanted the Heart Sutra, concentrating deeply on this powerful chant.[5]

In this memory of turning adversity into joy, balancing the potential derailers of spirit into buoying gratitudes, Chan Khong is in fact recounting an important lesson in coregulation—an important concept we will return to throughout this book. As we will see, *coregulation* is one of the miracles of human evolution, the ability of the body to mimic those around them and thereby discern the mood and threat level of the other. Being a calm presence in a storm can actually calm others.

We can also see in this story how Chan Khong is developing what psychologists call post-traumatic growth, turning adversity into a memory of empowerment. Elsewhere, she writes,

> My weeks in jail in Hue and Saigon were important lessons for me. I realized how much I take for granted so many wonderful things in my life. For example, in jail, I dreamed of climbing freely and happily on to my motorbike "like a bird flying in the air," with my long hair flowing, the cloth of my ao dai [dress] flapping in the breeze, and two giant bags of

> rice for those in the slums on top of the back wheel. I realized that having a motorbike and being able to ride it whenever I wanted was one aspect of living in Paradise.[6]

In this memory, again we can see Chan Khong practicing looking for the joys of life in every possible moment—a vital part of right effort. Although we don't have control over many difficulties that arise in our lives, we can use all the moments in between to look at the small joys of being alive. Each time some support is taken away from us, it can be an opportunity to focus on the gratitude for having that aspect as a part of our lives. In this way we are strengthening our nervous system against being easily hijacked, and at the same time, developing resources for later use. (We will explore in more detail how to create such resources in Chapter 5.)

Meanwhile, Thich Nhat Hanh was developing another practice important to the Plum Village tradition. Earlier, he had learned to count his steps to help himself out of a deep depression while he was hospitalized; now, he was refining this practice of mindful walking into a fine art. He published the book *A Guide to Walking Meditation* in 1984, teaching different ways to incorporate mindful walking into life, both to nourish joy and protect yourself from being carried away into traumatic response. As Chan Khong recalled, when the Buddhist nun Thich Nu Tri Hai was jailed from 1984–1988, she relied heavily on Thay's book and the practice of walking meditation to sustain herself, practicing mindful walking for five kilometers each day in her four-square-meter cell.[7]

Thay and Chan Khong both had a good start on understanding how to weave individual practice into daily life. Now it was time to take the next step. The war was escalating, and Thay felt an increasing need to bring the lessons they had been learning from their individual practice to larger numbers of ordinary people. He believed that people needed a spiritual practice to survive; these techniques of self-regulation could be a survival strategy.

On February 5, 1966, Thich Nhat Hanh founded the Tiep Hien order, or the Order of Interbeing, with Chan Khong and a handful of like-minded practitioners. It was important for them that those ordained were free to choose whether they wanted to live according to monastic traditions or as laypeople. The order was created to bring Buddhism right into the middle of social concerns, the renewal he had so long envisioned; including both lay and monastic options would enable them to expand their circle of membership.

The Order of Interbeing called for an *engaged* Buddhist practice—one that addressed the needs of ordinary people in the midst of a world spinning out of control. In her book *Learning True Love*, Chan Khong recalled practicing walking meditation while bombs were falling, and mindful breathing while caring for a child with bullet wounds.[8] This demonstrates the essential skills we will practice later in this book: becoming aware that our nervous system is dysregulated, and taking steps to calm it so that our actions will be intentional and clear-headed rather than simply a "flight or fight" reaction to stress. Chan Khong had a plan of action that was strong enough to override the impulse to simply *react*. For the initiates of the Order of Interbeing, this plan informed every action of every day. It became a lifejacket, buoying them to wake up in the morning, bathe, brush teeth, eat, wash dishes, walk from here to there, and so on throughout the day. In the years to come, they would develop a broad and sophisticated set of practices from the essential Buddhist teachings, applying them creatively in the most daunting of circumstances.

Bringing Buddhism to the World

Whether he had a premonition that he might not be able to physically support his young spiritual disciples, or he simply felt deeply how important it was to grow this new collective, Thich Nhat Hanh left Vietnam soon after the Tiep Hien ordination ceremony and embarked on an international speaking tour. He was not able to return for thirty-nine years.

During this next period of his life, Thay became an internationally renowned peace activist in exile. In 1968, he published *The Miracle of Mindfulness*, based on a series of loving letters he had written to his fellow SYSS workers back in Vietnam. After its publication in the US, it would become a foundational text for meditators and peace activists and position him as a champion of peace. He adopted his now well-known motto, "Peace Is Every Step," and brought his teaching everywhere, claiming that "man is not our enemy; our enemy is greed, hatred, and delusion." By the 1980s, Thich Nhat Hanh had spent a considerable amount of time in Paris heading the Vietnamese Peace Delegation—at the time, he was without a home in Vietnam. Along with Chan Khong and others, he decided to settled in the French countryside. There he created Plum Village, the place where they would continue their visionary experiment in living and breathing the way of awareness, understanding, and love. It would also become an important cultural and social refuge for thousands of Vietnamese refugees, providing a healing environment of harmonious community.

If you were to visit Plum Village today, with its cute songs and gentle approach to practice, you probably would have no sense of the origins of this lineage, born out of the traumas of war and violence. You might not be aware that these practices were developed in the midst of chaos and destruction—and now, having read this history, you might wonder how this all applies to you. Today some practitioners, laypeople, and monastics still need to explore the deep and subtle nuances of extensive sitting practices; but most of us just need a raft that will keep us afloat—whether or not we actually reach the other shore. This is why the Plum Village tradition, grounded as it is in essential skills of nervous system regulation, is so valuable for us today. In the next chapter, we look at nervous system regulation through the lens of modern neuroscience before we dive deeply into the neuro-informed Dharma that is the Plum Village lineage.

2 The Owner's Manual

The Science of Neuro-Informed Mindfulness

Before we go any further, let's pause and think about some of these concepts we touched on in the previous chapter. What does it mean to be "neuro-informed"? How do we know if our nervous system is regulated or dysregulated? And what do we really mean when we talk about trauma?

As children we are taught how to pay attention to our outer world, but we are rarely taught how to understand or cultivate our *inner* lives. And yet, that inner life strongly governs how we navigate the outer one. Although we are born with a complex nervous system that has evolved to ensure our physical and emotional survival, we receive little to no education on how it works. We are given no rules of the road, no owner's manual. In this chapter, we will get to know just how our body/mind operates.[1]

Evolutionary biologists say that humans first roamed the earth between five and seven million years ago. Evolution over millions of years has resulted in awe-inspiring complexities; our human existence is the inheritance of quadrillions of successful outcomes. Amazing!

Because the process of biological mutation and adaptation takes a very long time, we can safely assume that the nervous system we have today is essentially identical to that of our ancestors who lived some fifteen thousand years ago—a blip on the screen of an evolutionary timeline. Life back then was a series of infrequent emergencies, with a lot of concentrated work in between: hunting and gathering enough food to survive. The human nervous system was accustomed to mustering occasional big energy to fight or flee, and those who survived shook it off and went back to business as usual. That nervous system hasn't had time enough since then to evolve and adapt to the unrelenting stresses in today's world, and therein lies a very basic problem: we are navigating a twenty-first-century lifestyle using a nervous system that evolved and adapted to serve the realities of the hunter-gatherer.

EXERCISE 2.1:
Heightening Awareness of Outer and Inner Stimuli

PURPOSE: To notice how the stresses of today's daily life impacts our ancient nervous system
DURATION: 1 minute
FREQUENCY: 3 times daily

A few times each day, stop for just 1 minute and check in with your body. What's it like in there? Look around and notice what outer stimuli are impacting you. The point of this exercise is to see where your focus is, getting used to checking inside, noting the variety of stimuli, and experiencing your body.

Anatomy of the Human Nervous System

Our mammalian nervous system is a truly miraculous communication network. It consists of billions of nerve cells fed by chemical transmitters creating electrical impulses that result in what we think of as our "inner" experience. This nervous system is made up of our brain, spinal cord, and peripheral nerves that connect the brain to every part of our body. For the purpose of being able to understand and shape our inner experience, we will first just focus on the brain and one bundle of nerves. While this is an oversimplification, we can gain a mountain of insight if we start here.

The brain is made up of three main networks: the brain stem, for basic survival; the limbic network, for how we assess the relative safety of a particular situation; and the cerebral cortex, which coordinates what we experience with our senses, how we interpret it, and what we do in response. Each of these parts can communicate with the other parts by way of a super long nerve that connects the brain to all the organs called the vagus nerve.

The survival network, found in the bottom or stem of our brain, is an *automatic system* (also known as *autonomic*), which means it keeps our vital functions going without us consciously needing to do anything. That is a good thing as we would be hard pressed to do the enormous job of keeping all systems afloat (heart, lungs, digestion, body temperature, etc.) even if we knew how, which of course we don't. This survival network has both a gas pedal to go fast (the sympathetic system) and a brake to slow down (the parasympathetic system). The sympathetic system is what gets activated when you feel threatened, and it is sometimes thought of as the "fight-or-flight" state; your body gets ready to defend itself, and it puts other necessary functions on pause while you deal with the immediate danger. The parasympathetic system is the "rest, digest, and connect" state; your body feels a general sense of safety and is able to work on other crucial survival functions, including nourishing itself and socializing with others. The survival network responds to signals from the limbic network to go fast or slow depending upon what is needed. This survival network is fully functional at birth.

The emotional network (aka limbic system) is governed by two primary structures located deep inside the brain: the *hippocampus* and *amygdala*. The hippocampus is the memory center for our brain. It is responsible for converting our experience into long-term memories, creating new nerve cells, and learning new things. It also helps us navigate our world by orienting us in space. The amygdala uses those memories stored in the hippocampus to determine whether or not a stimulus is a threat and to alert the survival network to act accordingly. Once a stimulus has been identified as a threat or not, the amygdala signals the survival network to step on the gas or the brake, as needed. In a big emergency, the amygdala may turn off access to the hippocampus so as not to waste energy or confuse the situation with a flood of unnecessarily complicated information. This turning off can make our long-term memory a bit like Swiss cheese. (Have

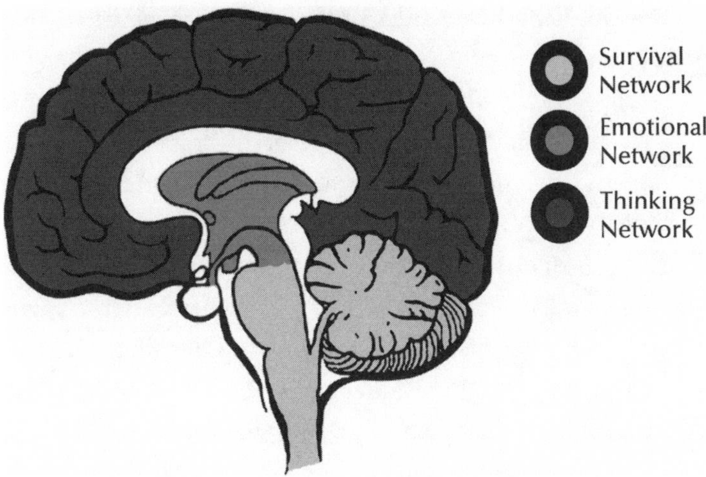

Figure 2.1: Brain stem (survival network), cortex (thinking network), and limbic area (emotional network)

you ever wondered why you have such a blurred memory of significant moments in your life where you felt you were thrown off guard? Personally, I find it comforting to know that this is just how we are built!)

Working together as the limbic system, the hippocampus and amygdala link stimuli to response, facilitating how we feel about our world. As the maker and keeper of memories, the limbic system helps us know what conditions have proved to be historically safe or unsafe and help us decide how to act accordingly in new situations. It helps us develop vast social networks, which were key to our survival as a species and which give us a sense of belonging, comfort, and culture. Under optimal conditions, the limbic system feeds the survival network information or impressions of how we might feel about a certain situation. It helps us make decisions about entering into emotional relationships or pursuing a calling and allows us to be open to adventure.

The thinking brain (aka prefrontal or cerebral cortex) is a thin gray tissue that covers the core of the brain and is responsible for what we call *executive functioning*. The basic activity of this brain region is to orchestrate thoughts and actions to manifest internal goals. The thinking brain is associated with higher-level processes such as consciousness, thought, emotion, reasoning, language, creativity, and what we generally think of as memory. Together with the vagus nerve, it is responsible for navigating interpersonal relationships, being empathetic, and being able to coregulate with other humans. That's quite amazing when you think about it!

More recently, neuroscientists have been very interested in researching large-scale networks that connect different regions of the brain. One of these is called the *default mode network (DMN)*, a network of interacting brain regions with fancy names that is active when we are daydreaming or not focused on the outside world. Conversely, it is at rest when we are focused on external tasks and goals. Much like the limbic system, it acts as a kind of check-and-balance mechanism. When well regulated, the DMN helps us step out of the way of the self by keeping cognitive functions from coming online, when necessary, thus helping us be sensitive to our surroundings: an optimal combination of attention and peripheral awareness. Importantly for us, it also acts as a liaison between the conscious awareness and the unconscious. But when it is switched on constantly, it can feel like a chattering voice in our heads that accompanies us everywhere we go. It can really wear us out!

I have experienced a sobering example of what it feels like when the DMN is in full swing: once while driving, I suddenly realized that what I was "seeing" in front of me was actually a story in my mind. The actual scenery around me—the road I needed to be paying attention to—had become so muted as to be almost be absent from my conscious awareness. Yikes!

Although research on the DMN is relatively new and not yet fully explored, now studies are showing that this area being overstimulated is associated with anxiety, depression, and even psychosis, and that meditation—specifically, mindfulness meditation—helps keep the DMN in good working order. In general, cultivating mindfulness in everything we do helps to keep the DMN in proper balance. This means trying our best to do things—like sitting, walking, talking, playing, eating, working—one at a time, and being mindful during the process.

POLYVAGAL THEORY AND COREGULATION

Polyvagal theory, as developed by the neuroscientist Stephen Porges, can help us better understand how the vagus nerve works with the thinking brain to perform this important function of coregulation.[2] The vagus nerve is the longest nerve in the body, running from the brain stem to almost all the organs of the head, chest, and belly. You can think of it as a busybody, or a go-between, or maybe the town crier, trying to keep all systems apprised of the overall goings-on.

One part of this nerve bundle is responsible for regulating our sense of safety. It does this by picking up on social cues like tone of voice, gestures, body language, and facial expressions. In this way it interprets the state of the nervous system of another person: whether their autonomic nervous system is in a sympathetic or "threat" state (fight or flight) or in a parasympathetic or "safety" state (rest, digest, and connect). This process is called *coregulation,* a neuro-relational phenomenon that occurs when two or more brains and bodies are in sync. When this happens, our nervous system automatically shapes itself accordingly, often outside of our awareness. In concert with a mirroring process that is as-yet unclear to neuroscientists, our musculature and nerves take on the patterns of the other, and we experience in our bodies what the other is experiencing. Amazing!

We know that success in one-on-one psychotherapy is largely due to the healing component of coregulation. The therapist first develops a strong bond with the client. Then, with time, the therapist can help maintain client stability with their own stability—coregulation—enabling the client to inch closer to difficult emotional states, like buoying someone up while they're learning to float.

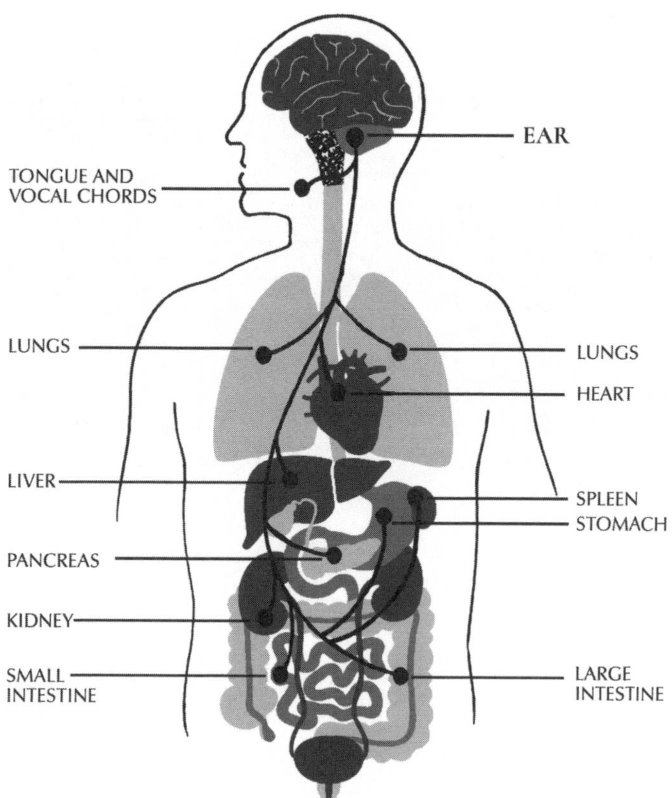

Figure 2.2: The vagus nerve

Here's an example of coregulation in practice. When I had my first encounter with Thich Nhat Hanh, at a large outdoor event, I was relatively inexperienced with meditation, and I was feeling skeptical. When it came time for walking meditation, Thay came down off the makeshift stage he'd been standing on and seemed to float past right in front of me. I remember feeling a jolt of energy, or as if I'd been shaken by a small earthquake. Later, I was able to understand that this earthquake I experienced was probably just my body coregulating with his. It would have been an abrupt jolt for my anxious, impatient, dysregulated body to attune to this peaceful person with a well-regulated nervous system effortlessly gliding over the grass before me. As we will learn in the following chapters, it is possible to befriend and balance our own nervous systems to access this kind of calm and clarity that comes with self-regulation.

Or consider another, dramatic story for a slightly different perspective on coregulation. (In order for you not to worry while reading it, know that no one was hurt and everything worked out in the end!)

Some years ago, I was hiking with a seventy-year-old friend in a tropical jungle, enjoying the fantastic vegetation and exotic birds in the canopy. We happened on some teenagers who were harvesting medicinal herbs and struck up a friendly conversation. Then, out of the blue, I felt on high alert, noting a sudden shift in how I perceived one of the teens. The experience was to see him split into two different people: one friendly, one dangerous, seemingly rising up out of the other. An instant later, I was down on the ground at knife point. Thinking back on that moment, I couldn't pinpoint any visual changes that would have clued me in to what was about to happen. Then, as much to my astonishment as the attack was the response of my seemingly frail elder. She began to yell and scream at the teens as they took off with my backpack; it was like she was shaking off my fear with her forcefulness.[3]

This is a good example of how coregulation can work in multiple ways. First, when I experienced this feeling of the boy splitting in two, I was picking up on subtle changes in his demeanor beyond my conscious awareness. Wanting to flee, but being restrained, I must have dissociated, creating a collage of images before my eyes of a few seconds of experience. What seemed at the time to be a quite mystical experience, now seems to make more sense to me through this notion of coregulation. Then, when my friend came to my rescue, my fear was neutralized the moment she became fierce—unconsciously, my energy rose up to match hers. My ability to coregulate with her had a healing effect, and I had no long-lasting traumatic symptoms after the experience.

NERVOUS SYSTEM RELEASE

When the nervous system prepares for action, a chemical and physiological preparedness takes place. When the action is performed, that chemical and mechanical input into the system is used up, and we relax. But sometimes the action cannot be fully completed, and so that tension stays in the body. We know, at least unconsciously, that this is the case—and so, at times, our bodies release that tension on purpose. For example, when we find ourselves crying at schmaltzy music or a sappy movie, the feelings arising aren't just from the music or movie, but from a release of accumulated tensions. Our bodies release tension in many ways: we cry, make loud sounds, experience shaking in our arms or legs, feel the rumblings of our digestive system. Rather than feeling worried or embarrassed when this happens, we can thank our body for being so smart!

Each morning as I get up to sit in meditation, I find that my mind is already raring to go, like a bucking bronco. I used to pull hard on those reins of attention in order to focus. But eventually, I learned to just sit there and watch the horse buck. When I did this, two things happened. First, eventually, my mental horse stopped bucking without me pulling on the reins. Second, I realized that not all of this bucking was coming from irritation or fear; some of it was actually a release of energy coming from joyful insight. When this happens, it reinforces my faith in just sitting, accepting whatever kind of pasture I seem to be in at the moment, rolling in the dirt and giving a nice whinny when the bell sounds.

EXERCISE 2.2: Your Portable Mini Nervous System

PURPOSE: Having a useful physical model of the nervous system ready at hand; helping build self-awareness of the state of the nervous system
DURATION: 1 minute
FREQUENCY: Whenever a reminder is helpful

Here is an exercise I love doing with children; it seems so mischievous! Hold out your arm in front of you and imagine the shape of your body on it, with your forearm representing your trunk and its internal organs. With washable markers, draw in the heart, lungs, stomach, intestines, kidneys and adrenals, and if you like, genital organs. These are the organs regulated by your autonomic nervous system or survival brain. Next, on your wide-open palm, draw a face that looks energized: big eyes, open mouth, lots of feeling. The five fingers wide open represent how we feel when we sense danger or excitement. The parts of the limbic system that are in charge here—the amygdala and hippocampus—are located deep inside the brain. Fold your thumb across your palm to represent this system.

Next, curl your fingers down over your palm to form a gentle fist. Here is the thinking brain or prefrontal cortex. You can draw a nice smiley face on your fingers.

Review what we just learned. Gently caress your forearm with your other hand, starting from the top of the fist and moving down, imagining that you are soothing this whole nervous system. This represents all the ways we will learn to nourish and rebalance our nervous system so that we can be fully present to our lives.

Now, open your palm wide; you can see how that calm smiley face, representing the prefrontal cortex, all but disappears when the limbic system is wide awake and on high alert. Once again, caress each finger back into place, and then move your hand right down through all the organs. This exercise can remind us that we have ways built right into our nervous system to "keep it all together" inside our bodies.

THE DEVELOPMENT OF THE NERVOUS SYSTEM

Even before we are born, our survival brain is almost in full swing, ready to activate when we take our first breath. In contrast, the amount of gray matter making up the thinking brain is minimal, and the strength of the emotional brain is dependent on how responsive and capable our caregivers are in keeping our basic needs met: safety, health, comfort, nourishment, rest, and human connection. In this way, both the thinking brain and the limbic system, with their billions of neurons, are pure potential at birth, waiting for stimuli to shape them.

Since babies don't have a wealth of experience for the limbic system to draw on, they may be disposed to be cautious of (or simply reject) anything new. Picture the classic scenario of a baby making a face and fussing after having their first bite of baby food. Much will depend on the ability of the caregivers to provide positive coregulation during these initial experiences of newness, setting the pattern for receptivity to the new. This is why we introduce babies slowly to new things, like solid foods, strangers, animals, sounds, baths: we need to respect their preferences and gently persist in offering newness calmly and with happiness.

The human brain is much like a forest floor in the wilderness. When we first encounter an untouched forest floor, we have to forge through grasses and around obstacles, which makes our progress slow and tentative. But if we tread the same route over and over, the grasses pack down, the way around obstacles becomes clear, and a path begins to form. Over time, the path becomes easier to follow, and the travel time is quicker.

The same is true of our nervous system and how it forms neural pathways. Each part of our brain is strengthened or weakened by the amount that it is stimulated or activated. The pathways that connect stimulus to response also become stronger depending on the amount of use they get—as the saying goes, "What fires together, wires together." When we do something that has a particular impact on us, the more we do it, the stronger the impact becomes.

This is true for both pleasant and unpleasant experiences. For example, simply recalling a special moment with a loved one can evoke a feeling of care and well-being—and your ability to feel this way will be strengthened each time you bring back this memory. On the other hand, if, as a child, you are frightened by a mouse you find in the cupboard, and subsequent encounters with mice are also met with screams rather than positive responses, every reaction will create a deeper sense that mice are frightening. Repetition of stimulus and response together can predictably create a stronger and quicker response; this is called a *conditioned response* or *conditioning*. Conversely, having a different reaction to the stimulus begins to weaken that habitual response. For example, imagine that someone introduces you to a pet mouse that you come to think of as cute and cuddly rather than scary; the more this sense of "cute and cuddly" is reinforced, the less likely it is that you will react with fear when seeing mice generally. This ability to strengthen or weaken a conditioned response can be transformative when used skillfully!

Understanding Stress and Trauma

If we're planning to go on a long journey, we know we're bound to encounter stormy weather from time to time. It is helpful to know the signs of a storm coming so we have time to seek appropriate shelter. On our individual journeys through life, big storms arrive in the form of stress and trauma—our biological inheritance since the time we were mere lizards. Let's pick these two concepts apart.

Stress is a response of our body/mind to situations that require attention or action.[4] *Stressors* are the circumstances, internal as well as external, to which the body is responding. Although we may not have as much control as we'd like over external circumstances, we actually have quite a bit of control over the level of stress we experience in relation to what we are encountering. Knowing the signs of stress and how we can regulate our own nervous system accordingly is one big key to a sense of well-being. In fact, experiencing stress and learning to manage it is *core* to our sense of well-being! Without stress, we wouldn't learn how to be resilient when faced with the inevitable trials of life. Without stress, we wouldn't learn how to explore new adventures of body and mind.

Beneficial stress can come from everyday activities; this kind of stress is necessary to mobilize ourselves, focus, and rise to the occasion. When stress hormone levels are mildly elevated, quickening the heart and lungs, it increases our ability to focus or to exert a little extra energy to get the job done. This may make us feel a bit tired, but we will recover when the stress subsides. In this way we build self-confidence, creativity, determination, and a variety of beneficial characteristics.

Where I live in rural northern California, our spring times are lush and replete with carpets of wildflowers and native grasses. The moss springs up after the rains of winter, and the blue oaks leaf out with a pink fuzziness. As the grasses reach knee height, I know it is time to get out the weed whacker so I can cut them back, to make sure I can see any critters (read: snakes) crossing the paths I walk on. I feel grateful that I can still handle the machine; the grass looks nice when it is cut; and the chickens really love the cuttings. It is hard work followed by a welcome nap. That's beneficial stress.

Tolerable stress is when the body's emergency brain is activated to a greater degree than beneficial stress; this happens when we perceive a significant threat to bodily, emotional, or spiritual well-being. (Tolerable stress can also result from beneficial or normal stress that lasts too long.) We feel tolerable stress in our bodies as we ready for physical or mental fight or flight. Our assessment of situations as posing a threat depends on a lot of factors, including our history of being in similar situations, whether the situation is time-limited, and whether there is sufficient interpersonal support there for us. With tolerable stress, the nervous system response subsides when the perceived threat passes.

As June approaches, I can feel the tension building: wildfire season is upon us. We've yet to have any wildfires in our neighborhood, but the close call we had last summer just down the road is weighing on my mind. I'm still doing the same work as in the spring, but I feel a bit of hypervigilance when I see folks walking along the road smoking—a fire hazard! This is tolerable stress as my body recognizes a potential threat that I'll have to respond to. Mostly, I can put this all out of my mind when the person disappears from view. This year, the neighbors have formed a fire-safe council. This sense of connection, that we've got each other's backs, has helped a lot to keep me calm when I sense tension rising.

Toxic stress or *traumatic stress* occurs when a perceived threat is extreme and frequent or long lasting; the nervous system is majorly activated and stays highly activated even when the threat passes. This kind of response is automatic, out of conscious control. In this situation, our body's emergency response system just can't shut off. Some examples of toxic stress are abuse (physical, emotional, sexual), chronic neglect, and exposure to violence, poverty, racism, or war.

By September, everything I see out our window reminds me of potential wildfire. Our irreplaceable keepsakes are now stored at our daughter's house, and the "grab-and-go" bags of extra medicines, clothes, and emergency supplies hanging at the front door are reminders of the now ever-present threat. We never leave the house without our dog. We have walkie talkies connected to the network of neighbors. My blood pressure is about twenty points higher on the average. This is potentially toxic stress: the longer I perceive this threat of imminent, disastrous wildfire, the more damage it can potentially do to my body.

Were the body to continue at such a level of activation, serious if not fatal damage could ensue: a complete blowout of the cardiovascular, respiratory, or emotional system. Fortunately—miraculously—our nervous system has a circuit breaker (the vagus nerve) that shuts down the system completely when it is overloaded. This is what we typically think of as a *trauma response* to lasting toxic stress. We may physically collapse, pass out, and/or dissociate for a period of time. We might walk around in a fog, or feel out of touch with our bodies. This shutdown can be total or partial, depending on the severity of our need to turn down our over-activated nervous system. We might think there is something wrong with us, but it is actually just the opposite: we're operating just as we've evolved to do.

It seems debatable as to whether our hunter-gatherer ancestors suffered extreme stress and trauma. We don't know if they, like the gazelle, could just get up and shake off a wild animal attack (extreme stress) without lasting impact (trauma). Still, it is clear that our common nervous system has evolved to rebalance itself after intermittent and occasional stress. What is also clear is that this same nervous system has not yet evolved to be able to handle the repeated or sustained overload many of us experience in our human-shaped world; the trauma response that may have at one point saved our lives can become a chronic situation, reactivated again and again. That said, with our current understanding, there are a multitude of things we can do to mitigate the traumatic effects of too much or too little for too long.

THE WINDOW OF MINDFUL OPPORTUNITY

Below is a diagram of the *window of tolerance*, a term coined by neuroscientist and psychiatrist Daniel Siegel. It is a schematic of the energy arousal levels of our nervous system. The two parallel lines show the upper and lower limits of this window of tolerance. In between, the level of activation of our nervous system is balanced enough to allow the nervous system to integrate all its functions well. The cortex and limbic systems and the vagus nerves are working in harmony to inform us of our inner and outer environments so that we can respond appropriately. This gives us a sense of well-being; we feel confident enough to handle everyday challenges and to notice the large and small delights that come and go.

Within the window, we experience differing levels of energy and potential for learning and growing. Within these limits we

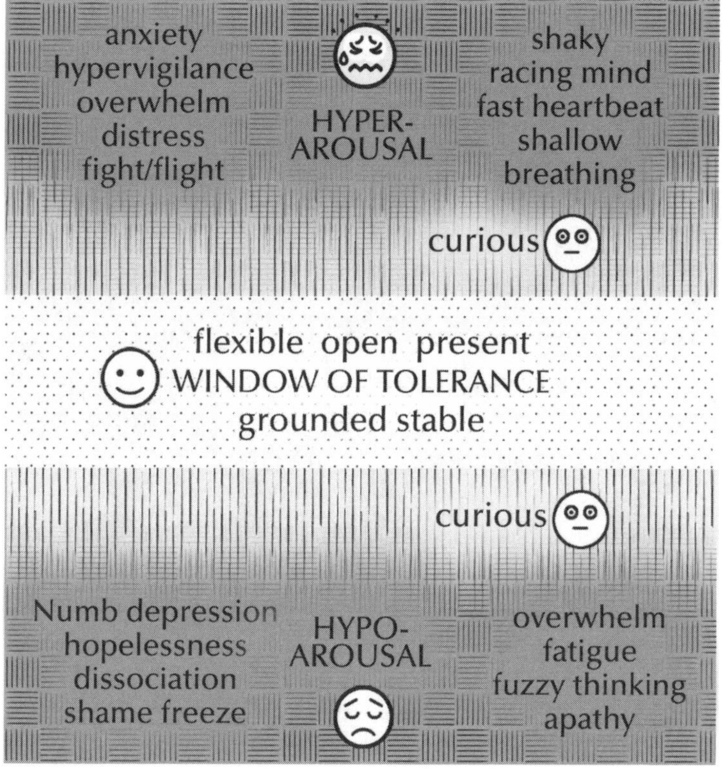

Figure 2.3: The window of tolerance/the window of mindful opportunity

experience the full range of emotional states: glad, sad, mad, afraid, surprised. The very center of the zone is where we feel the most comfortable and at ease. As we move upward toward activation of the sympathetic nervous system—the one that mobilizes us for discernment and action—we feel more on alert, ready for response. In the event that tolerable stressors occur, the limbic system kicks into place to automatically pop us out of the window, mobilizing us against a real or perceived threat. Initially, we may find our heart racing, we breathe faster, and hormones race through our blood to prepare us for fight or flight. Our minds may also race. We might feel unable to control our voice or arms or legs, as they seem to have minds of their own. This mechanism has been the one throughout the millennia to account for our ancestors' survival, right up to this very moment.

If this hypersympathetic response puts out too much of the stress hormones (cortisol and adrenaline) for the body to tolerate, the parasympathetic system can kick into high gear to counterbalance, and we get popped out of the lower frame of the window. Here, we might feel frozen; our mind may be quite foggy, we may feel very tired, or not connected to our bodies at all. We may literally pass out, or feel like a deer in the headlights. Feelings of hopelessness and despair may set in, and we feel immobilized and unable to respond. This, too, is a protective mechanism so we don't exceed our bodily capacities and actually do irreparable damage to our various systems. While it may feel horrible, it may also, literally, be a lifesaver.

It is in the areas approaching the upper and lower limits where curiosity becomes key. Near the limits of balance, we can see how our suffering is made and learn how to unmake it. These are the learning areas, the challenge areas, the areas in which we have the chance to grow and stretch that window of tolerance. With each successful stretch, we become more resilient, more able to find stability while stressed.

Another way to look at the window of tolerance is as a zone of concentric spaces nesting within each other.

The circle in the center of this diagram represents a "comfort zone," which doesn't really appear clearly on the first window of tolerance diagram. This center is a place of potential rest and recuperation. It is where we can return to restore a depleted nervous system when we need to or create added reserves to use in the future. The next concentric circle is an area of curiosity, learning, and challenge. The outer zone is a lifesaving arena at times, but it can be risky if we get stuck there for a while, caught up in dysregulated chaos.

The value of this diagram for me is in how it accentuates the pros and cons of the comfort zone. Although rest and restoration

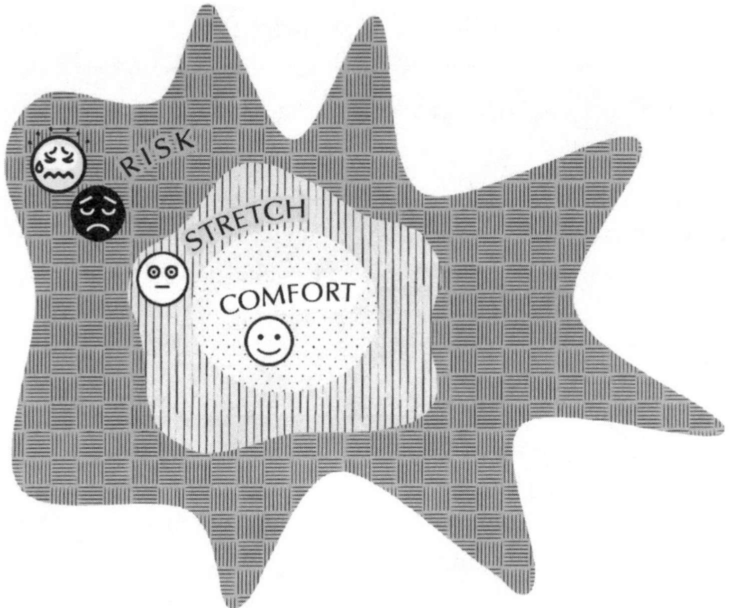

Figure 2.4: Concentric spaces of comfort and risk

are vital in maintaining a regulated and optimally functional nervous system, too much hanging out in the comfort zone is like never getting any exercise. We need to occasionally stretch and learn! If we are well rested and restored, yet remain in that comfort zone, we can get weaker rather than stronger; living in a smaller and smaller bubble leads to a lack of resilience. Over time, options for comfort become fewer and fewer, like Goldilocks always looking for what's "just right," or the princess who can't sleep if there's even a tiny pea under her mattress.

The concept of this window has been acknowledged and adopted by several healing modalities, which sometimes give it a different name. For example, in the Community Resiliency Model of the Trauma Resource Institute, it is named the Resilient Zone, or the OK Zone when working with children. Each name serves to highlight the purpose of its specific use. For our purposes in this book, I suggest we also consider an alternate

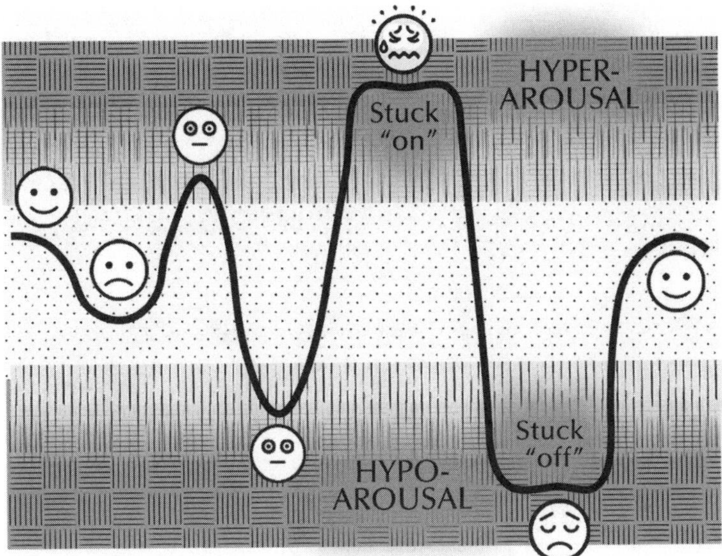

Figure 2.5: Window of mindful opportunity over time

name for the window of tolerance: *the window of mindful opportunity*. This puts the emphasis on *opportunity* rather than forbearance. Rather than think that we must grin and bear this process of *tolerating* things as they are, here we focus on the opportunities we encounter to learn and stretch. It's not that we *have* to explore our limits, but rather that we *get* to explore. Do you feel a difference inside between *have to* and *get to*?

Mindfulness is the optimal balance of attention and awareness that can best illuminate reality. It is a light that the contemplative person shines upon their inner experience in order to see things as they are. But the opportunity to truly learn, to expand our ability to see reality, is only available inside this window. Once we slip over the edge into the high or low areas, we no longer can maintain mindfulness. The automatic fight-or-flight or shut down responses that kick in when we get outside of the window skew our perceptions; the body is swept up into automatic action or inaction, and our thinking brain shuts down.

When stress is sustained without time to recuperate, the nervous system may get stuck into continually mobilizing the fight-or-flight response even when the threat has passed. At this time the nervous system may begin to hyperfocus on what's wrong in a way that creates constant misperception, a skewed balance of what we are encountering. This is what we commonly call *trauma*.

SUFFERING AND TRAUMA

Trauma is not what happens to us; it is what happens *inside* us as a result of what happened to us. (This includes when bad things happen that shouldn't and when good things that should happen don't.) Stress events leave a memory in our nervous system of what to do under threat, and when something triggers this memory, our limbic system can be automatically set

Figure 2.6: Signs of trauma

into action. Trauma is when the body goes into this automatic reaction even when there actually is no dire threat.

For the purposes of this book, it is important to acknowledge the difference between suffering and trauma: trauma is a kind of suffering, but not all suffering is trauma. Going back to our first diagram of the window of tolerance, think of what the difference might be between experiencing stress and suffering within the window and outside it. Within the window, suffering is manageable. We are not carried away by the limbic system's automatic responses; we can self-regulate and hold our impulses at bay, noticing the way our body feels, what our perceptions are, the thoughts and emotions that arise. As we do this, we settle, and the former habit energy is not reinforced. In contrast, with trauma, our system remains dysregulated.

Trauma happens when big or relentless stress and suffering befall someone who does not have the right conditions to deal with it, such as healthy coping strategies, supportive friends or family, or institutional help. Not all traumas are debilitating: some have a mild, ongoing impact on a life, whereas others pose more formidable challenges. Some traumas are our responsibility as individuals to heal, while others really require collective healing—racism, classism, homophobia, xenophobia, for example. (Is there anyone who doesn't need some collective awakening and healing from the shortsighted fallout of our current human limitations and development?)

Simple trauma describes the nervous system dysregulation that may result from a single, circumscribed traumatic event: an assault, an acute illness, a natural disaster. Its signs and symptoms are readily recognized. For example, someone who is attacked by a dog might continue to feel a persistent underlying fear—body tension, high blood pressure, irritability—even when there are no dogs around.

Complex trauma involves multiple traumatic-response-inducing events, or stressors that are experienced repeatedly over an extended period of time. The incidents may be large or small, but over time, they wear down the nervous system. Imagine, for instance, that you have grown up with the constant threat from a vicious dog next door; even if you have never been bitten by the dog, the cumulative impact of the fear it provokes can cause a lingering nervous system response in your body that is similar to a simple trauma response.

Historical trauma refers to what happens in the nervous system when toxic stressors are shared by a group of people within a society, or even by an entire community, ethnic, or national group. Historical trauma has three characteristics: widespread effects, collective suffering, and malicious intent on the part of the perpetrators. For example, if you are part of a social or ethnic group that has regularly had dogs used to control, punish, and otherwise terrify and oppress you or your ancestors, you might find that your sympathetic nervous system goes into overdrive when you encounter a barking dog, even if you have not personally had a bad experience with one. This kind of trauma frequently goes unrecognized even though it may impact large groups of people.

Intergenerational trauma (sometimes referred to as *trans-* or *multigenerational trauma*) is defined as trauma that gets passed down from those who directly experience an incident to subsequent generations. Intergenerational trauma may begin with a single traumatic event that affects an individual, multiple family members, or a community. Without support to heal these original traumas, the affected person or group may develop problematic coping mechanisms that they may pass on to future generations without being aware of it. For example, any of the previous examples of a trauma response to dogs may result in you teaching your children—consciously or not—to avoid dogs, even if your children may not understand where the fear comes from or why they should feel fear.[5]

Although this next story does not describe a traumatic event, it does capture how easily and unconsciously we can pass things from one generation to the next.

Three generations of a family are in the kitchen preparing a holiday meal. The youngest is putting the roast into the roasting pan when they are stopped by their parent, who warns them that first, they must cut the end off. When the younger child asks why, the parent says, "That's how we've always done it" and has to admit ignorance of the underlying reason or custom. The two of them then turn to their elders for an explanation and find out that the only reason for this "traditional" preparation method is simply that the pan the grandparents used to have, three generations ago, was too small to accommodate the whole thing.

So it is with intergenerational trauma: we learn behaviors and reactions easily and often do not question where they come from. In many cases, this is because, unlike a smaller roasting pan, the deeper, traumatic reasons rooted in our family history cannot be talked about, because those who suffered it do not have the skills to handle the overwhelming feelings that could surface. Those who *do* pass on the stories may become even more traumatized by repeating them, causing their wounding to become compounded.

SIGNS AND SYMPTOMS OF TRAUMA

If we look at the signs and symptoms of stress and then imagine them on steroids, those become the signs and symptoms of trauma. We can find these symptoms in our body as well as in the way we perceive things, think, and act. When we find ourselves overreacting to interactions and events in our daily lives, when we cope in ways that bring us and those around us suffering, chances are we are holding some trauma in our bodies. Depending on many factors, trauma might cause a person to go into fight-or-flight mode or begin to shut down from overwhelm.

ARENA OF IMPACT	FIGHT-OR-FLIGHT MODE	SHUT-DOWN MODE
Body/sensation	Physical pain Rapid heartbeat High blood pressure Breathing problems Tight muscles Insomnia	Numbness Fatigue Over-sleeping Weakness Loss of appetite Digestion irregularities
Emotions	Anxiety or panic Fear Anger Avoidance Irritability Guilt and shame Mood swings	Apathy Grief and sadness Feelings of disconnection Avoidance Hopelessness Guilt and shame
Thinking	Racing or intrusive thoughts Nightmares Paranoia Forgetfulness Homicidal thoughts Distorted thinking Lack of concentration	Confusion and slow thinking Nightmares Dissociation Forgetfulness Suicidal thoughts Distorted thinking Lack of motivation

This is not a definitive list, nor are the categories quite this distinct. Nevertheless, this chart may help us notice what is going on with ourselves or our loved ones—or for that matter, even strangers.

Additionally, another trauma response may be more difficult to notice than fight or flight and freeze/shut down: fawning. *Fawning* is an unconscious and automatic response of attempting to please someone—not out of caring or compassion, but rather out of self-protection. Because this can appear to be a more conscious response to perceived danger, it is more difficult to identify and address as an automatic trauma response. Signs of fawning include habitual apology, self-blame, lack of authenticity, and false enthusiasm. Fawning is a limbic response that appears to have both hyper- and hypoarousal characteristics, including both heightened activity to placate others and a numbing of one's own awareness of body, emotions, and personal needs. Seen through a lens of vagal response, we might think about it as being more aware of social cues while simultaneously being in a shut-down mode, which leads to a disconnection from the body. Fawning is common in cases of complex trauma, such as when someone has grown up in situations that involve drug/alcohol addiction or domestic violence.

Remember that during considerable stress, the hippocampus, the seat of what we think of as memory, is compromised, so explicit memories (vivid stories) may not form or be accessible. What is stored during toxic stress are *implicit* memories: the body remembers the way it responded, but you may not remember why or what the situation was that led you to learn this lesson. The surfacing of the memory is in the form of action rather than thought or story.

For example, when you are involved in an accident, the associated sense impressions—whether they are sights, sounds, smells, sensations, tastes, or thoughts—are stored along with the way your body automatically prepared to protect itself. If you were to encounter one of those sense impressions, it might automatically set off a response like the one you originally experienced that was intended to help you be safe, along with whatever internal mental states were present at that time.

Take, for example, the situation of a child walking by a fenced yard on a beautiful spring day, a sweet scent of honeysuckle in the air. They notice a dog inside the fence, put their hand out to pet the dog, and are met with growling and the dog baring its teeth. The child is immediately frightened and runs back home. Fast-forward five years; the child is now a teenager. They are walking somewhere when suddenly they feel very frightened and automatically decide to drop their plans and hurry back home. They are bewildered by this occurrence and feel embarrassed; they have no idea what came over them to cause such a reaction. In fact, what triggered the feeling was the same sweet smell in the air they unconsciously associated with the growling dog from years before.

POST-TRAUMATIC GROWTH

Toxic stress is seemingly ubiquitous in the world today: does that mean everyone ends up with damaging trauma? No! A good many people are able to get up after an extreme experience and, in a short while, shake it off without lasting impacts. Even those who do experience lasting impacts may find that what they have gone through has, in fact, deepened their resilience, their sense of inner strength.

The Japanese have an art called *kintsugi*, where broken ceramic is mended with gold to produce a new vessel of even greater beauty. Similarly, when we suffer and then overcome that suffering, we sometimes develop even greater confidence, resilience, joy, and creativity than we had in the past. This can be described as *post-traumatic growth*: feeling a greater sense of aliveness, more gratitude for the supportive elements in our lives, and a lessening of fear. When we begin to overcome these difficulties, a growing sense of freedom and faith comes with it—a feeling that we can handle whatever life brings us. These stories of overcoming can become a resource for us when we are stuck in doubt or despair, and they can bring us back to our core resilience.

Many revered Buddhist teachers are the product of post-traumatic growth of some kind: journeys through the hell realms that led them to fearlessness on their paths and an unshakeable determination to pass on the fruits of their trauma healings to others. The Venerable Thich Phuoc Tien is a touching example.

Tien came to the monastic life after witnessing immeasurable death and destruction during the Vietnam War. He saw the impermanence of life so clearly all around him: anything could be killed by a bomb or a stray bullet in an instant. Indeed, his own father was killed in front of his eyes, caught in the crossfire, an accident of war. The pain of his father's death was great, but with time, it began to subside and heal, in part because of the support he felt from his monastic life. In this way, he found he was also able to let other, ordinary types of suffering slip away. From this stark beginning, all forms of suffering seemed to be put into perspective for him.

We must remember that what has happened in the past has happened. That is not going to change. What *can* change is the impact that those events have on our present moment. Healing from trauma means that when difficulties arise in our daily life, our body does not automatically go into an automatic sympathetic response; it doesn't get hijacked by the emotional brain. Through our neuro-informed Buddhist practice, we can shift the response to the thinking brain so that we cultivate mindful responsiveness. Things that used to activate the nervous system no longer cause the same degree of dysregulation. Little by little, the grip of the trauma, known or unknown, begins to dissolve.

We can begin to heal from past traumas by paying attention to when they show up in the present: in the habits we wish to change, in reactivity that seems uncalled for, in relationships we'd like to improve, in fears we wish to overcome. In order to heal, it isn't necessary to relive the past or even know where these difficulties came from in the first place. Instead, it is more valuable to learn how to work with our trauma responses, here and now, and use them as doors to healing. The key to exploring what is on the other side of the door is your preparedness to step out into the storm that awaits you there. In Chapters 4 and 5, we'll discover how our practice can aid in this kind of healing.

In the late nineties, I was living in the highlands of southern Mexico. Shortly after moving there, I began having strange spells in my sleep. I would wake suddenly, feeling extremely agitated, and shaking with out-of-control blood pressure. I was away from anything familiar to me, and I had little medical or emotional support—it was quite frightening. During this time, my nervous system was completely dysregulated, close to the upper line of my window of tolerance. Although daily life kept my mind busy, the nights were challenging, and going to sleep became an act of faith; I'd cross my fingers hoping that I would make it through the night alive.

What got me through these nightly attacks was not figuring out the cause of these panic attacks—it was simply accepting the feeling that I might not make it through the night. Without even knowing the trigger for this dysregulated response, I was able to contain it within that window of mindful opportunity, observe it as it was, and eventually become less activated in its presence. This is the process of healing: when an automatic response no longer gets you stuck outside that window. I found a willingness to just *be* with the pure sensations; it was like giving in to the experience of a rollercoaster. Eventually I discovered something in those sensations that led to the way out. Since then, I have never had a morning where I don't wake up grateful to be alive; I have more confidence in my insights into my own health needs, I have a greater understanding of and compassion toward folks who have health challenges, and I have a heightened appreciation for life itself.

In this next exercise, we explore how we experience resilience in our mind and body. However, please keep in mind that this exercise—like many other exercises in this book—has the potential to produce tension or restimulate trauma. Please make sure to assess your capacity in the moment before trying them. If you do venture a try, start small: remember, though, that if it is *too* small, you won't experience much of the point. So, like Goldilocks, try to pick a practice that is not too hard, and not too soft—one that is just right for you.

EXERCISE 2.3: Overcoming Difficulty, Recognizing Resilience

PURPOSE: Experiencing your own resilience
DURATION: 15 minutes
FREQUENCY: Open

Settle yourself in a place where you will not be disturbed, and relax, noticing any signs of calm. When you feel ready, bring to mind a significant difficulty you have had that you feel that you've overcome to a large extent. This doesn't mean that you have completely gotten past it—but it should be something that you know, deep down, you've made powerful headway in overcoming.

Notice how your body responds to this memory. If thinking about this difficulty brings a sense of well-being, then you're on the right track. If you feel upset, then set this memory aside for now, and find some other example.

When you think of yourself before and after this difficult time in your life, and how you have worked to overcome it, what positive impacts do you see? Here are some ideas:

- Personal strength
- Improved relationships
- Future possibilities
- Appreciation for life
- Philosophical or spiritual changes

As you gain perspective on how this difficulty impacted you, notice what happens inside. If the feeling is pleasant, savor it for a few breaths.

Note: For our purposes in this book, savoring means paying careful attention to pleasant (or neutral) sensations for at least 20 to 30 seconds so that the neural pathways of the pleasant sensations have time to develop and strengthen.

3

Rules of the Road

Essential Teachings for a Neuro-Informed Buddhist Path

Back in the fifth century BCE, so the story goes, there was a prince who led a very sheltered life. One day, eager to get out into the world, he snuck out of his palace, only to encounter the shocking realities of life: sickness, old age, and death. Upset at his discovery of the anguish and suffering people were enduring, he became determined to find a way to end it.

This prince was a brilliant neuroscientist, and he set out in the laboratory of his mind to discover what suffering was, how it was made, and just how it could be ended. Basically, he set out to restructure his brain so that the areas that produced a calm presence could become dominant over those that created skewed perception. In fact, from all reports, he succeeded—just about nothing could rattle him! He was able to develop a nonjudgmental awareness and sense of calm so strong that he could see things as they actually were in the present moment, in the *now* in which they were fully alive. He was able to see how suffering developed, and he was able to develop the inner tools and processes to prevent or transform those sufferings. Of course, stressors in and around 500 BCE were a bit different than what we face today, but the nervous system was pretty much the same. With today's advances in neuroimaging, scientists are just starting to explore the mysteries that the Buddha was able to uncover in just a few short years—and with a very low budget, I might add!

Let's see how all the science we learned in Chapter 2 can be found tucked into the teachings, going back some 2,600 years, as the Buddha conducted his active search for understanding and overcoming the great suffering of his time. He found his way out. His way out was *in*.

The Essential Teachings: The Way Out Is In

The Buddha himself proclaimed to be *awake*, or as we might see it, immune to being bumped out of the window of mindful opportunity. But he never claimed to be anything other than a human. In fact, he made this a big point of his teachings: he was human, not a god, and he managed to figure it out—so you can, too. His teachings, practical and poetic guides to how we can follow in his footsteps, are called the *Dharma*. The community that practices his teachings is referred to as the *sangha*, which is just folks with a keen interest in mutually supporting each other to follow those mind experiments.

Together, the Buddha, Dharma, and sangha are referred to as the *Three Jewels*—the riches that come from the aspiration to live in harmony and with awareness. They are like lab partners in discovering the basics of how a human being functions. Together with ethical guidelines, these Three Jewels comprise a philosophical, experimental, and experiential path from which to craft a life. As practiced in the Plum Village tradition, Buddhism is not necessarily a religion. In fact, for those who have grown up in other root traditions, such as Indigenous paths, Islam, Hinduism, Sikhism, Judaism, Animism, or Christianity, it is recommended to incorporate the practices into your own religious tradition, or have them stand side by side (this is known as *double belonging*).

The Buddha got started in his investigation by discovering how to watch his mind. The tool he used is called *mindfulness*, the building blocks of which every human possesses in the forms of our limbic system, vagus nerve, prefrontal cortex, and some other areas of the brain with fancy names. The experiment he set out to conduct was to observe the mind in every possible moment and situation. Today these experiments are what are referred to as *practices*—exercises repeated numerous times to shape a nervous system and consciousness that operates optimally, to produce as peaceful and as fully engaged a life as we can.

This process of inquiry is called *mindfulness meditation*. It has three basic aims: to calm the mind so that the default setting of the brain is on "safety"; to continuously reregulate the nervous system to maintain that calm; and to look deeply, so as to see the nature of all phenomena as they truly are, in the here and now. In the process, we actually can strengthen or relax the various networks of our brain, fine-tuning them so that the higher functions can override the lower functions, taking us to a higher level than we generally are able to rise to.

EXERCISE 3.1:
Comparing Attention and Awareness

DURATION: 2 minutes

FREQUENCY: Once

PURPOSE: Understanding components of mindfulness

Cautionary note: While this exercise is an invitation to touch something very small, it is always possible that even this light touch may be more dysregulating than you might have imagined. In that event, take a break and return to another small issue later, or skip this exercise until after you've read the following chapters, where you will be given very specific tools to navigate this exercise. Put your entire attention on this part of your body, just for 30 seconds, to get a feel of very pointed attention. Now let go of that one pointed attention. Relax. Next, gently allow that same part of your body to come into your awareness and sense into this experience. What do you notice?

For me the two experiences feel quite different. Attention seems to require more of my energy; my whole body feels as if it is scrunching up tighter, like when I'm squeezing out a sponge, and as if every bit of me is pointing toward the object. Awareness is more like that scrunched-up sponge being released in a bowl of water where it can absorb everything. I feel my entire body relax. Mindfulness is a middle way between these two types of focus: being present, with just the right proportions of attention and awareness.

Each of these elements, attention and awareness, has its benefits and drawbacks. Too much attention can be exhausting; too much awareness can make us dreamily carried away or drowsy.

Armed with his powerful tool of mindfulness, and the resulting acute ability to see things objectively, the Buddha set out to help others discover these truths. He was not teaching the content so much as the process, to help people learn for themselves how to get beyond the normal skewed human range of experience.

Please note—mindfulness alone is just a tool; it does not lead you to the end of suffering all on its own. How you use this tool, what motivates you to pick it up, and what you are trying to accomplish with it are all significant factors. You can craft a mindfulness practice in the service of overcoming suffering, but you could also craft it to maximize individual happiness and ignore consequences of those actions on others, society, or the environment. (The same can be said for following the path of science!) The Buddha's intention was to help *all beings* overcome suffering and to attain deep, long-lasting contentment. It was not singularly applied to get a competitive edge over someone or something else. His teachings are all aimed to benefit all of life. How he focused, and what he did with that focus, is called *right mindfulness,* as we shall see in the following pages. Right mindfulness is a vital process that cannot be separated from the use for which it was intended: the end of suffering and increasing joy in life itself, both individually and collectively.

Neither mindfulness alone nor science alone can describe Buddhist practice. Buddhist practice cannot be reduced to a mechanical application of attention. What this practice offers is a way of life that is, first, grounded in an ethical system that provides a container, a purpose, and a vision of the rightful place and purpose of human embodiment. This noble vision is then supported by a step-by-step process (though it isn't actually linear) in the form of the Four Noble Truths and the Noble Eightfold Path. From here come all the specific teachings that support understanding and access to walking on that path.

What follows is a glimpse into how neuroscience and neuro-informed mindfulness explanations interact with the following basic teachings of Buddhism:

The Four Noble Truths

The Noble Eightfold Path

The Historical and Ultimate Dimensions

The Five Mindfulness Trainings

The Five Skandhas

The Four Nutriments

The Four Noble Truths: A Guide for Overcoming Life's Challenges

The Four Noble Truths are the most fundamental teaching of the Buddha. This concept was meant to inspire the seeker to see for themselves how suffering or ill-being is fundamental to the human experience of life. With direct experience, one would then be able to find a path out of that suffering, transcending the mundane or historical dimension, and transforming into a fundamentally different kind of human being: a completely free person, free of the traps of conditioning and awakened to the reality of life. Here are the four elements necessary for this liberation:

Recognize suffering. Life is full of suffering, which gives rise to trauma and other states of ill-being. If you know you are suffering, the good news here is that you are not broken, bad, or beyond fixing—you are normal! Lay down your shame and guilt. Suffering is a normal part of life, and accepting this is necessary to heal our individual and collective wounding.

Recognize the causes of suffering. Suffering arises because of specific causes and conditions. Everyone has basic human needs that, when not met, create a potential threat to physical, mental, social, or spiritual survival: these include food, shelter, belonging, nurturing, connection, and meaning. Through understanding our nervous system—how it operates, its messages, and its limitations—we will be able to see more clearly the mechanics of how suffering arises when our needs are not met.

Know that the cessation of suffering is possible. It is possible to overcome many of the habits that lead to ill-being or suffering, to transform and heal. Knowing why we are like we are, from a scientific perspective—how habits are developed, neural pathways reinforced or extinguished—leads to a method of undoing some of what ails us. This alone is cause for happiness—the possibility of some relief! When we have more capacity to regulate our nervous system, we can choose whether to be with suffering or well-being in each moment. Both exist, and both are necessary.

Follow the Noble Eightfold Path to transcend suffering. The path out of suffering is by following a practice known as the Noble Eightfold Path (also known as the Buddhist Eightfold Path and the Eightfold Path). The eight elements of this path show us how to change habitual responses that cause suffering—those automatic responses that have largely outlived their usefulness. The Eightfold Path is a journey for life, going beyond simple relief to provide genuine well-being on both an individual and collective level.

A WORD ON FREEDOM: MUNDANE, PRACTICAL, TRANSCENDENT

The concept of freedom is a complex one. In the US, freedom is often referred to as a list of rights: the right to choose our religion, to say whatever we want, to assert ourselves as individuals. But this kind of "freedom" actually may cause suffering when we practice it without considering how our choices affect others. This is not the kind of freedom offered by Buddhism. *Freedom,* in the Buddhist sense, is the ability to make wise choices that undo habits of body, speech, and mind, that reduce suffering, and that make us aware of the ten thousand things that delight us. Freedom is being alive to each moment.

When adopting a neuro-informed perspective, we talk about being *in choice,* meaning we have the freedom to choose for ourselves just how to practice. Choice is conscious action: we are conscious of the underlying feelings, perceptions, and motivations that relieve suffering and promote joy. In mindfulness, we also know that our choices affect others; our happiness cannot be separate from the happiness of others. If our actions create suffering for parts of the web of being that surrounds us, it ultimately creates suffering for ourselves. This is not freedom.

Freedom from habits that cause suffering requires awareness of how we make our suffering. In neuroscience terms, freedom is knowing how to prevent our nervous system from being hijacked. It is expanding our window of tolerance or mindful opportunity—fostering an ease with mild discomfort in order to see reality ever more accurately.

The Noble Eightfold Path

The Noble Eightfold Path describes the eight essential elements of Buddhist practice: right view; right thinking or intention;

right speech; right action; right livelihood; right effort or diligence; right mindfulness; and right concentration. This path can be pictured as a wheel, where the eight elements are each connected to the center by spokes—though it is difficult to talk about any of them as separate because each influences the other. This path is cyclical as well; each trip around the wheel carries us deeper and deeper into the realities of life.

Right view is a process of educating ourselves to understand the nature of suffering and how the universe operates. It incorporates our basic understanding of the nervous system, both its structure and function, as well as our own felt experience.

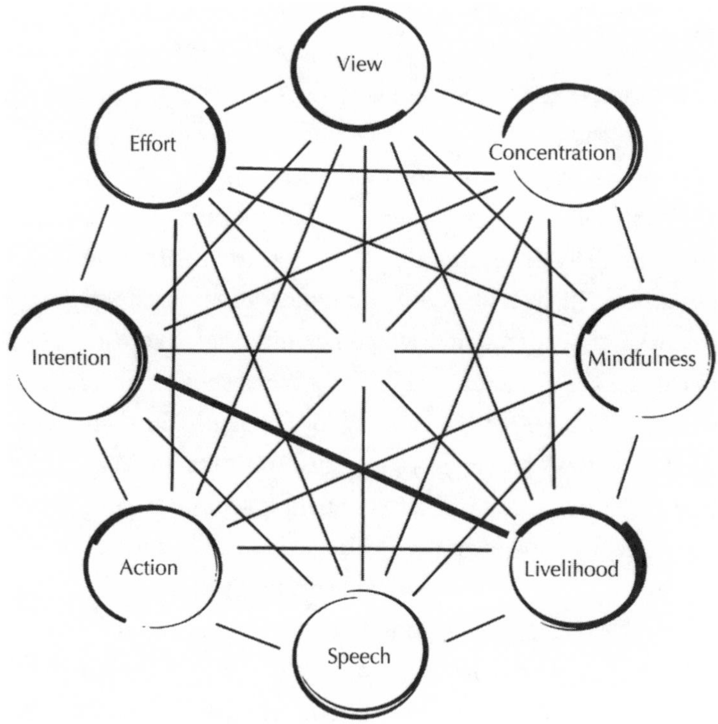

Figure 3.1: The Noble Eightfold Path

Right view can only be experienced when we are within the window of opportunity—when we can be calmly observational, not carried away with skewed view by our limbic (emergency) network. This process helps bring to the surface all the ways that we have misunderstood ourselves, our families, communities, and whole cultures. Right view enables us to truly see these fixed, misguided notions we've had about the nature of suffering, joy, and life.

When we are inspired to *change* those notions, we can say we are practicing *right thinking or intention.* In this way we can get past the habit, guilt, and shame that trap us in vicious cycles, creating nervous system imbalance, clouding the mind, and producing counterproductive reactions. Once we understand our motivations, we can accept and embrace the basic human needs they reflect. This kind of thinking is grounded in a cerebral cortex that is integrated with the entire nervous system. It does not lead to quick habitual action; there is space to consider what is the best path to travel.

Right speech arises naturally when our thinking is clear, based on deep understanding of the nature of suffering and of ourselves. This is a form of communication, in both words and gestures, that intends to overcome suffering in ourselves and in others. We understand that the way we speak can wound or heal, can blind us to the existing joys or highlight them. Right speech is a way in which we manage to coregulate in a healing way with others, creating a larger field of well-being in general. Right speech depends on our being able to self-regulate so that we can articulate what we are able to clearly see.

Right action is a reflection of our intentions and the way we talk. When actions come from a calm nervous system, they are the most skillful means we have in the present moment to bring about healing, transformation, and happiness, both individual and collective. These actions are not habitual reactions stemming from traumatic processes of the limbic system; rather they are calm, stable, and well-considered responses grounded in the thinking brain.

Right livelihood is using our actions to manifest our deepest intentions in a way that is beneficial to ourselves and others. It depends on seeing the big picture, on knowing when actions that seemingly benefit ourselves may actually have a negative impact in the long run, or may benefit some beings at the expense of others. We recognize here that what impacts the individual is not separate from what impacts the collective.

Right effort or diligence is the art of discerning what efforts to make and when to make them. We understand that in any one moment, we have thousands upon thousands of possible stimuli on which to put our attention. Right effort is the ability to discern where best to put our mindfulness and act accordingly to transform suffering and touch well-being. (See "Right Effort" later in this chapter for a more detailed explanation.)

Right mindfulness means living in a state of mind that maximizes transformation and healing, allowing clear understanding to emerge into consciousness. It is the optimal balance between attention and awareness in the service of ending individual and collective suffering.

Right concentration is the ability to sustain right mindfulness, building and strengthening neural pathways to develop insight into the nature of reality and to beneficial heart/mind states: loving kindness, compassion, sympathetic joy, and inclusiveness.[1] This, in turn, contributes to the deepening of right view—and so the cycle repeats.

The distinctions between each of these steps in the Eightfold Path are somewhat artificial; in reality, they coexist with each other. Contemplating the eight, you will see that each of them influences the others, so that while right view gives rise to right thinking, how we practice with right thinking may also change how we practice right view or right effort.

The Two Truths: The Historical and Ultimate Dimensions

In 2014, Thich Nhat Hanh gave a twenty-one-day retreat on the theme "What Happens When You Die." He opened with his playful smile, holding a kernel of corn and a little pot of dirt. He put the kernel into the dirt and gave it some water. Every day over the course of the twenty-one days, he talked to the pot as a plant began to grow from the kernel. Each time, he asked, Where is the little kernel of corn? Is it gone by the time the plant is fully mature? Is the plant the same as the kernel, or is it different?

Ultimately, he states, It is not the same, and yet also not different. We can no longer see the form of the kernel, and yet we do not mourn its passing. This is the truth of the interrelatedness of everything, what Thay calls *interbeing*. This is the *ultimate dimension*, where notions of before and after, birth and death, and being and non-being lose their meaning.

But in an everyday, practical sense, the kernel and the plant are of course quite different. Were we to bite into a big, juicy ear of corn, our experience would hardly be the same as biting into the kernel from which the ear sprouted. This view is holding the truth of the conventional or *historical dimension*. We as human beings would be hard-pressed to exist without spending a good deal of time hanging onto this historical dimension of reality.

Physicists tell us that on an atomic level, everything is made of the same stuff. What's more, all that stuff is always in motion, so things are always changing—whether we can see it or not. In fact, matter can turn into energy and energy into matter.

Ultimately, nothing is bad or good, right or wrong; it is all just stuff in process. Yet science also acknowledges the practical differences between substances like carbon and titanium; the various states of solid, liquid, and gas; the differences between electrical charges. There are laws of gravity, thermodynamics, biodynamics.

Buddhist teachings of the historical and the ultimate dimensions are very similar: everything is made of other stuff, and all that stuff is also made of other stuff. Everything is changing all the time, as do the surrounding conditions. At the same time, in order to interact with that stuff—to build, preserve, or use it—we must also count on it staying relatively the same over at least a short period of time. The trick, whether we are talking about Buddhist practice or scientific understandings, is holding both truths simultaneously.

We can look through these two lenses at mental formations as well as physical formations. In the historical dimension, a person may be quite angry, joyous, judgmental, or depressed. When seen through the ultimate dimension, as we understand that everything is constantly changing and made up of an infinite number of causes and conditions, those mind states become easier to work with. In this way, the ability to grasp the truth of the ultimate dimension helps us navigate the historical dimension, transforming unwholesome states of being. Likewise, working in the historical dimension gives rise to the truth of the ultimate. Balancing the two, we use these different dimensions to help us overcome suffering.

Later on in this same retreat, Thich Nhat Hanh suggested a simple way to understand the relationship between these two dimensions. He drew a picture of two parallel horizontal lines connected by a diagonal line, creating a big Z. He then told us that the upper line represents the historical dimension, the lower, the ultimate. As he slid his finger down along that diagonal, he said, "It is our mindfulness meditation practice that allows us to connect this historical dimension to the ultimate, right in the here and now." He added, "And now we draw the Zed of Zorro!" and pretended to slash a "Z" in the air with an invisible sword. Everyone laughed at this break in seriousness—and in relief in the knowledge that we all have the capacity to manifest this awareness, right here, right now!

The Five Mindfulness Trainings: Coming to the Eightfold Path with a Calm Mind

Historically, all spiritual paths have a code of ethics, and Buddhism is no exception. Without such a code, groups of people are a bit like newborns without swaddling, flailing around. Without a system of ethics, we risk developing coping habits that, while they may serve us in the short run, can be harmful in the long run, both to ourselves and others. In the West, it is customary for those interested in a contemplative path to jump right into a meditation practice without first appreciating and working within the ethical guidelines of that tradition. But allowing ourselves to be held within an ethical container is fundamental to this path, and it is wise to explore the Buddhist code of ethics right from the start.

Looked at in a neuro-informed way, the Five Mindfulness Trainings are a set of contemplations that aspire to train us in finding an optimal balance between safety and transcendence, between leading a life that insures our individual and collective physical and emotional survival while aspiring to touch the thriving embedded in the ultimate dimension. It is an invitation to recognize, discern, and resist habitual energies that overfocus on threat while cultivating reverence for life, generosity, love, harmonizing communication, and healthful life choices. Rather than suppressing experience, we are invited to discern in every moment from a place of mindful integration, just where that optimum lies—mindfulness in action. Ultimately this can lead to a deepening ability to live every moment with the awareness of the interbeing nature of every breath, of all life.

The community of the Buddha began with five basic commitments or *precepts*, and they continued to adapt their code to new needs that emerged out of living together.[2] They call for practitioners to refrain from

1. killing;
2. stealing;
3. sexual misconduct;
4. lying; and
5. intoxication.

The first four of these five precepts are fairly universal among most spiritual paths and secular ethical systems; the fifth, refraining from intoxication, was seen as a necessary ingredient for a path that strives to develop a clear mind. The basic code continues to this day, but they are typically not seen as hard and fast rules; rather, the precepts are meant as a set of guidelines that gives focus to our lives, calms our mind, and helps us stay on the path. The precepts allow us to contemplate our actions, to recognize and restrain behaviors that impede self-development, to form good habits, and to help us live harmoniously within our communities. They help us improve the balance of our nervous system, pushing us toward states of well-being: loving-kindness, compassion, sympathetic joy, equanimity.

In the Plum Village tradition, we call the precepts *mindfulness trainings* to reflect the opportunity they give us to cultivate mindfulness in our daily lives, as we make decisions and take actions.[3] Everyday decision-making might seem to fall within the historical dimension, but if we are looking deeply, practicing these mindfulness trainings, we run into the truth of the ultimate dimension as well. When practicing these trainings, the practitioner not only aims to cultivate virtues (reverence for life; generosity; commitment; loving speech and deep listening; simple, healthy living) but also an overarching and ever-present sense of connectedness: the interbeing nature of the entire web of life.

The Three Poisons: Greed, Hatred, and Delusion

Being the magnificent body/minds that we are, we've been gifted with strong drives that keep us safe from predators, well fed, sheltered, and tightly connected to each other. Were it not for these energies, we wouldn't have survived as a species. Yet too much of a good thing can unknowingly throw us for a loop. In Buddhism, we call the excessive form of these driving energies the *three poisons:* greed, hatred, and delusion.

Greed develops from our drive to go after our basic needs (food, sex, security, connection). Hatred develops as an excessive, short-sighted defense against perceived threats. And delusion develops from our ability to make generalizations or assumptions from the information available to us. These root abilities are essential survival skills, courtesy of our friend the limbic system (see Chapter 2), always there to keep us safe! We should not take the energies themselves as enemies, only the runaway processes that may accompany them.

These energies develop into poisons when we misperceive threats and, subsequently, fall prey to our habitual short-term response mechanisms. Fortunately, we do have an executive decision-making team in the form of the prefrontal cortex and vagus nerve (see Chapter 2), so we can discern between short- and long-term benefits and actually make wise decisions.

Getting angry at, or worse, shaming ourselves or others for simply having these drives is not going to get us anywhere. Being upset with ourselves because we've just binged on popcorn or yelled at someone will not solve anything; rather, it skews things all the more. Instead, mindfully being present, cultivating the ability to see what is actually happening, learning how to undo our bad habits will put us back on the right track.

The Five Skandhas: The Construction of an Inner Life

The five skandhas is a concept that describes the various components of inner mental experience to understand our inner life and how it affects our actions. When overwhelmed by a situation, I find it helpful to know that I can look inside at just one small piece of it. By exploring just a tiny bit at a time, we can illuminate each piece of our experience in a manageable way. We gain understanding without needing to take on more than we can chew in any one moment.

The five skandhas or experiences are body or form; feelings; perception; mental formations; and consciousness. In practice, each of these areas is ever-changing, and each is made up of smaller pieces. Let's look at them more closely.

Body or form is made up of the receptors of everyday experience: eyes, ears, nose, tongue, body, and mind. These come in contact with the physical world, causing us to feel sensations. This skandha helps us distinguish between the characteristics of sensations such as hard/soft, hot/cold, or wet/dry—in short, our direct bodily experience.

Feelings are our most basic response to bodily experience, interpreting sensations of the body as pleasant, unpleasant, or neutral. Pleasant feelings lead the body/mind to desire and to cling or want more. Unpleasantness leads the body/mind to want the experience to go away, to have less of that sensation, to avoid it. Neutral feelings produce little reaction or indifference. All of this, for the emotional brain, is in service of discerning our basic, immediate physical or mental safety.

Perception is what we make of an experience, as we recognize and interpret the meaning behind those root feelings of "like it" or "don't like it." The emotional brain searches for a memory of previous experiences, interprets what is going on, and provides our thinking brain with labels, concepts, and context for the experience—again, for the purpose of survival.

Mental formations are judgments based on that perception. When we combine the knowledge of our past experience with our ingrained habits, new emotions and mind states are created. These can create a sense of well-being or ill-being.

Consciousness is the element of awareness, a knowing or observing of all of these skandhas together.

Here's an example that demonstrates how these five skandhas work together.

Say that I feel a pain in my toe: The *form* of the pain might be described as sharp and hot, while the *experience* of it would be unpleasant. My *perception* of the pain is that it's my arthritis acting up—it's a pain I've felt before. My *mental formations* of the pain cause me to become anxious and worry that the pain will get worse; what if I need an operation? My *consciousness* is the awareness of all of these things together: the pain arises and I am immediately nervous, experiencing at once the unpleasantness, the memory of past pains, and the knowledge that it could get worse. But of course, this anxiety only exacerbates the pain in my toe!

ONIONS AND CURIOSITY

Let's look at a different example that's a bit more fun. There is an exercise in mindful eating that I offer when working with children. It is to eat a raw onion. I start by explaining that we might immediately think, "Oooo, I don't like raw onions," and squeal and writhe with the feeling that comes from just thinking about it. I challenge them to try not to focus on this world of "like" and "dislike," and rather to jump into the world of curiosity. (In fact, I suggest that it is even kind of fun to writhe—it's a very immediate form of nervous system release!)

When I first pose the exercise, almost no one is willing to try it. After all, children are already quite invested in discerning pleasant from unpleasant, and in exercising their autonomy. But as I continue to offer the experience, I begin to focus more on the "challenge" aspect of it. I explain that when we are caught up in "I like it/I don't like it," we really limit our ability to fully experience the world of onion. One by one, they come up to take their piece of onion. I try to make the challenge enticing, but not to pressure. Children can choose to take a piece just to smell, or even just to feel the temperature of that piece, or to pick it apart. The important thing is for them to get into the spirit of curiosity and investigation, even for a short time, and out of the "I like it/I don't like it" mode.

Once everyone has their piece of onion, I count to three, and say, "Go!" And they investigate: looking, touching, smelling, biting, tasting. I ask them a number of questions about the onion: Is it soft, or crunchy? How can they tell? Is there any sweetness? Is it dry or juicy? Is it mild or spicy? Where do they notice these sensations?

Often, by the end, there is not one child who hasn't eaten their piece of onion, and several will even ask for more. There's no right or wrong here. There is a place in life for each level of action. Of course, it is important to stay away from some things that we don't like, especially when they are injurious—but it is also important to challenge ourselves to a broader experience. When, little by little, we learn to balance practicality with curiosity, the notion of pleasant/unpleasant begins to fall away. The experience of eating a raw onion is transformed from our unhelpful, narrow experience of "I don't like it" into a neutral or even pleasant experience. It allows us to enter into the miracle that is *onion*.

Taking on a new experience might seem overwhelming, especially if you find that experience potentially dysregulating. But when you break it down into each of the skandhas, you can get a very full experience of onion, one chew at a time—and a full experience of yourself as well. Notice what comes up as you focus on each of the skandhas in turn: form, feeling, perception, mental formation, and consciousness.

EXERCISE 3.2: Exploring an Onion

DURATION: 10 minutes

FREQUENCY: Once

PURPOSE: Experiencing our five skandhas

Ready? 1, 2, 3 . . . INVESTIGATE!

Notice with each investigation what sensations you have. Take your time. Use each of your senses.

Start with the unpeeled onion and investigate slowly. Approach the experience as if you'd never seen an onion before. Notice any unexpected discoveries. Can you concentrate on just one sense at a time, without distraction, even for a couple of seconds?

Stay in tune with your body. Notice if your habit is to jump to "like" or "dislike," and how you experience that in your body.

Think for a moment about previous experiences with raw onions and what those experiences were like for you.

Notice your emotional state in the present moment and consider how your emotions are related to your bodily reactions.

The Four Kinds of Nutriments

When we can nourish each of those five skandhas in a way that brings a sense of well-being, we learn to fortify and balance our nervous system. There are four kinds of nourishment that help us accomplish this: *edible food, sense impressions, volition* (intention or will), and *consciousness*. Unfortunately, often we are unable to tell the difference between true nourishment and unwholesome forms of consumption. As we feed ourselves every day, are we aware of the impact it has on us? How can science help us understand why we reach for certain kinds of nourishment over others?

Let's start with *edible food*—a big source of both pleasure and suffering for us. As human beings, we are hardwired for survival to eat everything in sight. We recognize and crave the most densely calorie-packed foods we can find. But in the wealthier parts of the world today, we are presented with a practically infinite supply of densely packed calories, carefully crafted to promote craving—foods that don't necessarily bring us nutritional benefits. Additionally, we get so caught up in the sensation of liking or not liking the taste of a food that we get distracted from how what we put in our mouth is impacting our body. How does looking at ourselves through this lens impact the mental formations we have about ourselves with respect to what we eat? Personally, when I could see my poor eating habits as outgrowths of my hard-wired nervous system, I found a lot more understanding and compassion for myself. At times, when I'm eating mindfully, paying close attention to my bodily reactions, I am amazed at what I find. For example, I might find that what my body finds appealing is actually a crisp piece of romaine rather than a brownie. Another surprise is how this mindful eating satiates me on much less food than I'd imagined.

Sense impressions are just that: impressions that are left on our eyes, ears, tongue, nose, body (inside and out). As with food, sense impressions may be both wholesome and not so wholesome: this includes news, digital and social media, advertisements, books, films, games, and conversations. We know that our thoughts and emotions are made of neural pathways that are quickened and strengthened by repetition. In a society suffering from sexism, racism, economic manipulation, and political divides, what we consume on the level of sense impressions—often unconsciously—forms our implicit biases. Whether we think we are affected by these unrelenting messages or not, how could we possibly be immune to internalizing at least some of them?

One of the seemingly more benign ways we can damage ourselves is with the sheer glut of information available to us in the digital age. The incalculable bits of information (or misinformation) at our fingertips are a bit like the unlimited assortment of calories presented to us. If something grabs my curiosity, in a flash I am off to the computer to check it out—and my mind becomes distracted from whatever it was I was doing. Further, consuming great amounts of what seems like information waters the seeds of impatience and sometimes even my ability to sit with uncertainty. If I am trying to cultivate a proper balance between my attention and awareness, I'm kind of working against myself!

Knowing the potential impact of our consumption can really help motivate us to guard those senses, to avoid allowing an onslaught of sense impressions to forge unwholesome neural pathways. Additionally, we often overlook beneficial sense impressions as we are bombarded with consumer messages. Let those consumer come-ons be a bell of mindfulness to search out a couple of wholesome impressions to provide balance. Like going shopping for goodness, take time to inspect your item by pausing and really taking it in: spend maybe 15 seconds savoring it. Fill your shopping cart with a growing collection of bird sounds and laughter, smiles from strangers, courageous weeds growing up through cracks in the sidewalk, even a deep cleansing breath of gratitude for the air.

Volition or *intention setting* is a very powerful way to nourish ourselves. It is the visualization of what we intend to do or feel—imagining it as if it were happening. Visualizing an action actually micro-fires our muscles to create the sensation that we are actually accomplishing that intention; over time, it can even change the structure of our brain. (Remember that saying, "what fires together, wires together"?) Volition is an optimal collaboration between the amygdala (which evaluates and responds to the way we feel about a situation) and the cerebral cortex (which enables us to problem-solve and put plans into action). Together, they help us identify where we should best put our intention, selecting things to focus on that will be most likely to lead to the desired outcome. Being aware of our thoughts, knowing whether they point us in the desired direction, savoring the ones that send us there, and reining in those that do not are all key to nourishing wholesome intentions. We'll explore how to do this in the following exercise.

Finally, let's look at how our *consciousness* nourishes us. Thich Nhat Hanh describes our consciousness like a home that has a living room and a basement. The living room is our present awareness of the first four skandhas (body, feelings, perceptions, and mental formations). The basement is what we Westerners might call the unconscious, where we keep all of our potential mind/body states. These two parts of our consciousness are called *mind consciousness* (the living room) and *store consciousness* (the basement)—we'll talk more about these two parts later. The important thing to know here is that what we do to one part of our consciousness impacts the other.

EXERCISE 3.3: Creating a Habit of Intention

DURATION: 10 minutes initially / 1 minute thereafter
FREQUENCY: Multiple times a day
PURPOSE: To identify and strengthen a small change in lifestyle or habit

Please consider this an experiment: to simply become curious about intention setting and creating beneficial habits. Begin by settling into a sense of well-being, giving yourself time and space to ease into this exercise. Notice where you feel at ease in your body, what feels supportive; perhaps take a few slow, deep breaths. When you feel settled, notice what is going on inside. You can explore this territory from two perspectives: what draws you to the intention, and what might prevent it from manifesting. Either can come first. Each brings in your ability to remember and imagine. The challenge here is choosing one small habit you'd like to change.

What is your deepest aspiration at this moment? What is calling to your heart? Think about where this knowledge comes from: images, body sensations, thoughts, or emotions? Allow time for these experiences to surface in whatever manner they want. No need to force this—it may take repeated questioning to be revealed, in its own time. Just stay curious; savor whatever is going on. Notice how this process is affecting you inside. If there is some sense of well-being, allow your focus to dwell there for a few breaths. If there is *not* a sense of well-being, what are you experiencing? What is it made of? Think back to the five skandhas and use them to explore: you can use all of this information to deepen understanding.

Next, consider something you consider an obstacle to manifesting this aspiration. Be aware of what goes on inside you when you think about it. What might it be like if this thing were *not* an obstacle? Have you ever had any successful experience with this issue, even for a very short time? What is it like if you try to imagine yourself being successful, even for a brief time? Here we are trying to get one of those seeds of possibility to germinate. Whatever you encounter in this exploration is wonderful information, steps along the path to setting intention, raising your awareness in each encounter of the true nature of your issue. As you inhabit this space, allow its full impact to be the object of your mindful attention. Savor it for a couple of breaths. Consider the connection that might exist between the calling and the obstacle, as if they were two sides of the same coin.

Finally, think about an encounter in your daily life, one that occurs with some regularity, that can act as a reminder for you to return your thoughts to your aspiration. This reminder will help you revisit your inner determination several times a day.

Here's an example. I find that everything distracts me from writing when I'm not feeling clear or confident that I can do the job to my satisfaction. I want that feeling of relaxed satisfaction at a job well done. Bringing that to mind, I can feel the tension rolling off my shoulders and a burst of "can do" energy as my hands feel the urge to make the gesture of brushing each other off in delight at having accomplished the task I set out to do. Very pleasant, very relaxing! I press on with curiosity: why do I keep jumping up when I'm not feeling confident? As I sit with it, I can feel my whole body getting tense and constricted, scrunching up around my heart. I don't like the feeling, and moving my body distracts me from the unpleasant feeling. I decide that each time I find myself jumping up, I will pause and go back to that hand-dusting, relaxed, can-do feeling. In addition, I'm going to try and remember, when I go to sleep and wake up, to rehearse that feeling and remember how it played out during the day.

Right Effort

The principle of right effort is about the choices we have in every moment, every day, and about choosing to direct our effort toward ending suffering, to make the present moment real and alive.

When offering this teaching, Thich Nhat Hanh typically would draw a large circle to represent our consciousness, dividing it in two. The upper half is what Thay calls *mind consciousness*, the grand collection of all conscious mental states. The section below is the *store consciousness*, where lies, out of conscious awareness, the potential for these mental states. We might think of mind consciousness as the living room of our mind, while store consciousness is the cellar. Thay frequently used the analogy of a garden: the *bija*, or seeds, lie dormant under the ground (store consciousness) and are tended by a gardener, whose job is to grow a nourishing crop (mind consciousness). The seeds are watered and nourished by attention (both wholesome and unwholesome). Right effort is a kind of *selective* watering so that we don't water indiscriminately and strengthen our unwholesome ones as well.

Using our neuro-informed perspective, we might say that these seeds are our neural pathways, which produce the full range of human emotions. The strength of the seed, or pathway, depends on just how much use those pathways receive. When a seed or pathway is nourished, a corresponding plant or emotion grows up into the mind consciousness. Our conscious

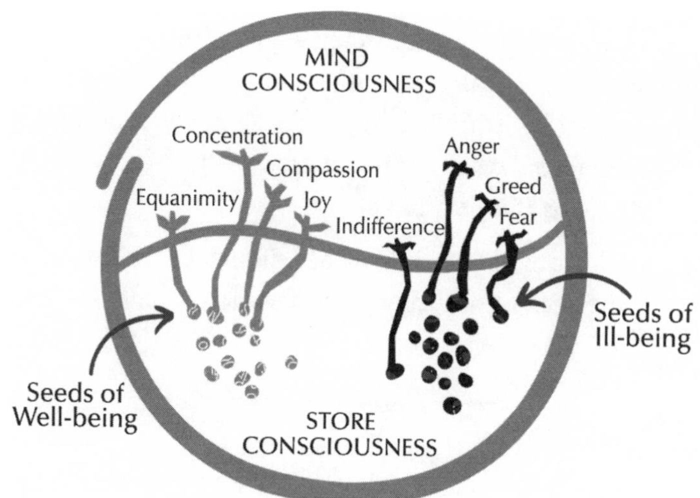

Figure 3.2: Mind consciousness and store consciousness. Mind/Store Consciousness diagram courtesy of the Plum Village app

awareness of these states can be wholesome—those that relieve suffering (like generosity, compassion, loving-kindness, or joy)—or unwholesome—those that cause greater suffering (like rage, resentment, hopelessness, lust, or despair)..

There are four elements of right effort:

1. As the "seeds" of our store consciousness grow into our mind consciousness, we must discern the wholesome neural pathways (and resulting mental states) from the unwholesome. *Wholesome* is experienced as producing a sense of well-being, *unwholesome* as ill-being. We focus and sustain our attention on the wholesome ones—truly savor them—until they naturally fade back into the store consciousness, now stronger than before.

2. We can then learn to call up the wholesome seeds from below at will. This practice forges strong neural pathways, making wholesome states of mind more easily accessible to us.

3. When we discover a seed or emotion that is unwholesome, we refrain from nourishing it further with our unmindful or habitual attention. Rather, we can simply see it for what it is and how it grows, without providing it with more fertilizer.

4. In this process, we learn what stimulates the unwholesome seed's growth and can now do our best to avoid helping that to happen.

This selective attention process is what constitutes right effort. However, keep in mind that there are times when we cannot properly practice this process: if we are stuck outside the window of mindful opportunity, it is impossible to access the mindfulness necessary to truly practice right effort. If our nervous system does not have the capacity to maintain the delicate balance we need to stay safely within that window, any attempts to remain present or hold the difficulty in a mindful way may only lead to greater dysregulation. The neural pathways that lead to regulation may still be too weak, and trying to push forward may inadvertently lead to more stress and a downward spiral of dysregulation. In those moments, we need to occupy ourselves with focusing on wholesome states of mind, where we can find them. This helps us build up stability for the future; eventually, we can return to looking at our unwholesome seeds without becoming overwhelmed. This process may take just minutes, or it might take months—or longer. If we keep getting pushed out of our window, it might also be a time to look to a companion or teacher to help us when the negative energy of an unwholesome state is too big for just one person to manage alone. We will look at the role of teachers, guides, and therapists in the next chapter.

The Middle Way

The Buddha, influenced by the ascetics of the time and perhaps put off by the opulence of palace life, went to extremes of denying the flesh in his early efforts to overcome suffering. On the verge of starvation, he convinced himself that such extremes were not the right path, and that instead one should follow what is called the *middle way*. Perhaps what the Buddha had discovered was the window of mindful opportunity—the awareness that our ability to truly practice mindfulness, to learn, and to expand our consciousness can only occur when we are not experiencing extreme activation of our sympathetic or parasympathetic nervous systems. Certainly, being on the brink of starvation will knock you out of that window, clouding the mind and forcing either panic or shutdown to take over.

Following the middle way does not mean compromising one's principles; rather, it is a way to guard against dualistic, black-and-white, all-or-nothing thinking. For example, let's return to the scenario of the corn kernel and the plant. Over the course of three weeks, as the kernel grows into the plant, Thich Nhat Hanh asks the questions, Where is the kernel? Did it die? Is the corn plant the same as the kernel, or is it different? Taking the middle way requires us to understand that these questions do not have simple "yes" or "no" answers, but that the answer transcends the level of inquiry. To say that it neither is nor isn't the same is not a compromise, but rather a deeper dive into the nature of reality.

The middle way is also a mandate to avoid strict rules that skirt the need for moment-by-moment awareness of each situation as it arises. For example, is it best to be a vegetarian or not? The commitment not to kill is very important on this path—it's one of the original five precepts, after all. Yet as one digs deeply into the question, we begin to see its complexities: for example, would we decline a nonvegetarian meal offered to us when traveling in a foreign country when doing so might cause offense? Would we refuse if we were starving to death? Following the middle way means avoiding rigid thinking (the declaration of being vegetarian, no matter the circumstances) and to interpret the question to fit each moment with its unique set of circumstances.

In the next chapter, we will see that such an approach not only applies to the extremes of mortification, but to the extremes of what may seem like purely beneficial mind states as well.

4

Navigating the Road

Understanding and Overcoming Obstacles in Mindfulness Practice

There seems to be very strong scientific evidence that mindfulness practice is a powerful vehicle on the road to peace, calm, and compassion. In order to drive safely, some rules of the road are in order. For our purposes, we'll call it a *neuro-informed approach*. Having a neuro-informed approach to mindfulness means learning to identify and adapt practices in a way that prevents us from getting hurt—it keeps us from getting shaken up when we hit bumps, get stuck in ruts, or crash the car when we encounter a pothole. That's what this chapter is about: identifying our own personal bumps, ruts, and potholes, understanding why they show up, and preparing for them. In Chapter 5, we'll learn lots of practical exercises and tips for what to do when we encounter them: how to ground, regulate, and stabilize.

Here, in their own words, is what one mindfulness practitioner discovered:

> Even through the distance of a TV screen, I can feel the aliveness of a gazelle, an animal I've yet to meet in their own habitat; it's their attunement to what is in front of them that touches me. And while it wasn't entirely conscious and it took some time to verbalize it, those images of wild animals were seeds of a yearning that I kept nourishing as I learned to connect to my body, mind, and heart. When I started a serious meditation practice in my early twenties, I did so because I thought meditation would take my pain away. And while I experienced beautiful moments, there was an underlying unease within my own skin that would not go away after 3 years of starting that practice. Whether they were suicidal ideations, ruminations of the same thoughts, anxieties, and a dissociation from my own emotions and my body, I didn't know how to transform them. I had huge challenges growing up that fueled this lack of ease, whether it was from my parent's bitter divorce and having to grow up at the age of 7 because of it, not receiving messages of affirmation from either parent, or moving to the United States at the age of 12, leaving friends and family and the only home I knew, an island archipelago known as the Philippines.
>
> It was through a neuro-informed approach to healing trauma that I started to realize that my body held the key to the healing I was seeking. During some sessions, I experienced the deep release of a body shake as I tracked sensations within my body. I learned to look around to notice colors, shapes, and textures rather than narrowing into a story. It was deceptively simple. Integrating a neuro-informed approach, I started to realize there are other aspects of myself that inform who I am and that my thoughts don't

define me. It got easier to accept the full range of emotions that flow through me. And while I've integrated other healing modalities since then and the work continues, as I reflect back on the person I was in my twenties when I first started, I think I've experienced more moments of what a Buddhist teacher calls mindfulness, a relaxed attentiveness in life. My face looks less anxious, my body knows what relaxed feels like, and it's a major part of my practice now and not just a yearning.

Basic Principles of a Neuro-Informed Approach to Mindfulness

In his groundbreaking book, David Treleaven identified five principles of what he calls "trauma-sensitive mindfulness":

1. Stay within the window of tolerance.
2. Shift attention to support stability.
3. Keep the body in mind.
4. Practice in relationship.
5. Understand social context.[1]

This approach focuses on easing problems that may arise for practitioners during mindfulness practice, specifically due to past trauma—we'll talk about this connection later in this chapter. But as we learned in Chapter 2, we don't need to experience giant traumas (like war, abuse, or life-threatening injury) to have our nervous systems activated! In this sense, "trauma" isn't really anything out of the ordinary—we're all "traumatized" to a certain extent just by going through a life full of external and internal stressors. Many of these things aren't frequently recognized as "trauma," like racism or poverty. The point is that although some of us suffer greater hardships than others, we all may find our nervous systems over-activated under certain conditions—and these will vary for everyone. With this in mind, I invite you to set aside "trauma" for now and instead think about these basic principles as simply providing an approach to mindfulness practice that provides us with the most benefit and does the least harm.

In this next section, I adapt Treleaven's trauma-sensitive principles and reimagine them as a neuro-informed approach to mindfulness practice.[2]

BEING IN CHOICE

First and foremost, each of us must use our own judgment as to what to practice, how to practice, when to practice, and how long to practice. We call this being *in choice*. Staying in choice is key to reassuring the nervous system that there is safety. When we hear that we *must* do this or that, or that we *will* experience a particular thing, our sense of being in choice may be threatened. When you're introduced to a practice, if something does not feel right, remember that ultimately, it is your body and your choice what to do with it! For example, if you are instructed to shut your eyes, but you find this distressing, you can slightly open them; if a posture is too painful for you, you can adjust it. Remember, too, that the suggested impact of a particular practice should be understood as just one possibility—if your experience is different, that's OK.

Invitational language is one way to infuse this understanding of choice into everything we do. Statements like "you are invited to . . . " or "you might find support in trying . . . " can be more inclusive and reassuring than "do this." Thich Nhat Hanh seemed to offer this invitation both in words ("you may like to . . . ") and in his gentle tone. When he gave instruction, it felt like there were no hard bits to chew on before swallowing! You may have already noticed invitational language in this book, but please do remember: all of the practices and exercises here are your choice to try as you like, when you like, and where you like.

KEEPING WITHIN THE WINDOW OF MINDFUL OPPORTUNITY

Understanding what the states of well-being and ill-being feel like is essential to a solid practice. When it comes to our nervous system, we all share the same basic setup, but each of us tunes in slightly differently to the signals it sends us. We need to know the signs that are unique to us of being in or out of the window of mindful opportunity. This is especially important when we get close to our limits of over- or under-activation, when we need to actively engage in nervous system regulation to bring ourselves back closer to the middle of the window.

The primary way we can tell whether we are in or out of the window is whether our actions and reactions seem under our conscious control. It might seem like a paradox, but simply being aware that we are near our limit is in itself a form of rebalancing. Just being able to ask ourselves the question, "Am I in, or out?" puts us back on the right track because the act of asking calls the thinking brain to come back online. In the next chapter, you will be introduced to a variety of exercises that can help keep you within your window. If we make a habit of doing these kinds of awareness exercises, they become both treatment and preventative medicine. They can build resilience so we are not so easily hyperactivated; they fortify us against living too close to the borders of the window; and they strengthen our ability to concentrate in a wholesome way.

USING SUPPORTIVE RESOURCES TO REREGULATE

One important method of keeping ourselves inside our window of mindful opportunity is identifying and using available *resources*. Resources are things that bring well-being to us without us having to make an effort. They can be real or imagined; a person(s) or other type of being; a place where we feel at peace; an experience we've had; a strength or talent; or a belief or spiritual path. The only criteria is that you know it feels good. Feeling good might mean a sense of safety, comfort, belonging, gratitude, connectedness, or competence; or you might experience this as feeling warm or cool in your body, feeling expansive or grounded, calm or excited. Our resources, and the way that they bring well-being to us, will be different for every person.

Bringing to mind these resources actually brings the body into reexperiencing the goodness from them. The more vividly we can imagine the resource, the more effective it is to strengthen the neural pathway and regulate our nervous system.

PRACTICING IN RELATIONSHIP TO OTHERS

Although it seems like this journey is one we must take alone, it is vital to have companions along the way. Companions provide witness to our journey: they show us by their presence that we matter, that we are worthy of understanding, respect, and caring. Companions can help us calm down in times of crisis, through the miracle of coregulation (see Chapter 2). Companions can help broaden our perspective, offer tips, provide a nonjudgmental sounding board, share words of wisdom, or simply offer . . . well, *company*. We are a social species, and we depend to differing degrees on experiencing coregulation with other humans.

When you are unable to stay present with what is arising in your life—internally or externally—it can be very helpful to have someone to help you follow these teachings. A guide can provide an extra eye to help you see where to hold focus. This guide would ideally be a skilled practitioner themselves, holding the energy of mindfulness with which the practitioner can coregulate. It is even more helpful if this guide (or teacher, or therapist) has familiarity with neuro-informed principles as well as mindfulness practices.

UNDERSTANDING SOCIAL CONTEXT

Every time I walk into a gathering, I assess the crowd. Whether I'm conscious of it or not, I'm looking for sameness and for difference: skin color, gender expression, dress, age, and body types. All the ways I have felt safe or threatened are imprinted in my habit of noticing; nothing is going to stop the nervous system from this survival tactic. Of course, I can be aware of entering that mind state, guard against being swept away by wrong perceptions, and manage my responses accordingly. Nevertheless, I do notice.

This noticing is also true for just about everyone else in the room, whether they know it or not. In order to really be neuro-informed, we need to learn to stay aware of the existence of unseen factors at play in any social situation we encounter. When a gathering lacks diversity (in any category), you can bet that is making an impact on some folks in the room. We can heighten our awareness of "the vibe"—the things our body is picking up on and coregulating with—and be curious about its source. Learning more about the variety of experiences people have due to differences of race, ethnicity, class, age, and gender expression is called being aware of *social location.* Chapter 8, "Journeying Together," will bring this more into focus.

Whether we identify with or feel different from another, we can guard against making assumptions of similar experience by remembering that no two people have identical social locations, not even identical twins! It helps to maintain "don't know" mind here, bringing forward our curiosity when we find ourselves assuming. This helps everyone feel respected and seen for who they are and the unique experiences they bring to the group.

INCREASING OUR TOLERANCE

If you've ever sat down to meditate with the determination not to move, inevitably you will be confronted with the urge to scratch an itch. Early on in my sitting practice I discovered the incredible joy of finally allowing myself to scratch some annoying itch that plagued me. To my dismay, however, the joy was short-lived, and my itch detector became ever more sensitive. Pretty soon, my whole body was itching in every place imaginable. Learning to live with an itch soon became a necessity if I was to continue pursuing meditation.

Out of this necessity came an important lesson in the power of attention: as I learned to choose an appropriate object of concentration (see "Developing an Anchor" in Chapter 5), it became easier to first ignore, then to tolerate that itchy sensation. Knowing that I could escape the intensity of the itch by focusing on my anchor gave me an island of safety, a reassurance that I could be a bit in control. From there, I was able to become curious about the nature of the itch. Being able to pinpoint the location of the itch, to consider the details of what an itch was, took my attention away from the urge to get rid of it. It was a bit like pulling the curtain back on the Wizard of Oz and seeing he was a little guy with a loudspeaker projecting his tiny voice—not fearsome at all.

Now, overcoming itches is not exactly a complete door to liberation, but it taught me a process I could put into place for other difficulties. The process of learning to make a once-intolerable sensation bearable is much like stretching the window of mindful opportunity. As we become more experienced, we are able to hang out closer to the upper and lower limits of the window without being hijacked by our nervous system. This broadens our ability to stay present, within the thinking brain, with more tolerance for discomfort. In this way, we can see more clearly what all these sufferings are made of—the key to undoing them. With time, we learn to hold the discomforts with more ease, and they become softer. This is *resilience*, an ability to be present with life's difficulties without being carried away, allowing us to be our most wise and effective selves.

Potential Pitfalls: Bumps, Ruts, and Potholes in the Road

If the principles we've just gone through are the rules of the road, then the pitfalls are one reason why the rules exist. In the rest of this chapter, we'll get a better understanding of the bumps, ruts, and potholes that can appear on a well-traversed road—and learn how to avoid them.

The truth is that some of us may encounter significant difficulties in following the practices exactly as they have historically been offered. In recent years, the idea that mindfulness practice is a straightforward route to overcoming suffering has been met with a substantial number of challenges. Some people may find practices more distressing than healing. Others come up against stumbling blocks years into their practice, finding that they suddenly begin to suffer in ways they hadn't before. As a result, numerous studies have revealed that a percentage of Buddhist practitioners—regardless of lineage, and including laypeople, monastics, and even Dharma teachers—also suffer from what appears to be adverse meditation-induced side effects.[3]

What happens if we *don't* find relief from our practice—or if it causes us to feel worse? Is there something wrong with us? How do we even talk about this with community members who devote their whole lives to practice, or with our teachers? How does this message, that mindfulness practice may create rather than relieve distress, fit with the notion of right speech, which guides us to contain our words to those that foster joy and confidence and hope?

Yikes! That's a lot to take in. How will we ever be able to just relax into the benefits and joys of engaged mindfulness practice while being on the lookout for all those potential pitfalls? For those who have begun this practice in search of the end of suffering, the idea that it may not cure all ills might be very unwelcome. But for others—especially those who may have had difficulties in their practice already—perhaps this inquiry is a breath of fresh air.

In fact, all of the above is good news. *What?!* Yes, while we as practitioners might stumble on the road in a few different ways, ultimately these stumbles are opportunities to deepen our understanding of the skills we need to make it through life: to be aware of whether and how we are struggling and to use reregulating tools to find our way through. What's more, we must do this type of deep looking into our practice—seeing both helpful and unhelpful aspects—in order to refine it and make it accessible to a greater number of people. All practitioners should be trained to be alert themselves to the possible hazards along the way. We do not want folks to be discouraged and not pursue the path the first time they hit a bump! Between what we now know about the science of mindfulness and the wisdom of the original teachings, there is a way out. We don't have to close the road in order to avoid the potholes and ruts.

Consider this: many of us take medications of all kinds that come with side effects. In many cases, the more potent the beneficial effect, the greater the risk of undesirable side effects. We know that even taking something as simple as an aspirin, which may have wonderful pain-relieving or heart-protecting benefits, comes with the risk of increased bruising or even cerebral hemorrhage! We weigh the risks against the benefits, learn the danger signals, and figure out ways to work with what arises.

Mindfulness practice also alters our physiology, strengthening some parts of our brain and relaxing others, as we will see in the next section. So why would we expect anything different? Especially considering how little we actually know about the intricacies of that nerve center on top of our spine! We need to get beyond an all-or-nothing approach that sees mindfulness meditation as either always beneficial or always risky. Can we set aside the fear and defensiveness that might arise with this line of questioning, and simply be open, be curious?

Before reading on, let's pause and check in with ourselves. What is going on for you, reading this? What's happening inside your body? What about your feelings and mental formations? Can we look at this problem with the openness encouraged by the practice itself?

MEDITATION SICKNESS: AN OPEN SECRET?

Is it possible that the Buddha just assumed that everyone would react to meditation practice in the same way that he did, sitting under that tree, just hanging in there? Did he leave room for the possibility that this might *never* lead to stability in the face of certain stressors? That there might be people who are wired differently for whom this approach would actually backfire?

In fact, references to "meditation sickness" can be found in medieval Chinese literature as old as 454 CE. These ancient texts note possible adverse effects of depression, anxiety, dissociation, suicidal thoughts, and even psychosis. Although some Buddhists defend these states as actually desirable to encounter, the medieval Chinese approach was meticulous in trying to mitigate these "sicknesses." (However, their methods are essentially incomprehensible to all but the most astute Chinese medievalist scholars.) Similarly, we might look to the *Surangama Sutra*, a compilation of a variety of sutras that enumerates fifty distinct types of *Skandha Maras*, or demons (which have been interpreted as representing difficulties in meditation practice).[4] This sutra, which is said to have been translated from Pali some twelve hundred years after the Buddha's passing, in part focused on how to identify and how to avoid some of these road hazards.

In more recent history, Hakuin Ekaku (1685–1768), the central teacher in the Rinzai tradition, wrote a lengthy account of his spiritual woes and how he overcame them, called *Wild Ivy*.[5] Likewise, the Tibetan tradition refers to "retreat lung," or "meditator's disease," which includes headaches, chest and back pain, and digestive problems. They caution that unless the problems are dealt with, this can lead to severe mental disturbances.[6] Clearly, adverse effects from meditation were not at all unknown throughout history, yet somehow this knowledge didn't seem to make it in Buddhism's passage from East to West.[7]

That brings us to the current research. Thanks to collaborations between monastics and neuroscientists, we now know that meditation can, indeed, make significant structural changes in the brain, strengthening or weakening neural networks depending on how much stimulation they receive. As a result of mindfulness meditation, the gray matter of the cerebral cortex actually grows in volume and density. This results in a stronger left hippocampus—a region of the brain that controls our ability to learn, have self-awareness, and feel empathy. Thus, these functions are better supported. The density of the posterior cingulate also increases, helping calm the default mode network (see Chapter 2), and produces better attention to the present moment without judgment, regret, or anticipation. The pons (part of the brainstem) and the temporoparietal junction are also strengthened. Meanwhile, the amygdala shrinks, curbing fear and anxiety.[8]

These changes generally have been assumed to be beneficial, leading to a heightened awareness and sensitivity of the true nature of reality. These changes hopefully help us overcome the mismatch between our nervous system's default settings and the ways in which we live today, or the values we may hold. But we shouldn't be surprised to learn that there may be unexpected difficulties—neuroscience is still a very young field, and we should be humbled by just how much there is yet to learn. What's important is to use what we *do* know to help us see the warning signs and learn how to better navigate and rebalance when we encounter bumps, ruts, or potholes on the path.

BUMPS ON THE TRAIL: REACTIVATION OF PREVIOUS TRAUMAS

Even though meditation sickness has been talked about in Buddhist circles for centuries, the thousands of papers published by modern researchers on meditation's beneficial effects have failed—until relatively recently—to mention adverse effects. As a neuroscience graduate student, Willoughby Britton—now a professor at Brown University—discovered, much to her surprise, that mindfulness meditation practice actually impairs practitioners' ability to get a good night's sleep. Although this was already well-known among meditation teachers, and routinely warned about in meditation retreats, it was not necessarily considered a big problem. Britton, thought otherwise, and over time, she has developed increasingly sophisticated research methods to understand the conditions under which all kinds of adverse effects happen to practitioners.

In 2008, Britton began offering occasional supportive housing for students returning from monastic to lay life and found that it began to especially attract those who were experiencing adverse effects from meditation practice. This grew into Cheetah House, a sort of recovery center or halfway house. At the time of its physical location closing, Cheetah House was bulging at the seams, with an ever-increasing number of people seeking refuge. In an attempt to meet this growing demand, in 2015, Cheetah House became an online community (cheetahhouse.org) offering a vast array of resources, research, and professional treatment as well as peer-support services. With increasing social and environmental stressors and the exponentially increasing use of meditation apps, the demand is quite significant, and their network of services is constantly growing. Britton and her colleagues also continue to embark on new research projects.

It is important to say, here, that for the majority of practitioners, the benefits of practice outweigh the drawbacks! Nevertheless, it is also important to be aware of and watchful for signs and symptoms of practice-induced difficulties. Meditation practice may exacerbate existing conditions, or bring up previously unhealed issues—for example, unresolved trauma may resurface during meditation, whether in the form of memories or unpleasant body sensations, thoughts, emotions, images, even smells. Here is a partial list of signs that something might be going wrong:

Bodily changes: Increase or decrease in breathing rate, heart rate, appetite, or weight; gut distress; feeling weak or faint; headaches; development of tics; insomnia or nightmares

Affect changes: Flattened or heightened facial expressions, gestures, or tone of voice; mood swings or unwarranted reactions; being unable to identify feelings; feeling agitated, irritable, panicky, or restless; altered speech

Perceptual changes: Things seeming unreal or distorted; hallucinations; hypersensitivity to colors, sounds, or smells

Cognitive changes: Trouble concentrating or making decisions; fuzzy, obsessive, or paranoid thinking; intrusive thoughts or mental chatter; extreme stillness with few to no thoughts when not meditating

Motivational changes: Apathy, hopelessness, or lack of ability to feel pleasure; lack of drive to meet perceived needs; the sensation of being an observer rather than a participant in your life

Social changes: Altered relationship to the sangha; withdrawing from others; having difficulty orienting to daily life

As lay people, we don't have a monastery routine or a community of fellow practitioners constantly around us who can remind us of a larger perspective. Most of us aren't even especially aware of just what may need rebalancing! It behooves each of us to get to know some of the signs when we might be getting tangled up in the weeds. If you think you may be experiencing some of these issues, consider seeking guidance in adjusting your practice and reestablishing more balance, whether with a sangha facilitator, a Dharma teacher, or a mental health professional.

But wait, you might think, aren't some of these issues signs of having reached nonattachment or "no self?" Isn't that a good thing?

No! This is not what is meant by the Buddhist concept of "no self." We understand that whatever we are, in terms of our bodies, feelings, perceptions, and mental formations, "self" is always changing. We also know that in the historical dimension, our body needs to eat; we need to know that certain people are our partners or friends; we need to experience emotional reactions to a loss. To lose our emotions, to experience a mind without thoughts or concepts, to experience distortions in time, where the past doesn't seem to have existed—this is *not* a healthy, functioning life. The practice is not an easy way to feel good about a bad situation, nor should it be an impediment to necessary daily happiness or functioning. You must discern for yourself if the practice is serving you.

POTHOLES ON THE PATH: OVERTRAINING AND THE MIDDLE WAY

The core teaching of the middle way (see Chapter 3) urges us to find balance between extremes: comfort and discomfort; hedonism and asceticism. This can be a fine line—or perhaps it is more like the swing of a pendulum, with the weight of the pendulum naturally pulling it back as it gets further off center. We have similarly learned how the three poisons of greed, hatred, and delusion (also covered in Chapter 3) emerge when beneficial survival drives are taken to their extremes; so, too, can the beneficial qualities we cultivate through our mindfulness practice become toxic if taken too far.

In the following illustration, the left side of the curve represents a low level of development of a particular desired quality: concentration, loving-kindness, compassion, sympathetic joy, equanimity, right speech, and the like. As we practice, over time we move to the right, increasing our facility with that quality—to a point. The top of the curve represents the maximum effectiveness for the quality, beyond which the benefits begin to decline. In Buddhism, this is what we call a *near enemy*, a quality that may seem similar to what we've been striving to develop, but which no longer has beneficial effects. For example, a near enemy of the quality of equanimity is indifference or callousness.

How do we get into these excessive states? One way is by gravitating to practices that are the easiest for us: the ones that drew us to or endeared us to a Buddhist practice in the first place, or the ones that we had already somewhat developed. It

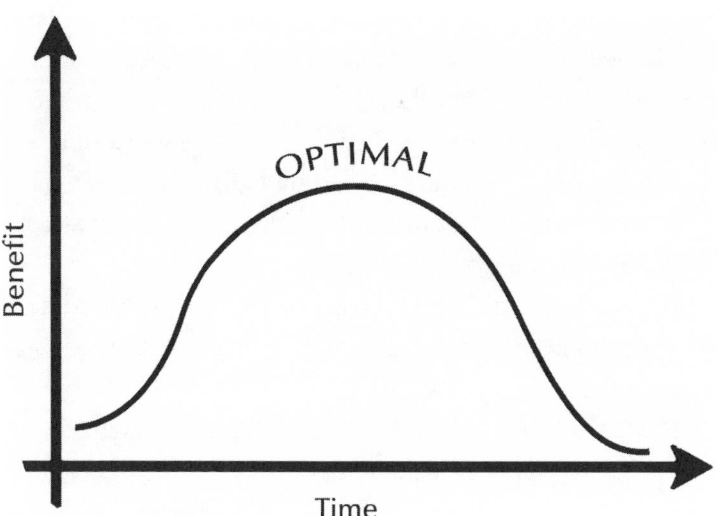

Figure 4.1: The curve of development through meditation

would make sense, then, that those might be the first qualities to reach their optimal training and go over the crest into the "non-beneficial" side of the curve. Of course, we all do this at times! It may be hard to tell, because it may simply look like really strong skill development. But in fact, when we overdevelop certain skills, we may be creating hideouts or rationales for not cultivating other aspects of our practice.

Too much concentration-focused practice can produce numbing or dissociation and can lead us to be narrow-minded, detached from our bodies, and unable to pick up surrounding information. To find balance, practice awareness of the body, the walking meditation, or the eating meditation; make better use of lazy days to be in touch with your body.

Too much compassion-focused practice can produce over-sensitivity, reactivity, or codependence. When we are over-whelmed by unrelenting compassion, we can become numb and dissociated. To find balance, practice sympathetic joy.

Too much joy-focused practice (especially outside of a strong ethical foundation) might lead to all manner of harmful behaviors. The extremes of joy can cause us to become overstimulated, creating imbalance in our nervous system and bumping us out of the window of tolerance. To find balance, practice compassion or equanimity—for example, contemplate impermanence, sickness, old age, and death; and study the Buddhist precepts (mindfulness trainings).

Too much equanimity-focused practice can lead to indifference expressed as apathy, depression, withdrawal, or numbing. To find balance, practice loving-kindness.

Too much loving-kindness practice may create attachment. To find balance, practice equanimity.

Even being in community, when taken to an extreme, can be a problem. For example, we might lose the ability to be on our own or make individual decisions. It can become harder to voice a view that is seen as counter to the norm, causing us to skirt important issues.

DISCERNING DISCOMFORT FROM DYSREGULATION

To cover all the earth with sheets of leather—
Where could such amounts of skin be found?
But with the leather soles of just my shoes
It is as though I cover all the earth! . . .

Shantideva (685–763 CE)[9]

This wisdom from the Buddhist philosopher Shantideva shows us that when we encounter difficulties, making inner rather than outer changes enables us to see reality more accurately and solve problems skillfully. Rather than trying to dominate our environment, we can adapt ourselves to reality in order to walk our journey with more ease, safety, and delight.

Western society has put a lot of energy into creating a culture of ease, and along with it, a fear of discomfort. We acquire more stuff or come up with workarounds to avoid discomfort, buying into a life of stress that then necessitates even more stuff to relieve the discomfort of those very stresses. This fear of discomfort can be an addiction. In our avoidance of discomfort, we become less and less accustomed to using our inner resources to become more resilient.

Let's return to an example we worked with in Chapter 2: Imagine a child has had a scary experience with a dog while walking home from school. When the child comes to their parent for comfort, the parent does their best to get the child to stop crying by distracting them or telling them there is no reason to cry. Wanting to help the child avoid being frightened is normal. Yet it may be just as motivated by the parent's inability to stay calm than it is by the immediate needs of the child. What might be best for the child in the short run is to cry, scream, run, or shake to complete the stress response.

Subsequently, the parent does their best to prevent another scary situation by finding a different route so their child can avoid the dog—which leads to trying to avoid dogs altogether. The child becomes preoccupied with situations where they might encounter a dog and their world narrows. Their experience of everything shrinks, and more things become scary in their unfamiliarity.

Given the same situation, could the parent respond in a way that would help the child stay safe and at the same time overcome their general fear of dogs?

First of all, the parent could stay calm and caring when their child comes to them. By way of coregulation, the parent's calm body helps bring the child into their own sense of calm. The child knows they are safe and seen. Once the child is reregulated, they can begin to take in their situation from a new perspective, slowly learning ways to stay safe with dogs. The child feels empowered by having overcome a fear, which makes them feel that they can overcome other fears the next time one arises. Further, and just as vitally, the child is able to expand their field of delight in the world: when they see a dog, they are able to enjoy its *dog-ness* rather than shrink away from it. This shift from fear to delight also inspires the child to create a habit of looking for other delights in their world.

In our practice we are encouraged to meet difficult situations with mindfulness, holding that difficulty tenderly, like a parent would a small child. As we do this, suffering can be transformed, and traumatic response can be avoided or healed. However, this assumes that we have the capacity to hold that suffering, which we might not always be able to do!

It is our job to discern our capacity to stick with a particular issue in each moment, to know if we're experiencing discomfort (in which case, we should stay with it) or dysregulation (which we need to pull back from). Of course, knowing the difference is not always easy. Becoming familiar with our own window of mindful opportunity can be helpful in this discernment process.

Inside and Outside the Window

In our original diagram of the window of mindful opportunity (see Figure 2.2), we can see a nice crisp upper and lower line, suggesting that it's easy to tell when we're in the window: we're either on one side of the line or the other. And it's true that when we're snug in the center of the window, it's pretty clear. You might think of this as feeling good, or blissful, or in the flow. Outside of the very center, however, there is much more nuance to consider. We could say that the dividing line between "in" and "out" is whether you are consciously in charge (in the window) or on autopilot, without much conscious control (out of the window).

Being too energized or too shut down is the result of the limbic system taking control of things. On the upper edge of the window, the mind races but doesn't necessarily make sense. Our muscles are ready to fight or flee, or both. On the lower edge, both body and mind are at a standstill, maybe even completely dissociated or numb. The true dividing line is whether we still retain some sense of *choice* in the matter, or whether we can recognize what's happening and get curious about it—like in my example of the intolerable itch. If you have a glimmer of awareness or can muster a little curiosity about your experience, chances are you're still in the window.

Let's think about it another way. Consider bird eggs: they are incredibly resilient, striking an almost perfect balance between fragility and toughness. Although their shell seems quite delicate, the shape of the egg bolsters its surface strength, allowing the shell to withstand the weight of the mother bird for weeks while also remaining thin enough for the tiny chick to easily peck its way out when it's time to hatch. What a worldly manifestation of the middle way!

So too, we must do our best to find the strength to handle the upper and lower limits of our window of mindful opportunity. This is not because it is pleasant to hang out there; it is because it is necessary. Little by little, it allows us to transform experiences from toxic to manageable, from unpleasant to neutral. This is how we avoid becoming calloused, indifferent, disconnected from life itself. In this way we can even transform the neutral into the pleasant—for example, noticing and enjoying the *absence* of a toothache. This is the first step to experiencing the pleasant sensations as awe-inspiring and energy producing, sensations of being fully awake.

But we can't do any of this until we know what it feels like to be inside and outside our window of mindful opportunity! This next exercise will help lay the foundations for all of the practices that will follow in Chapters 5 and 6.

EXERCISE 4.1:
Am I In or Out of My Window?

DURATION 5 minutes

FREQUENCY: As often as possible

PURPOSE: Forming the habit of asking and knowing "Am I in or out of my window?"

This exercise is quite clever because as you form the habit of asking this question, you are, just by asking the question, stretching the window of tolerance wider and wider.

At day's end, go back through your day, remembering everything that happened from the moment you opened your eyes: each activity or encounter you can remember. Now think about whether you were in or out of the window for each experience, or if you were approaching your high or low limits at any point.

For the moments when you know you were inside the window, notice, even savor what the experience felt like in your body. How close to or far away from the edge of the window was it? Appreciate yourself for noticing; feel the *enoughness* of that moment, your ability to take good care of yourself in the present.

For those moments when you think you were outside the window, look back on that event with compassion. Know that your actions were actually the result of being in habit mode, out of your control in that moment; remember that whatever happened was your limbic system trying to take care of you as best it could. Sustain that compassionate gaze for a few breaths. Do not get stuck in focusing on the bodily experience of being out of the window! If this occurs, bring your attention back to a moment you remember feeling *inside* the window.

5

Finding Shelter in the Storm

Exercises for Regulating and Grounding When Things Get Tough

Standing like a tree with my roots dug down
My branches wide and open
Come down the rain
Come down the sun
Come down the fruit to
A heart that is open to be
Standing like a tree.

—Betsy Rose, 1988[1]

Thich Nhat Hanh would often describe this scenario: He has gone out into the countryside to enjoy the day, having packed up some tea and perhaps a tangerine. He is happy to be out in the natural world, enjoying the blue sky, the grasses under his feet, the songs of birds, and the rustle of the leaves. After a while, he realizes the clouds are becoming thicker and the wind in the trees more vigorous. There is probably a storm brewing. Remembering that he has left his windows open and a manuscript loose on his desk, he decides to go back to his hut and settle in for the storm. He returns to find papers blowing around all over the place, and he sets about closing the windows, starting a fire, and getting himself warmed up. Then, when he's settled, he can gather up his pages and put them in the right order, bringing a sense of calm to his work.

This little story is the essence of what this chapter is about: what to do when you are caught unexpectedly in a storm. We need to recognize the signs that a storm is coming. We need to find sufficient shelter. And we need to know which of our immediate needs to take care of first. We cannot gather up our messy papers until we have shut the window and stopped them from blowing around!

Of course, we're not talking about a literal storm here. This chapter is about how to respond when your nervous system pops you out of the window of mindful opportunity. (We are talking here about times when hyper- or hypoarousal is *not* beneficial; that is, when we are not actually fighting off an immediate, physical threat.) We will try out lots of useful tools and exercises, including how to find and shape the anchors of our personal practice and how to adapt things along the way if they become too difficult. With practice, these reregulating exercises will enable us to stand up against that window, even open it a crack to peer out with curiosity, and still feel assured that we are safe from the storm.

This is how we practice when we have an inner storm:

- We return to our shelter (use our resources to anchor or stabilize ourselves);

- close the windows to the storm (shift our focus away from the difficulties); and
- warm ourselves (bring our attention to what feels stabilizing).

We will learn to create stability by where we put our attention.

Only when we are warmed up and cozy enough can we focus back on the work at hand. Once we regulate, we can begin trying to expand our window of tolerance and increase our level of ease with whatever has caused us stress.

This is not rocket science! We all have already developed our own ways of bringing ourselves into balance, either consciously or unconsciously. You may recognize that the exercises that I offer in this chapter are not really new to you, at least in principle. Yet it is sometimes very beneficial to have a conscious awareness of *how* we cope—and cope well. This gives us a more conscious choice of what to strengthen so that it is more readily available to us when we need it. In an emergency, we know we go on automatic; if we learn to strengthen good habits of balancing, then we will be able to reach for these tools automatically even when we are being swept away by that limbic brain.

The following reflection written by E. illustrates how regulating and grounding when conditions are stormy can make all the difference for herself and for her family. E. writes,

> My son is eleven years old and has developmental disabilities, including significant speech delays. He has experienced multiple medical traumas. In early 2020, when he was seven, he had to have a medical procedure with anesthesia at a children's hospital. In the procedure room, he pushed away the anesthesia mask and began kicking and pushing everyone around him. Five medical providers held him

down to put the anesthesia mask on him, which definitely traumatized him. He had two other medical procedures in the two years following at the same hospital, but in different procedure rooms. The anesthesiologists were understanding of my son's trauma and used IV lines instead of a mask. The most recent medical procedure was only six weeks ago. This time, I arranged for my son to be able to take Valium before we even entered the hospital. As a result, he sat by himself for the first time while the anesthesiologist placed his IV and seemed calm. However, when his stretcher was wheeled into the procedure room, he stood up. It was the same room as the one in which the five medical providers held him down in 2020. He recognized it and looked ready to run, despite the calming medication in his system. I sang to him a song about feeling safe and loved, and he started to relax, bending down and putting his hands on the stretcher. The anesthesiologist then gave him the anesthesia through an IV so the procedure could take place. He woke up with his parents by his bedside in the recovery room.

A few hours later, at home, he bit his long-time babysitter. He wet his pants twice that afternoon, despite being toilet-trained. He had insomnia and could not fall asleep until 11:00 pm. In the weeks that followed, he became violent toward my spouse and me. At first, he attacked us by biting, pinching, pulling hair, and scratching, up to eight times a day for a few weeks. It often took 5 to 10 minutes for him to calm down and stop the attack. I bought a Thai boxing shield and other protective gear. We tried the supplement L-theanine, to help him feel calmer. There were fewer attacks, but they continued. Then last week, my son had difficulty eating. He was feeling upset and "hangry," more than usual. During one hangry episode, he tried to bite me continuously for several moments. When there was a pause, I said to him, "Darling, you're trying to fight now because that's what you wanted to do in the hospital, when the doctors and nurses crowded you and held you down." He looked at me, stopped everything, and walked out of the room into the kitchen, where he ate a considerable amount of food.

Seeing his response, I burst into tears. His traumas had become my traumas. I needed my own release. In the days since then, he has still had difficult moments and gone on the offensive once or twice a day. I have calmly reminded him that he's in "fight mode" and that he wanted to "fight" the doctors and nurses at the hospital who held him down. Every time that he's registered what I've said, he's stopped fighting immediately. He is beginning to understand a connection between his bodily states during the traumas and his bodily states now. He is smiling and singing more; signs of a shift toward more balanced nervous system regulation.

These experiences have empowered me with a greater understanding of my own inner processes and my son's inner processes. I see more clearly how I can support my son on his healing journey, and also, how to support my own healing.

Writing down this experience felt cathartic. I could feel more calm in my body too, as I think that putting these turbulent events into written words helped me to release some of the emotional tension in my body. The takeaways from the writing experience are 1) there's power in authorship, 2) healing is possible in multiple ways, and 3) I can trust in transformational processes that I might not fully understand on a cognitive, intellectual level.

Creating Stability through Conscious Attention

There is a wonderful YouTube clip I love to show when I work with middle schoolers. It depicts two basketball teams that are passing the ball back and forth. The audience is challenged to watch intently and count how many passes are made by the team in white. After thirty seconds or so, I pause the video and ask the viewers, "Did you see the moonwalking bear?" Inevitably, those who took up the counting challenge completely missed the person in a bear suit dancing right through the middle of the group, in plain sight.

Of the thousands of stimuli coming at us in any given moment, our nervous system can only process a tiny fraction. Of that small fraction, we are only able to put conscious attention on a couple at a time. In this way, we create our own "reality" of sorts. This reality is a far cry from what is actually going on in that moment. When the limbic system is strong, we tend to be overactivated, giving the nervous system the skewed perception of threat. If, on the other hand, we are able to maintain our attention and concentration on the unthreatening elements, we can convince the nervous system all is well and it will calm down.

Consider the Rodgers and Hammerstein song "I Whistle a Happy Tune," calling for us to respond to fear by whistling casually, as if we're not afraid—fooling those around us, but also tricking ourselves into not being afraid! I'd say that is a prescription for a solid practice when difficulties arise: finding uplifting things to which we can shift our attention, at least temporarily. Let's explore more thoroughly some ways to maintain and reregulate a balanced nervous system.

Emergency Relief

Many of the tools we'll use in this chapter require at least some intention in order to muster up practicing them in a pinch. The more we use the tools in a relaxed situation, the more likely they will be habitually accessible in a stressful situation. Yet when we are too dysregulated to access those tools—when we're *really* stuck outside that window—we need to get down to the very basics. So before we go any further, let's first learn what to do in case of emergency.

When the nervous system gets hijacked, really stuck outside that window, at some point we know it. We may realize it right away, in the middle of it all, or only in retrospect. After a bit of self-compassion, and recognizing that we've been shaken up, it is crucial that we bring ourselves back into more balance. We do this by shifting our attention to what brings us to our senses, literally what brings us into the present moment. We do our best to limit our focus to things that we recognize as safe. We do this as long as necessary to reestablish a sense of calm alertness: it might just take a few minutes, or it might mean we must completely switch gears to a different activity, or take a rest.

Whatever we choose to focus our attention on, it is important to stay right in the present moment, using just one of our senses at a time. For example, if we are highly visual, we might scan the horizon for a simple shape; for example, we might pick out all the triangles we can find. This simple little focus can distract us from the bodily sensations that are snowballing inside. Sustaining this search for a couple of minutes can bring us down enough to remember that we have other tools available to us as well, such as body scanning, focusing on the breath, grounding, or resourcing (we'll get to all of these later in the chapter), to take us further down the path of reregulation.

Using each of our senses we can hone in on just one simple thing in a variety of ways. Here are a few suggestions:

Sight: Scan everything you can see, picking out a particular shape, color, pattern, movement, or type of item (like trees, windows, or chairs).

Sound: Notice sounds close by or far away; consider their pitch, loudness, or rhythm; hum to yourself, sing a song, or let out a loud noise.

Smell: Notice different smells and determine their sources.

Touch: Notice different textures around you, like smooth, rough, or crumbly; hold a hot cup of water, or put a cold washcloth on your forehead; put on hand lotion.

Taste: Take a drink or a bite of something, and savor the taste, following it down the throat.

Think: Count backward from one hundred; spell your whole name backward; count how many beats your heart makes in 2 minutes.

Big muscle energy: Take a walk or run; lean up against or push on a wall; lie down on the floor and put your feet up; wrap yourself tight in a blanket or shawl; bite a rolled-up towel.

Do any of these tools seem familiar? You probably have some things you do already, either consciously or unconsciously, that fit into one of these categories of self-regulating. You may be pleasantly surprised to find how clever you have been to discover these processes all on your own! Let's add them to the list—either things you do already, or other ideas you have for self-regulating.

Whatever approach you end up using, the important thing is to feel what's going on inside and help the tension release. Allow the body to do what it is geared up to do. If your arms and legs feel energized, do something with them. If you feel like yelling, release some of that into a pillow or a balled-up jacket, or growl, or bite your sleeve. Do what your body is yearning to do (as long as it is safe).

For all the exercises in this book, and especially for those in this chapter, it is important to try them out in advance, to practice them, noting how effective they are (or aren't) for you personally. Try the following exercise and note what feels helpful.

EXERCISE 5.1:
Emergency Relief

DURATION: 15 minutes
FREQUENCY: Once for understanding, regularly to master
PURPOSE: Discovering what works for you in a pinch

Begin by letting those around you know that you may be about to act a bit strangely! Then spend some moments getting comfortable, and remind yourself that you are okay and safe in this moment. You are going on an adventure; bring your curiosity toward your experience. You will finish up the same way—affirming in the beginning and affirming at the end.

When you are feeling comfortable in your body and mind, bring to mind something that is mildly annoying. Bring it to mind in some detail, and notice how you feel inside, what parts of the body and mind are affected by this issue. Notice how strong the initial feeling is.

Using the earlier suggestions, or some you have come up with on your own, pick one area of focus (sight or sound, for example) and try it out (counting shapes, focusing on a sound, etc.). Take a minute or so. Notice what happens.

Once more, return your thoughts to the annoying issue, and then try using a different tool. After trying five or six of them, notice how you are now feeling about the issue. Notice what is happening inside.

End with a couple of minutes of doing something that feels soothing to you to return you to a comfortable state within the window of mindful opportunity.

Extra credit: Each difficulty you encounter will have a unique impact on you, so each may require a different trick to bring you back into the window of tolerance. Try this exercise out on other annoying issues.

Developing an Anchor

An *anchor* is just what it sounds like: something we can attach ourselves to when we need stability in a storm. It's anything that brings us a sense of "okayness," or what Thich Nhat Hanh calls *home* (see Chapter 1).

Many contemplative paths use the breath as an anchor. The breath is always with us as a finely attuned indicator to what is going on inside. Using the breath can also be an effective way to switch on the parasympathetic nervous system with its calming effects. Breathing in deeply, and breathing out slowly, encourages the vagus nerve to alert the brain that all is well. The breath is something that we have conscious control over, yet it's easy to quickly forget about when we're ready to focus our attention elsewhere. In short, using the breath as an anchor is practical, handy, and effective; it has become the go-to tool for those of us in the Plum Village lineage to bring ourselves back into stability. That is, unless it doesn't work.

That was the case for me. When I tried to follow my breath, I couldn't focus for more than a few breaths. When I watched my breaths, I would start to feel that they were in some way never deep enough—it felt like I couldn't take a complete breath. As I would try to breathe deeper and more slowly, I would become impatient and fearful. Now, as I think back to childhood, I can remember struggling to get to sleep as a ten-year-old, feeling afraid of some scary thing I'd watched on TV, and feeling like I was unable to breathe.

Whether or not this memory was the root cause of my struggles to focus on my breath as an adult, it never occurred to me as a new practitioner to mention it—or that I was struggling at all—to anyone. And so, wanting to be a "good" practitioner, I spent years either faking it or white-knuckling it, feeling like an impostor. With understanding, I was slowly able to befriend my breath. At this point in my life, it is my go-to regulator, bringing me feelings of relief and both inner and outer harmony.

I tell this story to emphasize that you always have a choice. If you struggle with focusing on your breath—or any other specific practice—you always have alternatives. You don't have to try to fake it like I did! For example, if breath isn't quite working for you as an anchor, try attending to your heartbeat or a part of the body that feels pleasant. For some people whose bodies have suffered pain or abuse, focusing on *any* physical sensation may not feel safe; although this will eventually be an important thing to explore, starting with a different kind of anchor may be more helpful in the beginning. This could include a mental anchor (a pleasant mental image or memory) or an external anchor: tuning in to sounds around you, feeling the support of the chair or cushion under you, smelling incense, or gazing at a candle flame. Whatever gives you a sense of safety and alertness.

Because it is so commonly used, and so effective for many people, let's start by experimenting with breath—knowing that if it *doesn't* work for you, there are lots of other things to try! Whatever it is, bring your mindfulness to your anchor and note what happens in the rest of your body: does the body give this anchor a thumbs-up?

EXERCISE 5.2: Breath as Anchor

DURATION: 5 to 45 minutes
FREQUENCY: Daily
PURPOSE: Exploring our breath

As usual, find a comfortable place where you won't be disturbed. Sitting, standing, or lying down are all fine. Just bring your attention to your breath.

How many places in your body can you sense that breath? Try each place for 5 to 10 breaths. It may be that you want to just focus on one place today, exploring each section on a separate occasion. There's no rush.

Nostrils: Can you sense the air going in and out of the nostrils? What do you notice about the temperature of the air in and air out? Can you notice the pull and release of the air in your nose? Do you find any of this pleasant or neutral? Try keeping your attention on the pleasant or neutral qualities for a few breaths. What is that like for you? Follow your breath from the very beginning to the very end.

Chest: Can you tell whether you are breathing in or out? What cues you into this? Is your breath long or short? How can you tell? Play around with the depth and speed of your breath: What do you find most pleasant, energizing, relaxing? Notice the beginning, middle, and end of the in breath and out breath. Is one more effort than the other, or more pleasant? Allow the breath to do whatever it wants, and just be aware without too much effort.

Belly: Place your hands on your belly, with middle fingers barely touching (this is a bit easier lying down on your back). Notice your hands moving apart and together as you breathe. When we talk about "belly breathing," this means that your belly is rising and falling, rather than your chest rising and falling. (It tends to feel deeper and more calming than chest breathing.) Be aware of the rhythm of touching and separating, touching and separating.

Experiment with varying the speed and depth of breathing, noticing what is most pleasant or neutral. You may also try sucking in your belly on the out breath and trying to keep the breath coming in and out from the belly rather than the chest.

Extra credit: "4/7/8 breathing" is a practice of rhythmic breathing that may be effective in sending the vagus nerve the message that all is well. Breathe in a 4-second breath through the nose, hold it for 7 seconds, and then breathe out for 8 seconds. Try this for 5 breaths. This type of breathing may also be helpful to wake you up if you're feeling a bit drowsy.

EXERCISE 5.3:
An Alternative Anchor: Sound

DURATION: 5 to 15 minutes

FREQUENCY: As often as possible

PURPOSE: Finding an alternative anchor that speaks to you

Begin by finding a posture that allows you to be relaxed and alert. Take a look around, noticing things that bring you a sense of delight, beauty, stability, or ease. Signal that ease to your limbic system by taking a couple of deep, slow breaths. If it is authentic, smile when feeling your intention of taking good care of yourself.

In this exercise we will focus on sounds, both internal and external. If you find that the way you are paying attention isn't engaging enough to promote concentration, choose a specific characteristic to notice: volume, pitch, direction, or whether a sound is steady or intermittent. Sound has many elements. Try sticking with one at a time, noting each time the impact of the listening on the body. Do not go overboard in your efforts; just be aware of the sounds that arise rather than going hunting for them.

After a while, allow the sounds to recede a bit, and just feel the aftereffects of this listening on the body. If you find this pleasant or even neutral, allow your awareness to dwell there in the body for a while. The sensation may fade or shift—no matter! When you notice the urge to stop, try to sit with it for a bit longer, recapturing your sense of feeling relaxed and alert, until the urge to stop comes again. This will help you develop patience and give you insight into urges in general.

Cautionary Note: Before we put more emphasis on getting in touch with bodily sensations, let's remember what we learned about the anatomy of memory. When we reexperience sensations similar to those we experienced during situations we perceived as threatening, we form automatic responses to keep us safe. To keep us protected and stable, we may have a tendency not to not feel those parts of the body. If scanning the body becomes a trigger for these implicit memories, you may want to take note, continue reading on, and return to this experience when you feel you have the internal and/or external support and stability to explore further.

EXERCISE 5.4: An Alternative Anchor: Body Scanning

DURATION: 15 to 20 minutes
FREQUENCY: Once, or more if you enjoy it
PURPOSE: To spend time experiencing the body from the inside
MATERIALS needed: Paper, a variety of colored markers or pencils

Begin by taking a couple of full, slow breaths. On your paper, draw the outline of a complete body—it does not matter if the drawing looks like a starfish; this doesn't need to be fine art. You can toss it when you are done, if you like. Make the drawing as big as the paper will allow.

That done, settle again in a way that you like. Begin to scan the body for pleasant or neutral sensations. It is natural to be on the lookout for aches and pains, but right now, try to focus on the good feelings. When you find a good spot, even one as insignificant as an earlobe, enjoy it a while: completely savor it. When you are well-acquainted with the experience of that spot, choose a color and shape to put onto your body sketch that represents that spot in an appropriate size to match your experience. Stay connected to the experience of placing the color on the paper. No rush.

When you've done that, continue this process with as many pleasant or neutral sensations in your body as you find and have time for. You can keep this drawing and add to it in the future, or you can throw it away and start from scratch next time. (You may find these drawings helpful in the future to remember where and how your body was in a wholesome state, where you felt mindful presence.) The important thing is to savor the process of enjoying your aliveness.

Plum Village Practices That Strengthen Our Anchor

In Plum Village monasteries worldwide, when people hear the sound of a bell—whether it is a temple bell, a clock chime, or the ring of a telephone—they stop what they are doing and spend some time with their anchor. This simple pause not only reinforces your anchor, it gives you time to come back to yourself and check in to the now. It even encourages flexibility by bringing you to an unexpected stop. Finding some reminder in your life that happens fairly frequently—hearing a telephone ringing, stopping at a stop sign or stoplight, starting to climb stairs, or taking a sip of water—can help you develop this mindful habit of taking a breather. There are even apps that will interrupt your computer time with a bell sound.

I have found it deeply satisfying to find practices in my own root tradition of Judaism that hold a similar spirit to this Buddhist one. In Judaism we have a tradition of pausing briefly when we go into and out of a building (some take it so far as to pause every time they go into and out of a room!) to say a prayer, acknowledging wholeness (my personal interpretation).

We also place a ritual object at the door of a building to touch when we go in and out. This, too, can be an anchoring experience. If you have a root tradition you'd enjoy weaving in, this is a good place to play with it.

Awareness of the Body

When we consider how our perceptions tell us whether we are feeling safe or threatened, it's easy to see that where we put our attention has a big influence on the state of our nervous system. If we are able to hone our attention on sense impressions and thoughts that we perceive as safe, our nervous system will register "safety," and inform the rest of the body accordingly. If, on the other hand, we are habitually focused on what seems threatening, our nervous system will signal "danger," and create a fight/flight/freeze response. If we are to keep our nervous systems in balance, we need to know how it feels when our body is signaling to us that it is balanced or unbalanced. The first step here is to actually develop awareness of the various parts of the body. Our daily lives are focused on the outer world: interacting with others, sweeping the floor, doing our work, or even just crossing the street. We don't spend very much time tuning in to the subtle messages that are constantly being sent by our bodies.

If we make a deliberate effort to spend time noticing body sensations every day, we will become more aware of when we're regulated and when we're not. Spending time being meticulously in touch with our bodies can also be enjoyable, relaxing, nourishing, and energizing. For some, it might be a necessary part of healing and empowerment. In fact, the more you can build a habit of being in touch with your body, the less likely you will be to need these exercises, as your whole system becomes more resilient.

However, it is important to note that for many of us, distancing from bodily sensations was, and perhaps still is, a coping strategy to survive overwhelming stress, such as violence or serious illness. If you have a history of suffering in your body, this practice may be difficult for you or reactivate past traumatic memories; you may find certain parts of your body feel numb or inaccessible. Becoming reacquainted with bodily sensations needs to go at whatever speed is appropriate for you and your body, staying within the edges of your window. As you practice, remember that you can always return to your anchor or resource that you've developed in the previous exercises.

As you do this next exercise, your job is to remain curious about your experience.

All the information we need to assess the state of our nervous system is held in the body: breath, heartbeat, muscle tension. Pique your curiosity by asking, Where am I sensing this feeling? Is it pleasant, unpleasant, or neutral? Is it increasing, decreasing, or staying the same? Is there a temperature, texture, size, shape, or color I associate with this feeling?

There is no wrong way to do these exercises! The question is simple: Can you feel it? If not, that's fine; then the right answer is "no." Either way, ask yourself: How do I know this? Sit with that question, even if there is no answer; the question itself is a practice.

EXERCISE 5.5: Attuning to Body Sensations

DURATION: 5 to 45 minutes depending on your enjoyment and spaciousness

FREQUENCY: Daily to develop skill

OBJECTIVE: Attuning to your window of tolerance

Find a comfortable position, sitting or lying down, where you can be relaxed as well as alert for several minutes. It can be helpful to take a few slow, deep, purposeful breaths, and maybe even give yourself a bit of appreciation for taking this time for yourself.

First, notice the places your body is being supported by the floor (or chair, or cushion), and feel the weight of gravity at work. Take all the time you need to experience this weight, and ask yourself whether this awareness of weight seems pleasant, unpleasant, or neutral. Just ask the question and see if an opinion arises; the answer is not as important as the question to just help get yourself into a mindset of curiosity. As you become more attuned to whether or not something feels pleasant, you will be able to return to these experiences when doing so is helpful. We are hardwired to continuously scan for the *unpleasant*, so learning to hold focused attention on the pleasant or neutral can take some concentration. For that reason, it helps to practice this often and when you are relaxed, building your skill in advance so it will be ready when you need it.

Begin by focusing on your feet. Notice the sensations in each foot. You can check for temperature; the feeling of the foot on the floor or in your socks; muscle tension; joint sensations; whether the feet feel similar or different from each other; differences between your soles and the tops of your feet. Just take your time and be curious. Finally, ask yourself: Are these sensations pleasant, unpleasant, or neutral?

Don't worry if you cannot feel a certain part of the body, simply notice the lack of sensation. Certainly it is not a bad thing not to be able to feel every part. In fact, some parts only come into our awareness when there is something wrong, like a toothache or stomachache. Our focus here is on tracking our sensations, and noticing the impact of this tracking on the rest of the body, mind, and spirit. If this impact feels beneficial, savor it.

When you've explored your feet to your satisfaction, begin to move up your body: legs, pelvic area, back, internal organs, arms, shoulders, neck, head. From time to time, notice how this process of attending to the body is affecting the body as a whole. It might also be helpful to take a couple of cleansing breaths here and there.

End your session by dwelling on one or more pleasant or neutral sensations.

Although the purpose here is to become more attuned to body sensations and develop your ability to concentrate your attention, you can also use this exercise as an anchoring technique to help balance your nervous system if you find the exercise pleasant or relaxing (see page 130).

Cautionary Note: Don't allow your attention to be distracted by chronic aches and pains. Just note them respectfully and return to the exercise. This can be challenging, yet very beneficial. Once you know the discomfort is not an immediate threat, do your best to go back to the rest of the body. Hyperfocusing on aches and pains can actually skew our perception of the discomfort, dysregulating us more than rebalancing.

Plum Village Practices That Develop Body Awareness

Stopping at the Sound of the Bell: As you learned earlier, it is an important Plum Village practice to pause for a moment when you hear the sound of a bell. In fact, it doesn't have to be a literal bell—it can be the phone ringing, seeing a stop sign, or even flushing the toilet! The point is that you build moments into your day where you reflexively stop. You can use this moment to return to your anchor (see page 130 in Chapter 5), or you can use it to become aware of the body—perhaps taking two breaths to just experience it and another breath focused on a pleasant sensation you're feeling.

Blooming of a Lotus: *The Blooming of a Lotus* by Thich Nhat Hanh is a book of commentaries and guided meditations.[2] In this book, meditations 1, 2, 3, 4, 6, 8, and 10 focus on body awareness. In a way, they can become a resource for you. These short, guided meditations put us in touch with a variety of ways to focus on the body parts, elements, and functions. They are good stand-alone meditations or can be used for just part of a sitting—for 5 minutes, or repeated for as long as seems useful. You might like to record yourself reading them out loud to use during meditation; some of them can also be found on the Plum Village app.

Deep Relaxation: A guided meditation. Usually you lie down in a safe and comfortable space, and focus on a variety of aspects of body awareness and appreciation (see page 196; this meditation can also be found on the Plum Village app).

Walking Meditation: This practice involves having the same objects of attention as sitting meditation, but while walking (see page 183). You may focus on the act of walking, with attention on your feet and the ground; on the sunlight touching your skin; on the clothing hanging on your body; on smells; or on colors. You can choose one object of focus or allow the natural arising of sensation to dictate where you put your attention.

Eating Meditation: There is an endless list of possible focuses here: taste, texture, the changing state of the food in your mouth, or returning the attention to eating as you notice the mind wandering (see page 185).

Working Meditation: While doing chores or working, you let go of goals and focusing on body position, movement, degree of exertion, colors, shapes, and smells—an endless cascade of experience.

Resources of Well-Being

When things get tough, it is worth remembering these wise words from Thich Nhat Hanh: "There are always enough conditions for happiness." When the mind begins to run away in fear or anger or despair, this sentence invites us to remember our *resources*, conditions in our lives that make life worth living. Resources can include moments of deep connection with loved ones, or with other beings; experiencing the wonder of a snowflake, dewdrop, or autumn leaves; or pleasant memories.

Sometimes resources that bring us joy may be mixed with other emotions like grief, fear, or frustration. This often happens when we are in conflict or someone dear moves or passes away. In this case, the mixed emotions of the situation make the resource temporarily less effective. Resources can also turn into a problematic coping strategy: we find regulation in the short term, but the strategy itself actually creates more stress, so we feel the need to turn to it again, creating a vicious cycle. This is the mechanism of addiction (drugs, alcohol, sex, relationships, work, consumption). It is important to find a variety of resources that are effective without creating a longer-term problem.

Most of us already have our pet resources, even if we don't realize it. My pet way to reregulate is through music: I rarely need more than two bars of a favorite piece to transport my mood into one of complete well-being. This was my entrée into walking meditation, a discipline I had struggled with for some time given my poor concentration. One day I had the idea of walking meditation while listening to music. Having my heart opened by the music and synchronizing that with my steps was magical. By the process of "what fires together wires together," in short order I had developed a new, positive relationship with walking meditation. Today, if I'm feeling low and put on some music to make myself feel better, sometimes I feel the overwhelming urge to go out and practice walking meditation!

The strength of a resource does not necessarily relate to its perceived importance: simply watching a leaf float down to the grass or eliciting a smile from a passerby can be surprisingly satisfying! Collecting and savoring resources can be a wonderful pastime and can bring enormous benefits as long as you take the time—just 20 to 30 seconds will suffice—to stay with and reinforce that experience. Collecting resources can become a way of life, boosting our spirit and the immune system. You can look at this practice as shifting attention to something that brings well-being or as actually broadening your attention to see a fuller picture. This latter understanding of resourcing makes it closer to what we'd call right view (see page 75) as we expand our awareness to include more than just one skandha (body, feelings, perceptions, mental formations, and consciousness).

This next story is an example of skillful resourcing. Rahima was in her late twenties when I met her, in a class on regulating the nervous system. This class took place in a large Israeli city, and most of the women in the class were Muslim, living as second-class citizens in an Arab neighborhood that had a long history of marginalization, division, and violence; it was the water everyone swam in. On top of this, Rahima had been badly injured by a land mine as a child, and—were the bodily harm and pain not enough—the resulting disfigurement of her body prompted her parents to tell her that she was no longer desirable as a woman, and that her future prospects for marriage would be limited.

On this particular day, the topic was resourcing: finding experiences of well-being and learning how to intensify them in order to build resilience. At first, Rahima was only marginally engaged in the class. But midway through, during an exercise involving music and dance, she took center stage: in that moment, as she began to move, a spell overtook our circle as we watched her sheer joy as she was carried away by the music. That moment became a reference point for us as we witnessed her transformation, seeing firsthand how women can support each other and heal themselves.

Dancing also became an anchor for Rahima's healing as she found her way back to a sense of beauty and self-worth. She went on to write about her previous traumatic incidents from a new perspective of strength. When she shared her writing with the group, Rahima explained that when tension began to come up as she wrote about the traumatic events, she was able to calm her body by going back to her felt sense of dancing—a crucial resource.

EXERCISE 5.6: Resourcing Ourselves

DURATION: 10 to 15 minutes
FREQUENCY: Daily
PURPOSE: Increased sense of well-being

Allow time in each of the following sections of the exercise to fully experience and savor each enjoyable part.

Find a time and place where you can be uninterrupted. Bring something to mind that brings a sense of well-being—a memory, an imagined situation, or even a fantasy. Bring it to mind in as much detail as possible: What do you see, hear, smell—what's going on? What are the best parts of this scenario playing out in your head? Become aware of what you are telling yourself about it.

Allow yourself to experience this scene in any way that you can enjoy it, and notice what effect it has on your body. Where do you notice this, and is the sensation pleasant, unpleasant, or neutral? If it is pleasant, then this may be a good resource for you. Remember, some resources may create feelings of well-being as well as a bit of sadness, anger, fear, or bitterness; this often happens with the passing of some being or place dear to us. If the unpleasant feelings dampen or overpower the pleasant feelings of well-being, set this resource aside for now and look for another one. With time and healing, it may become more useful to you in the future.

What do you make of this resource? How is it significant for you? Again, notice how focusing on the resource impacts you inside. If pleasant or neutral sensations are rising, focus attention on them.

Extra Credit: Spend more time with your resource, mulling it over and focusing on the good feelings it brings up in your body. This is a way to intensify the experience, to grease that neural pathway so it becomes easier to access in the future. You might relive the experience as a way to fall asleep at night. You might enjoy sharing the resource with someone. You might even make a drawing or a short comic strip of whatever it is and hang it up someplace you'll notice it. These are enjoyable ways to ensure access to this resource when you feel bumped out of that window.

EXERCISE 5.7: Making a Resource Out of a Challenging Circumstance

DURATION: 15 minutes
FREQUENCY: As many times as you might enjoy
PURPOSE: Reframing difficult circumstances

Contemplate something in your past that was very challenging for you. This should be something that you have made progress on or perhaps something you have overcome completely; think about a time when you learned a new skill, resolved a conflict, lived through a disaster, or overcame a health challenge. Do *not* choose something that you are finding challenging at the present moment! Notice how your body and mind are responding to that situation.

While you think about this story—or perhaps write it down—put the emphasis on those ways in which you gained freedom; overcame fear; or gained confidence, skill, understanding, compassion, gratitude, or generosity. While keeping focus on the story (that is, stay settled in your thinking brain), continue to be aware of signals from your body. You are a storyteller in this process, calling up explicit memories. You are not the actor in the story—this would call up *implicit* memories or activate the limbic system. While thinking or writing, if you notice some sense of well-being, stop to savor it. If you notice tension, then use that moment to anchor, or take a break. After this contemplation, think about the situation again and compare what arises to how you felt about the situation at the beginning of the exercise. Has there been any shift in perspective? In bodily sensations? In what you now tell yourself about that event?

Plum Village Practices That Develop Resources

Underlying all practices in the Plum Village tradition is the concept of interbeing: the insight that we are inextricably connected with everything in the web of life, whether animal, vegetable, or mineral. This is the ultimate resource! You may like to explore these practices and adopt them as your own as you make your way on the path of healing and transformation.

Creating Altars: Building altars is a beautiful way to remind ourselves of the bounty of resources we have accumulated. Altars can include photos of loved ones and ancestors; mentors; places of beauty; and/or things that remind us of moments of nurturing, delight, or awe. Tending the altar can be a practice in itself.

Singing and Chanting: These practices (see Chapter 6) vibrate various parts of the body. Be on the lookout for the ways in which pleasant sensations may arise from the music, the words, or instrumental accompaniment.

Celebrations: These are a way of extending savoring over many minutes, hours, or days, honoring any variety of resources: family, friends, seasons, memorials, and so on. You can blend creativity and tradition and bring in cultural inheritance or visionary aspirations.

Blooming of the Lotus: Exercises 5–9 in *The Blooming of a Lotus* guide us in how to expand our appreciation of our bodies.

Reciting Gathas: *Gathas* (see page 188) are short poems that blend ordinary parts of the historical dimension with a deep appreciation of the ultimate dimension together with an intention for living mindfully. For example, a gatha might describe ordinary drinking water but reflect on the interbeing nature of clouds, rivers, and tears, as well as the preciousness of water and the desire for all living beings to have clean water to be healthy.

Touching the Earth: *Touching the Earth*, by Thich Nhat Hanh, is a book of guided meditations that invite us to heal our relationships through acceptance, deep looking, and forgiveness, and embracing our ancestors, parents, teachers, and ourselves.[3] The practice of touching the earth can be practiced alone or with others. The text is read while prostrating to the earth in a gesture of humility and letting go of blame or self-blame. can be deeply restorative. When some sense of freedom or relief of suffering arises, focusing on this wholesome feeling becomes a future resource.

Grounding: Establishing Solidity

Another method of rebalancing a dysregulated system is bringing a sense of solidity into the body. This is often referred to as being *grounded*. There are many ways to do this. Luckily, we have the earth's gravity on our side! We are looking for bodily sensations of strength, weight, or anchoring so that we feel unshakeable. Think of us as being like a mighty oak; although the winds may blow in our crown, moving the branches around wildly, our thick trunk is unmovable, anchored deep into the ground with a long, sturdy tap root. When we talk about grounding, we're searching for this feeling in our own bodies, or we're amplifying it if we can sense it is already there.

The process of grounding brings us quickly into the present moment: eyes open, fully aware. It doesn't matter whether we are standing, lying down, walking, or even swimming—a sense of *groundedness* is generally available for the finding, if we know how to look for it.

EXERCISE 5.8:
Exercises for Grounding

DURATION: 10 minutes initially, thereafter 90 seconds
FREQUENCY: Every few days
PURPOSE: Boosting groundedness, invigorating self-confidence

Try these for a couple of minutes each:

Sitting Down: Become aware of where the weight of your body is supported by the chair, cushion, or floor. Notice whether this feels pleasant, unpleasant, or neutral. Bend forward and back, side to side, coming to the place where the body is most effortlessly held upright. Feel how the spine supports the head, and find the right position for the head and neck for optimal support. You can do this all slowly, allowing your body to savor any pleasant sensations coming from the sense of solidity. In fact, sometimes we can notice even more subtleties when we pause an extra bit. Notice the difference in grounding with the in breath and then the out breath. Notice the effect of resting your hands on your legs or in your lap or placing them on the ground if you are sitting on the floor.

Each time that you notice a grounding effect, allow your nervous system to just marinate in those sensations.

Lying Down: Repeat the previous explorations while lying on your back, side, or stomach. Always allow time to come into full awareness of the body's reaction, and then allow more time to savor as the neural pathways become faster and stronger in the process.

Standing Up: Again, repeat the previous explorations. Experiment with how the arms and legs figure in to the sense of grounding. Try it with feet together, then shoulder-width apart. How does it feel different with your hands hanging by your sides, on your hips, or stretched into the air? Take time to savor; keep your eyes open.

Extra credit: Put on something weighted, like a heavy coat, or place heavy pillows in your lap, or convince an animal (or a good friend!) to sit or lie on top of you. These might be surprisingly pleasant ways to feel solid. Always respect your own boundaries and proceed at the speed of wise curiosity.

When I am teaching this concept to a group, I love to introduce it by pointing out the unconscious ways we all have for keeping ourselves grounded: some of us may cross our arms over our chest or cross our legs at the knees or ankles, some of us my shove our hands into our pockets, or lean on an elbow, and so on. I think it is miraculous how we do these fortifying gestures naturally. It reinforces my faith in our natural propensity for strength and resilience.

Mudras: Finding Regulation in Spontaneous Gestures

The word *mudra* comes from the Sanskrit word for "sign," meaning hand and finger gestures that capture the experience of certain mind states and virtues or values such as peace, friendship, wisdom, humility, generosity, respect, and so on. Think of the V-sign for peace common in Western culture. The mudras have been helpful teaching devices, pairing physical and mental states with various gestures as links to the experience.

As you develop the first three tools discussed in this chapter (tracking the body, resources, and grounding), as you come into the fullness of the experience, you may notice that you feel the urge to express yourself with your hands or by making other bodily movements. We do things like this all the time, consciously or unconsciously, yet rarely do we pay attention to them. We add hand gestures or body language to soothe ourselves in times of stress, to release extra tension when we're overly excited, or to give ourselves a sense of strength and protection when we feel our boundaries being violated. Becoming aware of these movements when they arise spontaneously helps us utilize them consciously during appropriate moments.

EXERCISE 5.9: Gesturing to Intensify Our Message

DURATION: 5 minutes

FREQUENCY: Once a week just as a reminder they exist

PURPOSE: Increasing range of expression

For each of the following, bring to mind a situation in which the corresponding feelings might arise. Then, after counting to three, make whatever gesture comes to mind. Now repeat it, and notice how it affects you inside. It may be helpful to explore a couple of gesture options for each of the following situations and their associated emotions. After each exploration, you may want to make a few notes for the future.

Imagine a situation in which . . .

- You might need some self-soothing.
- You have a lot of joy or excitement.
- You are trying to establish boundaries.
- You are standing up to protect yourself or another being.

EXERCISE 5.10: Expressing a Gesture

This is a deepening exploration of the "Resourcing Ourselves" exercise earlier in this chapter on page 144.

Choose a resource to revisit. Reinhabit that resource fully, savor it again, and then ask yourself: What are the best parts of this experience? What is so important about it? Notice whether you have any spontaneous urges to express yourself, whether through words, sounds, or gestures. If you are telling another person about this resource, they can help you notice the gesture or urge while you are expressing yourself in words.

If you notice an urge to make a gesture, allow yourself to do it very slowly, noting how it feels in the body to make it. Ask yourself what this expression has to tell you. Continue to be in touch with this resource and what it seems to communicate. Becoming aware of gestures and being able to put them into words can have a profound impact on your experience! If this gesture offers a welcome message, and you would like to be able to revisit the moment in the future, then you may find that repeating the gesture will imprint the whole experience. Then, later, simply making the gesture will return you to this experience.

Plum Village Gestures

Bowing: In this gesture, made to another person, we join palms, symbolizing the mind and heart together; it looks like a lotus bud about to open. Along with the gesture, we say to ourselves, "A lotus for you," as an expression of support and respect. Stopping, smiling, I close my eyes and concentrate my good wishes for the person I am bowing to. It is an acknowledgment made with the entire body and mind.

Flowers for Applause: As an expression of joy, wiggling your fingers silently is called *giving flowers*. A sense of excitement and delight can be conveyed without the undue or jarring noise of clapping hands—it goes over much better in the meditation hall, and I find it is a more accurate expression of the sparkle I feel than pounding my hands together.

Using Two Hands: To emphasize that we are completely present to the current action, we use both hands instead of just one to complete even seemingly minor actions like passing a book to someone or drinking a cup of tea. When we go out of our way to include both hands, a sense of reverence can arise that can turn an ordinary act into one of complete presence and deep intention.

Restorative Sleep

Sleep is foundational to our lives, and it has a great influence on our waking experiences. Having restorative sleep is necessary for a stable nervous system. Although meditation itself can be very restorative, it can also sometimes lead to sleep problems. Willoughby Britton, mentioned in the previous chapter as the founder of Cheetah House, began her research career wanting to show how meditation led to more sound sleep. Her study turned out to show quite the opposite: she found that mindfulness meditation actually stimulates the prefrontal cortex, causing sleep difficulties to quite a substantial degree.

Although some meditators may feel an initial sense of overcoming the need for sleep, sleep deprivation can lead to serious consequences. With this in mind, here are a few tips for getting a better night's sleep that pertain specifically to practitioners:

- If you find yourself dropping off to sleep and then bolting awake during evening meditation, you may find it hard to fall asleep afterward. Try meditating with your eyes open, taking a few deep breaths periodically, and holding for a few seconds on each inhalation. If you know that falling asleep during meditation is a perpetual problem for you, try meditating in bed, lying down if you become too drowsy, and simply allow yourself to fall asleep naturally.
- If you are having disturbing dreams or body tensions, try doing some form of deep relaxation to drift off to sleep. Pick an exercise from this chapter that feels soothing, and notice and savor its pleasant effects. Bring these effects fully to mind, and then let them naturally drop out of your perception, following them as if they were the sounds of a bell reverberating into silence.

- Be aware that foods with a high glycemic index may make you feel drowsy after eating, but they tend to make you more wakeful during your sleep. This is especially true of beverages containing sugar or alcohol.

EXERCISE 5.11:
5-4-3-2-1

DURATION: 10 minutes or much less
FREQUENCY: Nightly
PURPOSE: Falling asleep with ease

When all else fails for me, I practice what I call "5-4-3-2-1," something I learned from Nancy Napier's book *Getting Through the Day.*[4]

To begin, allow five things to come into your visual awareness—don't go searching, just let them emerge on their own. Name them to yourself. If you find your eyes want to close, remember what you were noticing just before you lay down. Next, identify five things you can hear. Again, just allow the sounds to alert you rather than hunting for them. If a sound persists or repeats, don't count it more than once in a round. Lastly, focus on five sensations you experience inside, again, counting sensations only once.

That was the first round. Now do a second round, counting four things this time; in your third round, you'll count three things, then a round of two, then one. If you are still awake, start again with five.

If you find your mind-wandering or forget which number you are on, that's a good sign that the body is beginning to relax—let it! Just make a guess as to which number you had reached and be reassured that you are doing it just right; this is not a concentration practice.

Exploring the Edges of Your Window

Let's bring it all together! This next exercise is the heart of our practice of looking deeply: exploring the edges of our window of mindful opportunity. It is the culmination of all the previous exercises in this chapter, so it's best to make sure you're familiar with all of the reregulating tools you've learned so far. You might find it beneficial to explore the exercise through writing, drawing, or just sitting with it.

EXERCISE 5.12:
Creeping Up to the Edge of Our Window

DURATION: 10 minutes
FREQUENCY: Daily with one small focus
PURPOSE: Gaining a method to look deeply

Begin this exercise from a place of well-being. To do this, start by using one or more of the tools you have learned so far: tracking pleasant body sensations, grounding, or savoring a favorite resource. This starts you off on solid footing and is a reminder of where you can return to refresh yourself when needed.

When you are ready, bring to mind a tension-producing situation that is still a bit fresh. Start with something small; you can always pick something more challenging in the future. Include the surroundings, who and what was there, your sense impressions, and the details of what was transpiring. What did you tell yourself about this situation at the time? What emotions surfaced? Notice what parts of your body are responding to this memory; one part at a time, go through what is happening, and whether it is pleasant, unpleasant, or neutral. Check out your shoulders, back, belly, and jaw—as well as any other part of your body that feels right.

Now you can answer the following questions:

- What parts felt unpleasant?
- For each of these unpleasant parts, do you have voluntary control over letting go of that tension?
- If so, experiment going back and forth between the tension and letting it relax a bit. What do you notice? End this part with a bit of time just letting go.

As a next step, you can use grounding and/or resourcing as islands of refuge, spending time in that zone close to the edge of the window, then retreating to the island for a break. Go back and forth, sustaining the time you spend with one aspect of the difficulty, then going back to the island.

Finally, check back in and see if your current response to the difficulty has changed. Can you bring the difficulty back up while letting go of those tensions? What do you notice? How might this be helpful for you in the future?

We started this chapter learning what to do in a storm, when we find ourselves bounced out of the window of mindful opportunity. Each of the exercises in this chapter help us come back into that window, to a place where it is possible for us to have a mindful perspective. This is not the goal of mindfulness practice—it is the beginning! The goal is to gradually widen our window so that we are able to investigate and learn to tolerate conditions that were previously dysregulating. Stretching that zone is developing our resilience, our ability to remain unshakeable. Stretching that zone is a vital part of our self-regulating process.

From here, we can make a conscious effort to be with challenging circumstances, to unpack them one skandha at a time, and in the process, learn how we have contributed to our own suffering and find some freedom from it. The painful circumstances we have experienced may not change, yet our suffering can decrease. This is practice. Arming ourselves with these profound experiences of suffering and understanding how suffering comes about and how it can be overcome will, bit by bit, enable us to gather wisdom. It leads us directly into an ability to be compassionate with others, knowing they too are dancing with human-made sufferings.

Together these exercises form a system that strengthens our spirit when practiced as a daily routine; acts as a stabilizing mechanism when practiced in the face of unexpected or uninvited difficulty; and functions as a healing and transformational practice when deliberately used to move closer and closer to the edges of our window, stretching it millimeter by millimeter toward *unshakeability*. That's the theory, anyway! I know from personal experience that each millimeter I stretch sure feels satisfying, helping me build confidence and soften into a more openhearted, vibrant life.

6

Converging Road Maps to Nowhere

Exercises for Regulating and Grounding When Things Get Tough

Now that we have a notion of the foundational teachings of how to overcome suffering, and a heads-up as to some of the potential pitfalls of putting the teachings into practice, how do we proceed to carefully craft a life that will point us in the direction of overcoming some of the trials of this human life? In this chapter, we'll dig deeper into the essential teachings, through our neuroscience lens, and explore the *sutras*—multi-level teachings that are used to deepen insight and hone skill in training the mind—and more of the formal practices found within the Plum Village tradition, including sitting and walking meditation. Here, our focus is on how these teachings and practices can be used to keep our nervous system regulated enough, within our ever-widening window of mindful opportunity, to stay present in order to see the true nature of things deepening day by day, circumstance by circumstance.

Because I have been trained in a number of healing modalities, over the years it has struck me how similar various healing approaches are to each other. When I realized that these healing protocols were also similar to the foundational teachings of the Plum Village tradition, I felt excited to explore the parallels. Although they may use different terminology, or look through various lenses, healing modalities all stress similar processes in keeping with our neuro-informed mindfulness principles (see Chapter 4): a good relationship with a guide (coregulation); being in touch with the body; having access to beneficial states of mind (self-regulation); finding and maintaining an internal place of safety and calm (window of tolerance); and being able to identify and explore difficulties safely.

What Is a Sutra?

Sutras are said to be the Buddha's discourses, passed down orally for hundreds of years. These teachings travelled from the Buddha's birthplace in India all over Asia, to regions known today as China, Myanmar, and Tibet, and they were finally written down in a number of different compilations, depending on where they landed. The sutras are multilevel teachings used to deepen insight and hone skill in training the mind.[1] Here, our focus is on how these teachings can be used to keep our nervous system regulated enough, in an ever-widening window of tolerance, so that our ability to stay present in order to see the true nature of things deepens day by day, circumstance by circumstance.

Although we are focused on how the foundational teachings speak to handling those formative difficulties, studying the teachings and practices can be done on increasingly deeper levels. Those deeper levels are not within the scope of this book.

Thich Nhat Hanh's teachings on the sutras alone constitute a full bookcase of scholarship, not to mention thousands of hours of recordings of teachings that drew on entire libraries of foundational translations and commentaries on ancient texts. What follows is a brief look at the ways Plum Villagers recognize how to understand and be guided by the sutras from a neuro-informed approach. If you would like to study the actual sutras for deeper understanding, two books of commentaries are written by Thich Nhat Hanh: *Breathe, You Are Alive!* and *Transformation and Healing*.[2]

Three sutras will be our focus and most basic starting point:

> **The Anapanasati Sutra**, or Full Awareness of Breathing, is an itinerary of the journey for stopping and resting the mind, followed by looking deeply into the nature of the body/mind.
>
> **The Satipatthana Sutra,** or Four Foundations of Mindfulness, is more of a street map that shows us how, and to what, we can apply the Anapanasati, taking the meditations off the cushion and into our 24/7 environment.
>
> **The Bhaddekaratta Sutra,** or Knowing the Better Way to Live Alone, outlines the impetus to stay on the path in the present moment—a cautionary note to practice just within the window of mindful opportunity.

The application of all sutras depends upon your ability to recognize and maintain yourself within the window of tolerance. Within the window is where the practices are effective. Rather than exact "how to" instructions, the sutras are written in such a way as to point one in the right direction. It is still up to you as the practitioner to discover what is effective, to have your own insights on just how to benefit from the guidance they give.

The Full Awareness of Breathing Sutra (Anapanasati Sutra)

I was so happy that day I discovered this sutra. I thought I'd discovered the greatest treasure in the world. Before, I'd been content to simply gain knowledge. I didn't know how to enjoy the present moment, how to look deeply into my life, and how to enjoy the positive conditions that were all around me. This sutra is so basic and so wonderful. There are many great sutras, but approaching them without this sutra is like trying to reach the top of a mountain without a path to go on.

—THICH NHAT HANH, BREATHE, YOU ARE ALIVE

The Anapanasati Sutra is a clear roadmap to cultivating our ability to be curious and stay within that window of mindful opportunity. This teaching, which is made up of sixteen basic exercises, begins with the quest for well-being in the body, followed by the emotions and mental agilities, as we sleuth out their quirks and intricacies. As you will see, there is a parallel between these exercises and the self-regulation tools we learned in Chapter 5. Although the exercises build on each other, you don't need to do them in order. Each exercise has a different object of concentration for sitting meditation; the exercises can also be practiced in the off-cushion life, any time you decide to focus this way.[3]

In this sutra, the teaching begins with an introduction setting the scene. The Buddha is speaking to a group of students, who are being guided by respected senior monastics. This opening part of the teaching reminds us that trusted guides are foundational for proceeding on our journey. The students and monastics described in the sutra practice together as a community, which enhances their coregulation and allows them to learn tips from experienced community members.

Next, the Buddha brings the students' attention to their already diligent and successful practices. He reminds them of their own beneficial and wholesome states, and how well-developed they are as a community, nourishing their self-confidence and providing inspiration. He then instructs them to find a place of comfort and learn to adopt a stable, alert posture for meditation practice. All of this serves to create a sense of safety, confidence, and familiarity before the sixteen exercises are introduced.

In these exercises, we combine the awareness of our breath with awareness of a number of other elements. They are divided into four sections: Body, Feelings, Mind, and Objects of Mind.

The Sixteen Basic Exercises

Body

1. Long breath
2. Short breath
3. Whole body
4. Calming whole body

Feelings

5. Joyful feeling
6. Happy feeling
7. My mental formations (the fifty-one mind states, including emotions)
8. Calming my mental formations

Mind

9. Focus on my mind.
10. Make my mind happy.

11. Concentrate my mind.
12. Liberate my mind.

Object of Mind

13. Observe impermanence of all mental phenomenon.
14. Observe disappearance of desire.
15. Observe cessation.
16. Observe letting go.

My understanding of this sutra is that all the practitioner needs to do is ground themselves in the breath. Eventually, as concentration builds, the body will settle all on its own. As the body settles, the practitioner becomes aware of the settling, and gladness arises automatically. As they continue this cascade of calming and joy, one thing leads to another as the mind relaxes to reveal its various mental formations; from this still place, they experiences the very nature of mental formations.

Perhaps the Buddha was able to find many students who, through their diligence, were able to enter this wonderful cascade. But what about those of us who find it difficult getting into that waterfall of wonderfulness? Are there some things we might do purposefully to support ourselves in having these experiences? This is where understanding the teachings through a neuro-informed lens and learning to self-regulate can be very helpful.

The focus of these exercises is twofold. The first objective of the practice is to help the mind settle, to stop the hectic activity, and to help calm and cultivate focus so that the thinking brain can be relaxed and clear as it moves into the second objective, that of looking deeply into the nature of all phenomena. These exercises help us return to a state of pleasant or neutral experience. With whatever difficulty is troubling us, little by little, we ease ourselves into letting go of the habitual response, widening the window, and easing into freedom. If you put the stabilizing exercises of Chapter 5 side by side with the sixteen exercises and squint a bit so that the edges of each becomes a bit fuzzy, you may see a strong similarity between the two groups. Each of the exercises interprets its impacts by referring back to the body; each has a component of discerning the unpleasant from the pleasant and neutral; each contains the search for the pleasant and neutral and sustaining that experience; and then each has a small celebratory aspect of appreciating the outcome of the exercise.

SIXTEEN NEURO-INFORMED PARALLELS FOR UNSHAKEABILITY

1. Establishing an anchor calms us, such as the effect of a deep breath on the limbic system of our body.
2. Deepening familiarity with the anchor allows us to experience mind/body connection.
3. Maintaining body awareness can enable us to track our sensations.
4. Using tracking of pleasant and neutral sensations can help us calm our nervous system.
5. Sustaining awareness can intensify calmness.
6. Sustaining this calmness can create a sense of well-being.
7. Using the body as an anchor, we can become familiar with mind states.
8. Sustaining the mind states within the window of mindful opportunity opens the window wider.

9. Within the window, we learn to distinguish the impact of mind states on our nervous system.
10. Learning how to maintain ourselves within the window with difficult mind states maintains well-being.
11. Developing concentration relaxes the default mode network so we can sustain awareness of the present, focus, and deepen understanding of the workings of our mind.
12. Deepening understanding reveals and corrects misperceptions that create suffering.
13. Seeing all mind states change moment by moment helps lessen the perception of the threat.
14. Gaining the ability to observe the mechanics of desire without succumbing to habitual responses begins to break the autonomic patterns of undesirable habits.
15. Having agency over unwelcome habits creates joy and happiness, and gives us energy to continue growing.
16. Continuing to experience awareness and letting go of habits continually widens the window in which we operate.

Let's return to the exercises of the Anapanasati Sutra in more detail. The first section focuses us on our body. As with all stabilizing exercises, we practice to strengthen our ability to focus on the body when we are calm, and we use the strength of that practice in stormy weather to reestablish that calm. So each section has the elements of strengthening and preparing for eventual difficulties.

Beginning with a long breath activates the vagus nerve in a way that signals to our limbic system that we are not in danger. Being curious, we entice the thinking brain to come online. How does that affect the rest of the body? What happens naturally as a result of just being curious, being mindful? Looking for the impact on the body is a search for those parts that feel pleasant or neutral. If and when we discover parts that are pleasant or neutral, we sustain the attention on those parts and see if that further calms the body. We maintain a sense of curiosity. Sustained concentration on the experience creates neural pathways to this sense of well-being and makes existing pathways stronger and faster—and therefore more easily accessible when we need increased stability.

The next set of four exercises goes through a similar process, this time with the emotions, or mental formations, as the focus. As we notice what emotions we are feeling, we return to the body to ask where these emotions are sensed in the body and whether they have the quality of being pleasant, unpleasant, or neutral. As we do this, we may find that just the act of curiosity, of questioning, brings some calming or uplift. To heighten this experience, we can deliberately bring up some memory of well-being, again noticing where there may be pleasant or neutral sensations as a result of the remembering. Then, we are invited to drop the story, and merely rest in the results of the exploration. Gradually, we learn how to calm our body while experiencing these mental formations. This allows us a full experience in the present moment of our mental formations.

With a heightened awareness of the bodily states that are pleasant, unpleasant, and neutral, we shift attention to the mind in the third set of exercises. Here we develop an ability to call up pleasant sensations by calling up states of well-being—just like we did in Chapter 5 when we were developing resources. By becoming very familiar with the states of well-being, and by being able to call up and sustain them, we ready ourselves to encounter states of ill-being. Here we ground ourselves in mindfulness: we pay attention to the bodily sensations of well-being, and at the same time, awareness of ill-being. This is what Thay refers to as "holding like a mother." In this moment, it is possible to stretch that window of tolerance to somewhat calm the reaction due to the ill-being with an anchor of well-being.

In the final set of exercises, focusing on the objects of the mind, we become aware that it won't last forever; it is impermanent. This makes the task of being with the difficulty less burdensome, when we learn that it, too, will pass. This changing and passing of suffering can be such a relief, the cessation of suffering can be experienced as a reality in body, mind, and spirit! Finally, concepts fall away and are replaced by pure experience, to see deeply that nothing exists separately. This exploration will bring the insight of interbeing itself.

These exercises can be practiced straight through, 1–16, in one sitting, or you can take the first exercise and practice that for a year. We are experimenting, adapting, and noting where our explorations take us. They are good for stabilizing us when we sit on the beginner's cushion, and they are just as helpful when we sit in the seat of the senior student.

The Anapanasati Sutra is not a stand-alone teaching because it does not address what happens if we cannot accomplish an exercise, or if, in a more extreme circumstance, the exercise backfires due to one of the pitfalls mentioned in Chapter 4. We remember that the Buddha was inventing this practice from his personal experience, and the subsequent teachings were not necessarily given in some logical order, but rather they surfaced because of particular questions or difficulties he encountered during the next forty-five years as he unfolded the path. Because the teachings were passed down orally, the amount of information a student was required to remember in any one teaching needed to be limited. The student found that practicing the teaching right away was helpful so they could have a personal experience of it from which to draw.

The Four Foundations of Mindfulness (Satipatthana Sutra)

If the Full Awareness of Breathing provides a general itinerary for meditation, the Four Foundations of Mindfulness (Satipatthana Sutra) is a more detailed roadmap, telling us how to proceed in looking into just about everything there is, both inside and out. This sutra helps us understand how to focus our attention while doing nothing—and while going about our normal lives, doing the various activities necessary for daily life. It helps us apply the sixteen exercises of the Anapanasati Sutra not just to sitting practice, but also to doing: walking, eating, working, talking. The Plum Village tradition asks us to practice day and night, mindful of our every action and interaction.

There is a teaching story from India about an elephant that compares its big trunk to the mind, always curious about whatever comes its way. If you want to walk an elephant through a crowded marketplace, the story goes, you'd better have that elephant trunk under control. The wise keeper knows to offer a small twig of bamboo to the elephant, thus keeping the trunk occupied with a small task; then nothing else gets too disturbed. So it is with our minds: the mind always needs some sort of anchor, and depending on the situation, having a variety of twigs can be helpful. This is what the Satipatthana Sutra offers us; it gives the mind wholesome, doable tasks so that it doesn't go crashing through the marketplace of life.

The four areas of focus described in this sutra are the same as in Full Awareness of Breathing, only they are broken down into much smaller pieces.[4] The body (1) and its sensations here includes the physical makeup and experience of every part of the body; the resulting feelings (2) of pleasant, unpleasant, and neutral are considered in greater detail as awarenesses of grasping, aversion, or indifference. For the mind (3), we now consider all the mental gymnastics of every kind of mind state, emotions, and thoughts, how those come to be, and their characteristics. Finally, the objects that the mind is focused on (4) now include the general nature of phenomena, internal and external, and how they all interact with each other.

Here is an example just to show how very detailed we can get here. We can feel the sensations of our eyes. We can note under what conditions various sensations might be pleasant, unpleasant, or neutral and the different elements that make up our eyes. We might further consider what happens to our eyes under various physical or mental states; we can think about the functions of our eyes and whether these give rise to particular mind states; and we can note the effort we need to put forth to concentrate on one object with our eyes. We might ask ourselves questions: Can the focus of our eyes impact mind states? What happens when our eyes are not functioning optimally? How do we take good care of our eyes? And on and on. Why would we ever need to do this?

This is the first answer that comes to my mind: We must do whatever it takes to keep the mind occupied in a wholesome way. When we go about our everyday lives and don't necessarily need to employ our mental faculties—when we are walking, eating, resting, for instance—the Sutra suggestions can be handy twigs. This keeps a more optimal balance between concentration and awareness and helps us keep tabs on the default mode network (DMN) so it doesn't become overworked, distracted or unfocused. At the very least, this mind-wandering can be exhausting and also add to dysregulation.

I am reminded of a silent movie with Charlie Chaplin called *Modern Times*. In this film, Chaplin is a factory worker on an assembly line; he is in charge of tightening an endless stream of giant nuts with two giant wrenches. You see him go through his day: he punches in and then tightens nuts as they come, fast and furious, until the whistle blows. With that, the conveyor belt stops, he puts down his wrenches, and as he leaves the factory, you can see that his arms are still tightening with those very same motions—still working but without context. Poor Charlie; poor us!

The bottom line is that having a wholesome focus is like giving the elephant that piece of bamboo: it helps the trunk of our mind be calm and steady. Along the way, if we are paying attention, we are going to learn something, see patterns, have insights into the nature of whatever our focus is on. In this way we can learn how to avoid misunderstanding the nature of things, acting on those misunderstandings, and actually making our own suffering.

What I also experience in this regard is that the mundane moments of life take on a much fuller flavor. Sometimes, when we attend to these seemingly unimportant moments, we even begin to notice that what used to be unpleasant has moved into a more neutral experience, and what was seemingly neutral begins to have nuances of pleasantness and delight. What might once have been drudgery may even become awe-inspiring. In this way we learn just how much we have to savor, thus increasing our energy and creativity.

The Discourse on Knowing the Better Way to Live Alone (Bhaddekaratta Sutra)

I feel excited when I find ways in which neuroscience and the Buddhist teachings as encoded in the sutras point to similar, if not the same, human phenomena. As I go deeper into this study,

I can actually tell that I'm reaching the upper limits of my own window of tolerance. I can recognize that even delight can get to be too much at times and it too can have a dysregulating effect. Now I'm walking around—or sitting around—seeing this connection in every talk I hear and every meditation I do! I could go on like this forever. But that might be a bit much for this book. I just can't leave this discussion without mentioning the Discourse on Knowing the Better Way to Live Alone, the Bhaddekaratta Sutta, Majjhima Nikāya 131. It begins:

> Do not pursue the past. Do not lose yourself in the future. The past no longer is. The future has not yet come. Looking deeply at life as it is in the very here and now, the practitioner dwells in stability and freedom . . .

This Sutra focuses on the neuro-informed principle of knowing when you are in or out of the window of mindful opportunity and doing your best to stay within it, even if you tread quite close to the line. The teaching cautions against being "lost" in the past or future and even against being "swept away" by the present.

If you are pursuing the past, future, or even the present, it is important to do it in a way in which you are not "burdened." (Read: out of the window!) Of course, in order to live life, we must think about the future and the past so we can plan how to best take care of ourselves and our surroundings and so we can learn from our experiences. The key in this sutra is that we must discern, in each moment, whether this pursuit is burdening us. In the language of neuroscience, are we experiencing the limbic system coopting our ability to have that optimal integration of all the parts of the nervous system, or are we in a mindful state in which that integration is optimal?

The realization here is that only through becoming unshakeable, staying within that window of mindful awareness, can a practitioner see life as it truly is in the present moment. How to stay there is for us to learn from our own practice while maintaining our curiosity.

> "Knowing how to live alone" doesn't mean you have to live in solitude in a cave, separated from other people. If we sit alone in a cave, lost in our thinking, we aren't really living alone. "Living alone" means living to have sovereignty over ourselves, to have the freedom that comes from not being dragged away by the past, not living in fear of our future, and not being pulled around by strong emotions caused by the circumstances of the present. When we are masters of ourselves, we can grasp the situation as it is, and we're in the best position to handle whatever may arise. When we dwell in mindfulness day and night, then we are truly practicing "the better way to live alone." This is true whether we are surrounded by friends and family, or when we are living a solitary life.[5]

In this teaching, the emphasis is not on living with others in community or living by yourself, rather it is on the most intelligent way to live regardless. The thrust of this teaching is that only the present moment is really available for direct examination. If we aren't sitting in the present moment, then our memory of the past, or our fantasy of the future will hardly be an accurate reflection of the way things really are. This is a clear mandate to do whatever it takes to be present and not be carried away.

What does it mean to be "carried away"? It is when we are burdened by thinking of the past or the future, or when we are burdened with interpretations of the present moment. It is when we cross the line between being able to see clearly and being dysregulated by those thoughts. It is when we are hyper-focused on potential threats, skewing our perceptions through a lack of noticing all of the other nonthreatening elements around us. We are carried away from the present when what we are thinking about seems like it is happening right then and there. If we think of this burden as being outside the window of mindful opportunity, then this teaching is all about being mindful of our body/mind state and staying regulated. There is no injunction on thinking about the past or future, as doing so has the potential to deepen our understanding—but instead, we must simply be aware of whether or not we are staying in the middle of the lane or whether we are starting to drift outside of it. We can think of this sutra as being like the rumble strips at the edges of the highway, alerting us when we are too close to the edge. This sutra encourages us to find internal rumble strips to keep our mindfulness ever available.

Formal Practices

With these three teachings—the itinerary, the roadmap, and the rumble strips—let's see how this can play out in our life with specific practices. The rest of this chapter details formal practices within the Plum Village tradition, each of which has an informal counterpart to adapt and integrate into our daily lives.

SITTING MEDITATION

Finally, let's get down to what most people think is the sum-total of mindfulness practice! Although by now you know differently, sitting meditation is still a foundational and beneficial experience.

I like to begin each day with a sitting practice to prime my nervous system for calm. I sit there long enough that my whole body and mind settle and become clear enough that I can see things as they really are. Sitting practice also gives me a daily baseline of comparison to know when I am veering away from the intention of staying in the present, remaining calm and serene (or at least relatively so).

This sitting practice has three modes: stopping and resting; developing understanding of the body/mind; and looking deeply for healing and transformation of suffering.

The first steps are **stopping and resting**. Just what does that mean? What is it that we are stopping, when should we stop, and what is doing so good for? When the chatterbox in our heads (the DMN) is especially active, it takes our attention away from the present moment. This might look like planning for the future, or ruminating and grieving about the past. Whatever it is doing, it doesn't leave much room for being in the present. If we want to be able to look deeply for a sustained period of time to see just how suffering is made, we must first be able to attend to the present moment, rather than forgetting what we're doing and lapsing into mind-wandering. That means the first step is to slow down this default mode network. We call this *stopping*.

We also know that for change to happen in the nervous system, whether we're extinguishing old habits or developing new neural pathways, we need to repeatedly stimulate what we want to grow. This is where the *relax* part comes in. Relaxing is sustaining the stopping. We do this by finding arenas in which stopping can be easily sustained: we stop moving, or stop following our thoughts. We can't really consciously stop thinking, although stopping whatever we are doing and taking a moment to relax and breathe with awareness does slow down our thought processes in the right environment.

This is where the idea of 24/7 practice comes in. As lay people, I doubt if many (or any) of us actually succeed at practicing continually. For one thing, our worldly life environments are simply not conducive to this! Still, our practice encourages us to form habits of stopping—that is, stopping the chatterbox. We do this by focusing on *just* walking, or *just* eating, or *just* sitting. It is a "just" practice!

Having a morning sitting practice can point us in this direction of stopping. It can nourish our volition as well as jump-start the optimal balance between attention and awareness that mindfulness meditation cultivates.

As we learned in the Four Foundations of Mindfulness Sutra, the mind will settle when we give it a very small task. This task, or anchor (see "Developing an Anchor" in Chapter 5), becomes the object of attention in our sitting. We set our intention to settle, and everything else unfolds from there. Sitting with your trusted anchor, you can begin to just be. As we sit and attend to our anchor (whether the breath or another supportive focus), we maintain a small awareness of the chatterbox, smiling to it when we see it stirring. *Aha, I caught you.* Little by little, we learn to catch it as it first starts to whisper. Sometimes it will sneak up on you unexpectedly, to which we should respond with a smile. *Aha, okay, you got me! Let's keep playing.*

As the DMN becomes more balanced, less hyperactivated, the prefrontal cortex becomes more able to gatekeep our thoughts and keep them from intruding on our attention. This isn't a process of forgetting—the memories are still there. The choice is simply more under your control, giving you time and space to explore. By helping the chatterbox calm, we expend less energy, giving us more energy for the other aspects of our practice.

Understanding is the next step in the meditative process. As we just sit and observe something, the mind will do its thing.

By just watching, we learn how the mind behaves. We see what happens when we chase a thought. We see what happens if we just sit there with an emotion; we see what happens in the mind as a result of our awareness of the body; and we see what happens in the body as a result of thought. We notice when we are tired or agitated and what seems to increase or decrease those states. We notice how the body reacts when pleasantness arises and when aversion arises. This understanding will lead to a wider acceptance of how we are and how others are, to empathy, and ultimately to compassion for self and others. Even if we never consciously or completely heal our variety of wounds, this understanding will gradually wear away some of our suffering, bringing a bit more happiness into our lives. A moment here or there builds faith, confidence, and the intention to keep going.

Looking deeply is the next element of mindfulness meditation. To look deeply we need to be relaxed, know how the mind works, have some ability to concentrate, and know when we are in or out of our mindful window. While sitting, we can either bring up something that bothers us, or welcome it when it comes spontaneously and just be with it. Just watch from within that window, continually assessing your body signals so you are aware of when you are close enough to see clearly, and when you are so close that you might slip over the edge. This takes practice; sometimes it takes coaching and/or accompaniment from others. There is no timetable for this. You may jockey back and forth between deep looking and self-regulating during one sitting, or over a number of sittings. The pace is always up to you.

Roasting the Marshmallow

Learning to stay close to the inner edges of the window without slipping out can be an art, like roasting a marshmallow. To roast a marshmallow to perfection, you want to transform it from a tough white blob into a golden crusty ball of liquid sweetness. You must hold it close to the fire so it melts, but not so close that it bursts into flame. Sticking it all the way into the flame guarantees that it will catch fire suddenly. You hold your skewer just the right distance away and rotate it so your marshmallow browns just a bit on each side. Little by little you learn just how close to hold it and for how long.

You can use this image of roasting the marshmallow as a guide for how to approach difficulty: take it one side at a time, keeping it not too close and not too far away. As a sitting practice, you allow something that's bothering you to come up, and you take it one skandha at a time: starting with body sensations, just noticing each part of the body that feels involved in this particular difficulty. Just be curious about where you feel this; how far the feeling radiates; how intense it is; whether it is increasing, decreasing, or staying the same; and whether it is pleasant, unpleasant, or neutral. This is like one tiny side of the marshmallow being held to the flame.

When you sense that the difficulty is melting or browning a bit, before it gets too hot (before you get to the very edges of that window), shift your attention to a trusted sense of well-being. Here is where the resources you've been collecting (back in Chapter 5) and intensifying within your practice come in handy. Allow the edges of the marshmallow to cool by enjoying whatever resources you can savor. This may be noticing another part of your body that feels relaxed or strong, pleasant or neutral. Or your attention can go to humming a favorite tune, or bring to mind a personal strength, or a place or person or animal that brings that sense of well-being.

Toasty on one side, you can now go back for more, either in this sitting session, or at another time. Gradually you move your marshmallow in and out of the campfire. You roast that glob into a sweet transformation. In the therapeutic method known as Somatic Experiencing, this is called *pendulation*. The Tibetan Buddhists call it *Tonglen*. This is an element of *right effort* or *right diligence*: you're not running away, and you're not throwing yourself into the fire.

In subsequent sessions you might continue to just focus on bodily reactions to the difficulty, or consider approaching it through another skandha, such as perceptions (what you tell yourself about this thing), or mental formations (emotions arising and passing away). Slowly you will develop a rhythm of exploration that will serve you in countless other situations. As you practice, you will be able to have a more integrated experience of your difficulty or object of attention. You will be able to see it more and more as a whole, approaching right view. This can open to a new relationship with an old wound.

Here's an example. I remember a time when I was convinced that I would be much happier if I lost several pounds. I went on a fast for five weeks, at the end of which I felt a freedom I hadn't experienced before. I felt like I could walk differently, carry myself with more esteem, dress and do things differently. It was like taking off a heavy coat and letting the sun touch my skin—such freedom. I meditated on this feeling of freedom. Then in a flash, there on the cushion, I realized that this feeling had nothing to do with my actual weight, but rather a childish notion that only thin people were entitled to such feelings. More specifically, this was a notion my mother had passed down to me; the coat I took off was one I'd put on in childhood, one that had been handed to me by someone else. The big takeaway was that wearing that coat had nothing to do with the shape of my body; rather, it had to do with the shape of my mind. My mind had held me captive. In fact, I was constantly putting on and taking off coats. With this realization I had a choice to put that coat on or not. What freedom.

Once I could see this, I could then search my mental closet for all manner of constricting clothing and, one by one, toss them in the rag bin.

Let's try this practice, beginning with a small difficulty, just to experiment.

EXERCISE 6.1: Cleaning Out the Psychic Closet

DURATION: 10 to 15 minutes
FREQUENCY: As you are moved
PURPOSE: Discovering false beliefs: repurposing old psychic clothing that has outlived its usefulness

Any one of the three elements of meditation—stopping, understanding, and looking deeply—can be the main focus of any one sitting, or you can combine them. No matter what your focus is, begin and end your practice session by consciously entertaining a sense of well-being so as to be gentle and caring to yourself by keeping the entire nervous system in balance.

As usual, allow yourself to settle into an uninterrupted space and set your intention to be curious. Then begin your time by focusing on a resource of well-being.

When you feel settled and open, bring to mind some issue in your life that has bothered you over an extended period of time. This is going to be a partial exploration, so there is no pressure to be with it longer than you can maintain your curiosity.

Bring the issue to mind, taking a brief "tour" to look at how this has cropped up in your life over time. You may like to begin by noting body sensations in just one part of the body or one thought that surfaces—your choice. Allow your attention merely to rest here without needing to change anything. It may help to ask questions about your experience: Is it constant or changing? Does it have a color, shape, or texture? Each question ignites a spark of curiosity.

Notice your activation level; try to stretch it a bit but not overdo it. When you feel that this has been enough, go back to the beginning resource of well-being and resettle.

You can then go back to the "same side of the marshmallow" or come at it from a different angle: thoughts, emotions, images. You are invited to swing back and forth for as long as you like, as long as you can stay within that window of mindful opportunity.

As you get ready to bring this exercise to a close, touch the issue again and notice any changes in your inner experience. If you find welcome changes, savor this. If not, savor the fact that you were willing to try something new.

Finally, bring this session to a close by ending as you started, with a sense of well-being.

Healing the Inner Child

Another approach to meditating on difficulties that arise during practice is what Thich Nhat Hanh frequently called "healing the inner child." His use of this concept demonstrates his continuous search to find the intersection between Buddhism and Western psychology, to give voice and direction to specific healing practices that acknowledge childhood sufferings and trauma in all its forms: individual, cultural, systemic, intergenerational.[6] Like the metaphors of roasting a marshmallow or cleaning out the closet, healing the inner child is another way we can look deeply and practice staying within our window.

Thich Nhat Hanh's plea here is that we do not fear our suffering or fall into a victim role. For years I felt what he was saying was too simplistic, but now I hear it differently. If you want to untie these knots of suffering from your past, first you need to not be carried away by fear, to not fall victim to that limbic system that tries to protect you from a threat that is no longer there. Thich Nhat Hanh gives us many ways to self-regulate by finding various ways to go *home*: a set of mindful exercises, books of chants and songs, and the admonition to find small joys (there are always some around, he says). All these practices may resource us if our habit energy, developed from practicing regularly, is strong. Just like the tools for rebalancing a dysregulated nervous system, these formal and informal practices help us loosen and untie the painful knots. Fortified by the ability to stay within the window, Thay encourages practitioners to have a rich inner life that interacts with the inner child, holding them and listening to them when they are crying.

Not all difficulties, of course, have to do with our wounded inner child. But no matter what the difficulty is, we are nevertheless encouraged to hold it like a mother holds a crying baby. This image may not be immediately relatable to everyone. Here, Thay is encouraging us to see what the situation is made of. The Buddhist notion of emptiness, that everything is made of nonthing elements, is very helpful here to avoid overwhelm while looking deeply.[7] When a difficulty arises, we can explore it one skandha at a time. What are we seeing in our mind's eye? What do we hear? What is the perception, what are we telling ourselves? We explore slowly, at the speed that maintains our balance and body regulation, staying in the window.

WALKING MEDITATION

The formal practice of walking is quite simple, but it is a tad more complicated than sitting. Even before we begin to walk, we start being mindful. We bring our attention to noting how the body is readying to stand. We do our best to maintain connection to our anchor as we direct our mindful attention to our feet and the act of standing up, then walking. This is already way more complex than just sitting. In walking meditation, you may find it helpful to recite some words that help maintain focus (see "Gathas" later in this chapter). This is primarily a practice that keeps the mind calm and maintain contact with the body. It helps us inhabit a wholesome state as we walk.

Walking meditation can help you ground, heightening awareness of the body, so you can ease into formal sitting practice. Sitting can also be anchoring, a way to prepare for walking meditation. As usual, this is up to the experience of the practitioner.

Informal walking practice can be very beneficial; literally, it helps us walk through our day with more ease. Chances are that when we walk, we are usually not really present; rather, we're preparing for some other activity, working out this or that—the mind is in constant motion. These walking ruminations can be exhausting! To establish a habit of instead using walking meditation as a pleasant break, you might find one place you walk each day and make a deal with yourself to focus just on walking for those moments. This could be on the way to get a drink of water, or from home to the car, or down a particular set of stairs. Allow yourself that minute or two to let go. When walking in public places, feel free to find a pace that allows you to feel relaxed and inconspicuous. You, needn't walk like a zombie to benefit from and enjoy the walking.

Begin by setting your intention; pick some words if you like, and let it unfold. Some folks make a deal with themselves: if their mind wanders from that short walking meditation, they will go back and do it over. To end, notice how this walking left you feeling inside. If it was pleasant, savor it before going off to do your next thing.

As I mentioned in the last chapter, I didn't always find walking meditation to be pleasant or to bring me a sense of well-being, Although I was aware of the elements of resistance, that understanding on its own wasn't yielding beneficial results. Then I stumbled onto a way of walking with music that opened my heart. This gave me a whole new appreciation for just walking. I then learned to slow my steps to just the right speed, bringing myself into a mindful relationship with my walking. From there, little by little, I was able to broaden my repertoire of ways to enjoy walking meditation, like synchronizing with another person or noticing the wind on my face while walking, feeling the textures of what was under my shoes, the sound of the walking, being able to feel the impact of my steps up my spine, even to my cheeks. I sometimes focus on a feeling of gratitude that these knees are still willing to carry me around!

That's all there is to it—and yet, there is so much more. Walking meditation was a crucial moment of discovery for Thich Nhat Hanh, as I mentioned in Chapter 1. Thay found that walking meditation really helped to serve him in settling from overwhelming stresses, and he would spend many hours just walking. He developed many variations of walking meditation to keep him solidly grounded within his window. If you'd like to read more about the joys of walking meditation, I recommend his book *The Long Road Turns to Joy.*[8]

EATING MEDITATION

Eating meditation can be more complex than just walking, but there are many similarities in how we practice it. It can be done formally in a group or alone: formally, you may start with some bells, breathing, using words of reflection and intention-setting; or informally, by just taking a moment before you eat to remember your intention to be present for each bite.

Remember the onion exercise in Chapter 3? Eating can be a great way to explore how to temper the discriminating mind, noting but not over-focusing on the reactions of *I like it*, or *I don't like it*. Think about the textures to explore; the functioning of parts of the mouth; the senses of sight, smell, arm movements, sound. We can focus on those around us as well as the food; we can think about its impacts on our body, the bodies of those who grew the food, or on the environment. As we discussed before, every present moment is made of a myriad of elements. Here we train ourselves in calming the mind, being present with what is, and then looking deeply into the interbeing nature of what we are doing by eating.

We might also reflect on both the harms that we've experienced in relation to eating and the ways in which we may have used eating as a coping mechanism in the past. For example, we may have grown up with not enough nourishment to feel and think our best, or we may have experienced the harms of a fat-phobic culture. We may have experienced family dynamics or gendered components to our eating, or maybe even class or cultural issues, even ethical issues as our personal needs or desires can seem to conflict with those of the greater society or the well-being of the planet. On the flip side, eating is a great coping mechanism: we eat to find respite in an emotional storm; eating can feel nurturing or empowering.

On retreat, eating meditation is traditionally a silent practice. While the silence provides less distraction from the focus, for some, silence can be quite uncomfortable, surfacing memories of not-so-pleasant silences of the past. For many of us, eating is a minefield; our experience of just sitting down to a good meal may be anywhere from daunting to delightful. Because of this, becoming mindful of body and mind during eating can be downright activating! We need to know these things may be at play so they don't catch us by surprise.

All this sounds so very serious, and it is. But here, as always, there is plenty of room for lightness and enjoyment. It is serious business to make sure we don't let the misfortunes in our lives completely overshadow the delights. Every once in a while, I will focus my attention on my tongue while eating. Over the years I have collected over fifty different tasks this miraculous organ can accomplish; I have come to see the tongue almost as a separate little mindful worker-being. Even the tongue takes time out to savor what it's doing quite naturally. Thich Nhat Hanh himself enjoyed relating his mindful consumption in his childhood of a cookie, which could take him a good long time to consume, so entranced was he with savoring that treat. Enjoyment is not the same as grasping, and noting the bodily sensations of that difference is in itself an important practice.

A contemplation before eating may help to maintain mindfulness while eating. These are the Five Contemplations Before Eating:

> This food is a gift of the earth, sky, numerous living beings, and much hard work.
>
> May we eat in mindfulness and gratitude so as to be respectful of life in and around us.

May we recognize and transform unwholesome mental formations and learn to eat in moderation.

May we eat in such a way so as to preserve our precious planet and all its living beings.

We accept this food in order to nurture our kinship and nourish our ideal of serving all living beings.

At meal's end, notice how that was, always making time to savor the beneficial.

Given that digestion is optimal when the parasympathetic system is activated and the sympathetic system is offline, eating mindfully generally has a beneficial effect on our physiology, improving how we eat, what we eat, how much we eat, and how satisfied we are when we're done—and it probably benefits the planet as well!

CHANTING AND SINGING

Chanting is a practice of putting music to intentional words or sounds, combining listening, vocalizing, breathing, and contemplation. It is a very sophisticated practice. In addition to mastering a melody and lyrics, the experienced chanter becomes aware of the entire community while blending their voice in pitch and volume so as to create a harmonious sound. While doing this, the chanter allows the intention to penetrate their being, body and mind. Although neurobiological research is just beginning to explore the world of chanting, it is thought that the vibration from the vocal cords has a relaxing effect on the vagus nerve, starting from the ear on down.

As more Westerners were drawn to the Plum Village tradition, Thich Nhat Hanh encouraged practitioners to compose chanting melodies that were more familiar to the Western ear, perhaps further increasing this relaxing effect. It is interesting that the Plum Village tradition, in addition to having a vibrant chanting practice, has developed a community singing practice, composing music that helps embody Buddhist principles specifically (see the following section on gathas). In many cases, chants take the form of well-loved popular songs with similar themes, or sometimes we may change some of the words to match the practice. We may all have certain music that seems, almost instantaneously, to produce a sense of well-being. Research has shown that such music stimulates parts of the brain that release oxytocin (the "cuddle hormone," providing feelings of connection, bonding, and trust) and dopamine (controlling our sense of pleasure). In addition, the rhythms of music stimulate motion centers in the brain, which can add an uplifting or soothing element, depending on the song. So before beginning walking meditation (or even working meditation, in monasteries) singing is part of the routine, helping to start us off on the right foot.

GATHAS

Many spiritual paths employ words or phrases repeated throughout the day to help us maintain our mindfulness. In the Buddhist tradition, we call them *gathas*. Plum Village also uses words to focus the body/mind: words can be an anchor to keep our mind from becoming distracted, but even deeper, they can help us keep the heartful intention of whatever activity we're doing front and center in our awareness. There are community-wide gathas that we use as poetic reminders, and we are also encouraged to create our own. Like the five contemplations before eating, words can coax the heart open when turning on the water, washing our hands, sweeping the floor, going to the bathroom, turning on the light, walking, driving the car, answering the telephone, or bowing to others. This delightful blend of the mundane and the sublime, mixed with creativity and warmth, sets a tone for everything we do.

Gathas are a wonderful way to integrate our spiritual intentions with our work. There are numerous little poems that help point us in this direction. When turning on the faucet, we can remember the gatha "Water flows from high mountain sources, Water runs deep in the earth, Miraculously, water comes to us and sustains all life."[9] This helps us be present with the water while cultivating reverence for life—firing together, wiring together.

Gathas are also a way to reset the nervous system, bringing a bit of uplift to an otherwise slightly tension-producing activity. Constant resetting gradually creates a stretching of that window of mindful opportunity. Here's one I made during the height of the COVID pandemic.

Gatha for Putting on a Mask

Putting on this mask
I touch the seeds of compassion
And realize the insight
Of interbeing
With every mindful breath.

Thich Nhat Hanh wrote many gathas; a whole collection of these gems is in his book, *Present Moment, Wonderful Moment*.

BELLS

The first time I experienced a Soto Zen sitting, they slapped two pieces of wood together to get our attention. It got my attention, all right. A bolt of adrenaline went through my body that alerted my brain that I'd better watch out for other sudden intrusions. (Granted, that's the intention of this practice—to be alert!) It wasn't quite as jarring the second time.

In the Plum Village lineage, we use a somewhat gentler version of this attention-getter: bells. Temple bells are a major means of communication in the monastery. They inform us of scheduled activities, of meals, of waking up, of the beginning and endings of practices. The bell is a friend inviting you to return to that safe inner island. So the language of the bell needs to be gentle and welcoming.

One of the hallmarks of the Plum Village lineage is an almost childlike sweetness that is infused into daily life: kindnesses to the body, kindnesses to the mind. Right from the first bell, there is thoughtfulness about how to make the bell sound. Rather than "striking" the bell, it is called "inviting the bell to sound." Additionally, one doesn't just strike the bell: first it is "woken up" with a gentle half-sound to let everyone, including the bell, know that a sound is about to emanate. Sometimes the wakeup sound is barely audible, and a slightly firmer one follows—a wakeup sound for the wakeup sound!

The bell is invited after reciting a special gatha. The sound that emanates is intended to be one of pure resonance and can demonstrate (to the discriminating listener) the degree of mindfulness of the person sounding the bell. The experienced practitioner is able to coregulate with that mindfulness through the pure sound of the bell and the pause between sounds. This practice of care in ringing the bell is a sharp contrast to other lineages where the bell is meant to be jarring. In Plum Village, every precaution is taken *not* to be jarring; life itself provides plenty of opportunities for that without us needing to add to it.

As mentioned in the previous chapter, in the Plum Village tradition, hearing the temple bells—or any bell—can be a signal to stop and take a break, to interrupt the "doing" self and go back to your anchor for a much-needed pause. It gives us an opportunity to check in with the body, enjoy resetting back to a more relaxed state, and look around for delightful or supportive conditions right in the here and now.

EXERCISE 6.2: Personalizing Your Temple Bell

DURATION: 1 minute
FREQUENCY: Numerous times during your day
PURPOSE: Forming a beneficial habit

In Plum Village monasteries worldwide, when people hear the sound of a bell—be it a temple bell, a clock chime, or the ring of a telephone—everyone stops what they are doing and spends some time with their anchor. This simple pause not only reinforces your anchor, it gives you time to come back to yourself and check in to the now. It even encourages flexibility by bringing you to an unexpected stop. Finding some reminder that happens fairly frequently in your life can help develop this mindful habit of taking a breather: turning on a faucet, going to the restroom, waiting in line for your turn, starting to climb stairs, or taking a sip of water. There are even apps that will interrupt your computer time with a bell sound.

Bring to mind some small occurrence that happens frequently in your normal day, like hearing the sound of a phone, or opening a door, or being at a red light. Imagine yourself in the situation and stopping, taking a deep, cleansing breath, perhaps putting a small smile on your face or looking around for some small delight. Savor this moment, maybe for as long as three breaths, just long enough to strengthen the neural pathways to your habit of mindfulness and resilience. Then, take the next several days to lay in wait for opportunities to practice this. You might even want to write a little gatha that goes along with this, like "Hearing the 'ping' of my phone, I have choices of how to respond." It is especially helpful when the situation is slightly tension producing, turning on a faucet, going to the restroom, waiting in line for your turn. You can experience right away the healing and refreshing results.

I have found it deeply satisfying to find practices in my own root tradition of Judaism that hold a similar spirit to this Buddhist one. In Judaism there is a tradition of pausing briefly when going in and out of a building (some take it so far as to pause every time they go in and out of a room!); we pause and say a prayer, acknowledging wholeness (my personal interpretation). We also place a ritual object at the door of a building to touch when going in and out. This, too, can be an anchoring experience. If you have a root tradition you'd enjoy weaving in, this is a good place to play with it.

SMILING AS A PRACTICE

We know happiness can often elicit a smile. What we may not realize is that, in reverse, a smile has the potential to invite us into a state of happiness. As Thich Nhat Hanh used to say, "Sometimes your joy is the source of your smile, but sometimes your smile can be the source of your joy."

Right from our first sitting meditation practice, we are encouraged to begin with a half-smile. Why? Smiling alerts our nervous system that all is well and reminds us we intend to maintain a state of safety and relaxation in our practice.

Have you ever given or received a smile and noticed it seemed fake? A smile is a very particular configuration of facial muscles. It is really the upper half of the face that shows friendliness; the lower part of the face is actually more expressive of aggression. The following exercise plays around with our awareness of whether smiles—our own smile, and those we observe—are genuine or not. It is best done with another person, or you can also try it with a mirror.

EXERCISE 6.3: Smiling as a Resource

DURATION: 1 minute
FREQUENCY: Play this game anytime you want a chuckle.
PURPOSE: Awareness of the effects of a smile

You will need a partner for this exercise. One person, A, attempts to make a genuine smile. The other, B, watches them, remaining expressionless. Each person carefully notes how their body responds to these separate tasks—smiling and watching someone smile—looking for pleasant bodily sensations. Person B then lets A know if and when they have received what they perceive to be a real smile, and person B confirms whether or not they, too, felt their own smile to be genuine. The hard part of this exercise is doing it without one or both of you breaking out in laughter before you can complete it! If you fail to complete this exercise because you cannot stop laughing, then congratulations! You may not have been able to use the experiment to confirm two-way smiling effects, but you can now put this experience in your list of resources to bring about a state of well-being.[10]

Making Space for Rest, Creativity, and Play

Thich Nhat Hanh recognized the importance of rest, creativity, and play to bolster himself in daily life. He was a diligent relaxer, he packed a hammock to bring along to enjoy at every opportunity. A daily nap after lunch was routine, an opportunity to deeply connect with and restore his body and appreciate the ways his body was supporting him. He was adamant about pacing himself. While in the US on a rigorous speaking tour, he warned his new assistant, Jim Forest, ". . . you have to be good at saying no. Every third day for me is a day of mindfulness. On those days under no circumstances will I give any talk or participate in any meeting, no matter how important it may seem. On those days I need someone who can be a stone wall. Can you do that? Others have said they could but in actual practice could not. For them the proposed event was too important."[11]

This underscores how Thich Nhat Hanh saw rest as not only fundamental but as a skill—it is not easy to say no. Recognizing that unrelenting work, stress, and trauma would lead him back into depression, Thay made sure that balancing work with rest was more than just a way to sustain himself to work more. Life is more than just a hyperfocus on what keeps us alive!

For Thay, creativity—specifically, calligraphy and poetry—was also an important part of practice. Slipping into rich images of forests, rivers, skies, and seasons was a way to touch the wonders of life even in the midst of suffering. In this poem, called "Breathing," Thay outlines the trajectory of a healing path, a prescription of the way out:

Breathing in, *I see myself as a flower.* *I am the freshness* *of a dewdrop.* *Breathing out,* *my eyes have become flowers.* *Please look at me* *I am looking* *with the eyes of love.*	Resourcing oneself

Breathing in, I am a mountain, Imperturbable, still, alive, vigorous. Breathing out, I feel solid. The waves of emotion Can never carry me away.	Gaining stability and establishing strong intention, becoming unshakeable
Breathing in, I am still water. I reflect the sky faithfully. Look, I have a full moon within my heart, the refreshing moon of the bodhisattva. Breathing out, I offer the perfect reflection of my mirror-mind.	Calming body and mind to stillness brings insight
Breathing in, I have become space Without boundaries. I have no luggage. Breathing out, I am the moon That is sailing through the sky of utmost emptiness. I am freedom.[12]	Transforming the suffering leaves one free of conditioned responses, healed and awake.

Finally, a third important aspect of Thich Nhat Hanh's practice was play: taking good care of the silly, spontaneous child inside. Getting in touch with childish delights and wonders may take some practice if you have lost that in the process of growing up, but it can be a powerful protection against pitfalls in our practice.

Jim Forest tells a delightful story by about taking advantage of unexpected free moments. Once, while accompanying Thich Nhat Hanh on a speaking engagement, he and Thay decided to take an unplanned trip to nearby Yellowstone National Park.

> Once inside, a surprise awaited us, a sort of welcoming committee: a mother bear in the deep snow with her two playful cubs. I stopped the car so we could admire them. Then one of the cubs clambered onto the hood and began licking the window. The mother bear came closer—she was carefully guarding her child. Thay began laughing, then kissed the window at the spot where the bear cub's pink tongue was engaged.[13]

Thay also had a way of offering pithy sayings like, "To be or not to be, that is not the question," and then pausing with a gleam in his eye. I think he was waiting for our reaction so that he could delight in the delight of others; he could see the continuation of his own insights lighting up the world. This was a deep teaching for me and permission for us all to savor what tickles our fancy while inhabiting our insight of interbeing.

DEEP RELAXATION

"Deep relaxation" can be just another way to describe a nap after a nice meal. What more can it be?

As a formal practice, deep relaxation incorporates the body scanning we explored earlier in Chapter 5, which heightens our awareness of body and highlights how focusing on the pleasant impacts our physiology. But the practice of deep relaxation goes a step further: it is a deeper contemplation. Whether we are focusing on how we are caring for a particular part of our anatomy, or on how that part is supporting our lives, the practice of deep relaxation provides us with both insight and inspiration to be reverent and kind to the organs, muscles, blood, and bones that we depend on for our breath of life. Further, we can invite the contemplation of the physical makeup of our organs, muscles, blood, and bones by identifying the physical elements of earth, water, fire, and air within each of them. In this way, we sink deep down into the interbeing nature of our bodies; the boundaries between inside and outside fade.

Deep relaxation can be a self-led formal practice, a practice led by someone else, or an informal way to take a break and put your feet up. You can do this sitting or lying down, beginning with the intention to just relax as deeply as possible. You can really indulge here with a comforting blanket or pillows; personally, I enjoy a bit of quiet background music, but it's not necessary.

Deep relaxation is a full body scan, maybe starting far away from the pesky mind, at the feet. You needn't put in great effort here, just gently notice what there is to notice: texture, temperature, tension, various parts, whether the experience is relaxing, noticing any sensations of ill-being. Do not be concerned if there are occasional parts of the body that do not have a felt sense. It may take time to become aware of our bodies after extended periods of ignoring them for the outer world. For some parts, this is good news that we can't feel them. In certain parts, we only have sensation when something is wrong, as in our teeth or our liver. In other circumstances, we may have unconsciously removed awareness of this part, perhaps because it was the source of previous suffering. We may restimulate that suffering unintentionally. This may be gently noted and explored at a time when we have both capacity and safety.

Whatever the experience, we can end the focus on any particular part by asking two questions: What has this part done for me? (Pause here to appreciate the part, to savor it.) And what have I done to take good care of this part? (Pause here to recommit to self-care.) In this way, we bring ourselves into nervous system balance. If you end up dozing off, no problem.

LAZY DAYS

Some years ago, I became concerned that the underlying tensions in my body were really problematic. After I had explored various approaches, a friend encouraged me to try neurofeedback. The particular style of neurofeedback I tried consisted of hooking my scalp up with a dozen or so electrodes, which were connected to a computer monitor. I was then shown clips from movies—normal, mainstream movies—but the clarity of the screen changed according to my brain waves. The screen would brighten and clear when I was putting out beneficial brain waves that would help relax that underlying tension. I was put into the position of having a sustained yet relaxed attention. After just a couple of sessions, my body began to relax in a way that it could sustain those relaxed states without the screen to guide me, even in the face of potentially agitating situations.

How might one accomplish this as a practice? One idea is to practice a whole day of being lazy, watching life go by with this same kind of relaxed attention. Lazy days, either once a week or over several days after intensive work and practice periods, are essential to preventing everyday burnout, and they're at least a partial antidote to overtraining pitfalls (see Chapter 4). It is a practice in which the object is to just be lazy, whether it is with hammock time, meal time, cloud watching, or noticing how a tree just stands there in the sun or rain. Here's an example of how I enjoy a lazy day:

I begin with a bath, washing off the week's physical and mental tensions, paying special attention to each part I freshen up, readying it for *nothing*—twenty-four hours of aimlessness, whether I like it or not. I don't make plans. I lie in bed as long as I feel like it (until the animals insist on being fed). I might listen to some guided meditation or a Dharma talk on the Plum Village app. I vow not to do anything that feels like work to my body or mind, not even clearing up or taking care of a few undone details of worldly life.

This may sound luxurious, but it can actually feel like a major effort! Fear arises that I will be bored, or succumb to empty pastimes. But over the years, I have developed a faith that something is in me that wants to come out, if only I can be patient. If boredom arises, I can sit with it and be curious about it. At some point in the morning, my energy shifts, and I can enjoy the rest of the day watching clouds, inspecting the woods for tiny flowers, playing music—whatever. I find added strength to do this practice from my ancestors, who diligently lit candles and demarked the do-nothing zone of *Shabbat*, following the religious commandment to honor the Sabbath and keep it holy. By the time I wake up on Sunday morning, I'm raring to go with fresh energy, and this is always amazing! Perhaps this poem captures a similar experience:

Drops of Emptiness[14]

My heart is cooled
By drops of emptiness.
Suddenly I see
My boat has crossed the river
And reached the shore of non-yearning.
Soft sand, empty beach,
Old promises. . . .

Journeying Together

The Sangha as Teacher and Container

I am in the kitchen in Deer Park Monastery, on the cooking team for the day. We gather in silence, and someone lights a stick of incense on the tiny altar sporting two tangerines and a lemon. We stand silently, setting our intention for the day to serve up three wholesome, nurturing meals by way of joyful work. We look around our group of six, sending smiles to each other. I can feel my upper body expanding with a sense of excitement.

We have worked as a group for three months now, and I know the talents and shortcomings of each person on my team. I love breakfast prep. It is much the same every day, and there is a soothing rhythm to it: wash the fruit, start the oats, load up the condiments from the fridge. Working with Nate, I notice how he just likes to make oatmeal. He seems so curious watching the water bubble, stirring in the oats so slowly—it is like a waterfall of snow into the pot as he pours them in. My body relaxes just watching for that moment.

I begin by washing my hands, watching the soap go down the drain as I remember a gatha by Thich Nhat Hanh:

Water flows over these hands.
May I use them skillfully to preserve our precious planet.[1]

I pile up a bowl of fruit to wash, drain, and slice. I take a deep breath, remembering, *ah yes, breathe*. Knife and cutting board ready, I put a damp washcloth under the board to prevent slipping. Actually, this little trick, learned from Thay Phap Vu, brings me repeated joy every time I do it. I take time to enjoy this micro happiness.

Next to me, someone is slicing bread. They seem to be having a hard time, from the sound of the knife banging on the board. I notice a grimace on their face. I can feel my own body wanting to tense up, so I make an audible sigh—both for my own self-regulation and for the bread slicer. There is no need to say anything: by the glance and smile they give me, I know they appreciate this pause. I notice that the bread they are slicing seems to be a white loaf, not whole grain, and I feel judgment arise—*not very nutritious*. I acknowledge my reaction and use it as an opportunity to work on looking deeper into the sources of my judgement and possible reasons to be supportive of this choice.

By lunchtime I myself am having a hard time, running behind on preparing my dish. But I only have to take a pause and look around; there's always someone who can help out where I may be falling short. Because we all share the same intention, there is no resentment that I need help, and because we are a big enough team, someone inevitably has the energy and skill to come to the rescue.

At day's end we are tired, sitting in our dirty aprons together, enjoying a cup of tea and some yummy biscuits. It is almost like we are sharing one large smile.

What Is a Sangha?

Among all of the lineages of Buddhism that have made their way from East to West, the Plum Village tradition stands out as having a very strong emphasis on the sangha as an essential part of practice.[2] A *sangha* is a community of practice, practicing in order to overcome certain human conditioning that brings a sense of ill-being. It is a group that has a common approach to this task.

Although the sangha is important to all Buddhist paths, and certainly was central to the Buddha's original teachings, few Western Buddhist convert lineages stress sangha life and practicing as a collective as the foundational core of the path. The sangha, whether a monastic or lay community, is the foundation of all practice in the Plum Village tradition, highlighting our intimate and reciprocal relationship with the entire web of life and all phenomena. The sangha can be the epitome of engagement. It provides vital support for the beginner and serves up increasingly advanced practices as we get farther along on our path to freedom. In the Plum Village tradition, waking up cannot be seen as an individual aspiration; the nature of the individual and the collective waking up are inextricable.

Trudging through the deep snow of the human condition, an individual can sink down and may even become stuck. The collective has the potential to be like a big snow shoe. When the collective is functioning optimally, the impact of the weight of our human shortcomings is spread out and the supportive nature of others can carry us beautifully on our journey. The sangha provides a conducive environment to transcend our conditioning, a place where we can take advantage of role models to see and feel how things may be experienced differently, through coregulation, implicit learning, and havens of safety and support. This is what can potentially be found in a sangha, a community with the intention and practices that lead to living in harmony and awareness.

Of course, such a community must be made up of individuals, so it is impossible to tease the individual journey from the collective one. As Thay often said, the sangha is a "rock tumbler": each practitioner, as a pebble, becomes polished as life tumbles us together, rubbing off our rough bits. This tumbling, over time, produces a mutual polishing, allowing individuals to shine brightly and the collective to become a treasure chest. Or we could think of it as a petri dish, an ideal laboratory environment in which to grow our individual selves. Or yet another analogy might be a formation of flying geese: alone or in too small of a group, we would become exhausted quite quickly on our journey, but with the larger collective of the sangha, we are able to rotate through, providing support for others and taking a break, gliding on others' updraft so that no one needs to be fighting the headwind for too long.

Defining a sangha is a bit like defining a family today—we've got so many configurations! There are single-parent and multi-parent families, polycules, "blood" families and chosen families, extended families living under one roof. These days some of us even have a sense of Zoom families! Similarly, sanghas can appear in all shapes and sizes. It does take a certain amount of energy to be a support for others while also taking care of yourself, so perhaps it's helpful to start with at least five people's worth of energy to have a healthy sangha—from there, the possibilities are just about infinite.

Most commonly, we make a distinction between two primary types of sanghas: monastic and lay. A *monastic community* is a group of people who bond together with the agreement that their highest priority is to awaken to the present moment in all its forms. They have a common path of practice. They do their best to have a set of clear agreements (or at least, as clear as we humans can try to devise). Generally they live together, figuring out a way to get food and shelter and sharing domestic work alongside providing spiritual service to a lay community.

Lay sanghas come in a variety of shapes and sizes. Some come together virtually, some in person. Some meet daily; others weekly or monthly. Some have a facilitator or rotate facilitation, while others have teachers. Some come together based on a particular affinity: geography, ethnicity, race, gender expression, age, or language. Some come together seemingly by chance. Some sanghas see their purpose as being a refuge and support system for lives lived quite separately, helping to find moments of calm to remind themselves how to practice during the week. Some come together because they feel called to help heal some particular aspect of human existence: family isolation, social injustice, environmental degradation. In some cases, lay people may also live together under one roof or offer practices to others in the community. Lay practitioners or sanghas may also temporarily join monastic sanghas for retreats, brief periods in which they, too, adhere to the formal practices of monastics.

Recognizing that occasional formal retreats are not enough to develop and sustain a practice, the sangha-centered lineage of Plum Village strongly encourages everyone to commit themselves to this path by participating in some community life in a regular ongoing way. Weekly get-togethers for practice can become the hub of a spiritual life. Over time the sangha can develop all of the four pillars of the Plum Village tradition: study, practice, work, and rest/play.

Numerous formal practices take on added dimensions when we do them with a group of kindred spirits. Sitting, walking, and eating together provide us with a constant reminder of what we intend to do. The collective stillness during meditation practice is powerfully coregulating, helping us to melt away tension and helping us to settle.

Does it always work this way? Well, no. The person sitting next to you may be squirmy or annoying. Your tablemate may have so little on their plate, you might wonder why they're skimping—might they have secret stashes of goodies in their room to circumvent the meal regimen? (Oh, what the mind can conjure up!) The silence at meals might be tension-producing, maybe a reminder of dinner-table tensions from childhood. But these moments of difficulty are perfect grist for the mill: without them, we cannot experience the process of grinding them into a digestible nutrient, seeing clearly just how we make our suffering. Without this, we do not learn how our minds and nervous system work together to trip us up.

The collective nature of practices holds us in there, where alone, we might not be so carefully swaddled. Although you are always free to get up when you need to and leave the meditation hall, it is less likely that you will do so in a group setting than when you are home alone. The added container of being part of the sangha gives us more opportunity to sit with and recognize the impact of whatever is disturbing us, as well as a chance to reflect on the responsibility of the individual to hold that container of silence and stillness. It helps to practice how you are going to deal with uncomfortable mind states and create space to access your options for reregulating, to breathe, to open that window a bit wider.

The practitioner sits or walks or eats or works surrounded by models of alternative ways to inhabit common experiences. They learn from others by example, of what is beneficial, and what is not. When one sees oneself in others, learning can happen.

I am with my sangha having lunch on a Day of Mindfulness. I find myself preoccupied with thoughts of a recent difficult interaction; as Thay says, I'm "eating my anger." I glance at the person across from me, who is arranging tiny morsels onto their spoon. They have arranged it like a small decorative platter of noodles, tofu gently dipped in hot sauce, and topped with a sprig of mint. Their mouth opens like a great garage door and in goes the vehicle, chew, chew, chew. I am suddenly back in the room, smiling at my table mate, and at myself. I've just been reminded of the abundance that sits on my plate, and gratitude replaces anger. Ah, sangha!

Sangha support has many dimensions for me. The sangha can share the burden of decision-making so it doesn't rest all on my shoulders. While writing this book, I was gifted countless hours of conversation and ideas by my sangha siblings. The sangha also allows me to absorb states of well-being less developed in me by means of coregulation, my body effortlessly mimicking those who have better-cultivated states of compassion, kindness, joy, and inclusivity.

The sangha is a place where I ease into a sense of belonging and feel accepted. With time, everyone in my sangha has gotten to know most of my shortcomings first hand. Because we have looked deeply at ourselves and others, these inevitable shortcomings can be accepted more as part of the human condition and less as a reason to be rejected. As we will explore in this chapter, formal and informal practices help us fully acknowledge the gifts the sangha offers, promoting safety, belonging, and acceptance. Because I am aware of coregulation, I also feel this safety, belonging, and acceptance in the way my body relaxes and opens up. For example, I've conditioned myself to relax when I hear the bells ring during our meditation practice, really taking in the *stopping* through every cell and sinew. And when I forget, I can direct my attention to those around me, seeing how they are responding and relaxing. This is my springboard to freedom: freedom to be my authentic self, freedom leading to creativity.[3]

One Buddha Is Not Enough: Developing the Mind of Love

An awakened being is one who is able to embody all virtues at once, one whose presence is in itself healing and transforming. Such a being embodies *bodhichitta*, which Thich Nhat Hanh interpreted as meaning "mind of love." In his definition, bodhichitta is not so much an emotion as the ability of a person to act in accordance with the four heavenly abodes: loving-kindness, compassion, joy in another's joy, and inclusiveness or equanimity. Thay had the ability to manifest and hold all of these qualities, and transmit them, so that others could enter into this experience, become acquainted with it, befriend it, and inhabit this same mind. You could sink into the safety of this presence, being held in a coregulated state and being able to experience this possibility within your own body/mind.

Yet Thay never claimed to be a Buddha. In fact, he repeatedly proclaimed, "One Buddha is not enough." Whether we are talking about lay or monastic life, most of us do not have the opportunity to be in the presence of truly great beings. What can we do to create conditions in which we can all benefit from great presence, from experiencing bodhicitta? In lieu of having this complete mind of love manifest in just one individual, might it be possible for it to take the form of a sangha—where each of those particular qualities could be held by different individuals, all within the container of a collective?

In the Plum Village tradition, we walk the Buddhist path, as much as possible, in the context of others. Whether that is on retreat or in weekly meetings, while carrying out projects or enjoying social occasions, we utilize both the power of the individual practice and the witnessing, accepting, modeling, and coregulating effects of being with others who are also practicing. At any one moment, the group holds an energy made up of the collective energy of individuals. When modeling is needed, it is accessible. When witnessing and acceptance is needed, there are practices. When we cannot hold the mind of love, someone else can hold this space for us to bathe in.

We might think of the sangha, like all organisms, as being composed of cells, each with their own contribution to the health and functioning of the sangha body. This means that the individuals in the sangha can be treasured for their unique gifts, skills, and insights, and that no one individual needs to be fully realized. Each is respected for their contribution. Each realizes that all the cells hold the same aspiration: the overall health of the body.

Thay liked to give this example: imagine that you are hammering something, and the hand wielding the hammer accidentally smashes the thumb on the opposing hand. Immediately the hand puts the hammer down and goes to take care of the other hand. The injured hand does not grab the hammer and hit the other back. Because all the parts are connected, there is a natural caring response. Might this be the healing power developed in a deeply committed sangha, one in which everyone does their best to be conscious of this interbeing reality and put it into practice? There may already be effective solutions to many of the problems, large and small, that we face today; the problem is that we lack the ability to collaborate with each other, preventing those solutions from being skillfully put into place. Were we able to deeply see and act as one organism, the difficulties facing us now would, indeed, take on a more manageable tone.

Each retreat that Thich Nhat Hanh gave closed with his urging the participants to go home and form a sangha. He would always point out that the tiger on the mountain endangers itself if it leaves its refuge. So too, does the practitioner compromise their intention and potential for awakening without the benefit of a sangha. Retreat after retreat, baby sanghas are born, taking nourishment from the collective body of sanghas in the form of retreats, practices being developed, or books being published.

In this way, practitioners become sangha builders, creating groups that strive to follow the basic Buddhist precepts and set them into a context of both individual and collective suffering, while seizing all possible moments of beauty and joy along the way. This is healthy nourishment to build a strong sangha body.

I am a bit out of sorts one morning. It is a Day of Mindfulness, and I have made a commitment to attend. When it is time for walking meditation, I am not particularly in the mood—but I'm there, so I show up. We begin circling up for some songs. The songs are familiar, and I can focus on the goodness of the words, but I notice someone is off key. With proper attention, I try to be compassionate; I fail. I look around the circle of familiar faces and focus on someone who looks like they are in that kind of heart space I'd like to be in, in this moment. I notice my spirits shift a little. The fact that we are walking together helps me flow along, not needing to think about the speed, just focusing on my steps. I recognize and resist the limbic urge to hyperfocus on the negative. Because we are a group, I can attend to the spirit of the moment in a variety of ways. I can pick up on cues of contentment, calm, companionship. I have an abundance of wholesome states to choose from, like a smorgasbord of good-enoughness.

INTERGENERATIONAL SANGHAS

Although there should be absolutely no pressure on children to walk a particular spiritual path, children can find a lot of support practicing in a community that honors and respects their personhood, one that is confident in their abilities to touch their own beautiful nature. As we touched on in Chapter 2, we can see how beneficial it is to promote and develop well-being skills in young people to help them access the healthy balance of wholesome physical and mental states. When done in community, with abundant loving energy, magic can happen.

Although the Plum Village lineage is still making its way into the Western world and very much in its formation, we are already seeing a generation of young leaders emerging out of the nest provided for them through family and teen retreats at monasteries, children's programs in various lay sanghas, and regular contact with monastic and lay practice. We have already read examples of this in Chapter 1, about Thich Nhat Hanh's and Thich Phuoc Thien's childhoods in Vietnam, and how those early years of exposure to Buddhist practice supported them through incredible difficulties.

When children are part of a community of practice, adults benefit as well. When we listen to Dharma talks aimed at younger children and teens, the sweetness of the messages can open our hearts wide. Children's curious comments during community gatherings can be welcomed as moments of delight rather than intrusion; children often ask questions and raise issues that the adults have thought about, yet might be too guarded to bring forward. Simply being around children provides us adults with a living connection back to our own childhoods and those of our ancestors, opening opportunities for healing. Finally, integrating children into the sangha also allows parents the ability to have a spiritual life and find much needed support for their parenting. It takes a village to raise a child, so the saying goes, yet how many people actually have a village to rely on, one that shares their ethics and practices embodying a wisdom tradition?

In short—everyone benefits from having an intergenerational sangha!

SANGHA COMMITMENTS FOR SAFETY AND HARMONY

Just as the individual benefits from the guidance of an ethical code, in order for a group to get along well, they will also benefit from some agreed-upon behavioral guidelines to help put ethics into practice. Group commitments help everyone know what is expected of them, reminding us about direction and aspirations. As mentioned in Chapter 3, sanghas begin this crafting of an ethical container with the Five Mindfulness Trainings, the Plum Village version of the Buddha's original five precepts: to refrain from killing, stealing, sexual misconduct, lying, and using intoxicants. The Five Mindfulness Trainings are written in a way that is more detailed than the original precepts and tailored to today's challenges. They focus on understanding how to prevent the suffering caused by transgressing, as well as how to create the harmony needed for walking together on this path. Together they promote the lived experience of interbeing, the connectedness of all of life.[4]

Just as these five trainings are a guide for the individual, a set of Fourteen Mindfulness Trainings is a foundation for the healthy functioning of the sangha body. These trainings include openness; nonattachment to views; freedom of thought; awareness of suffering; compassionate, healthy living; taking care of anger; dwelling happily in the present moment; true community and communication; truthful and loving speech; protecting and nourishing the sangha; right livelihood; reverence for life; generosity; and true love.[5]

In the West, lay people often consider meditation to be the entry point of Buddhist practice—but this is a Western convert adaptation. In Asian traditions, practitioners more often begin by focusing on the precepts or trainings, to first settle the body/mind as a foundation for deeper practice. Rather than a list of "thou shalt not's," the trainings are perhaps better thought of as contemplations leading us to see how we may create suffering or happiness by all our actions—not only for ourselves, but for others as well. They are an invitation to fully embrace life as a work in practice: they support us in staying open and letting go of fixed views so we can embrace the validity and vitality of differing views, be aware of oppressions and power dynamics (both internal and external), become increasingly comfortable with our own discomfort and that of others, and guard our body, breath, and spirit so we can listen and communicate openly. With this agreed-upon ethical base, sangha members have a basis for working through difficulties that inevitably arise in groups.

RETREATS: A 24/7 PRACTICE

The most well-known of all collective practices is, of course, a *retreat*: a period of time when the sangha gathers together for a 24/7 experience of all the teachings in a living laboratory, taking pause from worldly distractions.

A retreat is made up of lots of elements that are not specific to retreats, like relationships, organizing, infrastructure, food, and other worldly things. What is unique about a retreat is that our focus and intention are held *collectively*. When we are "out in the world" it is much easier to forget we are practicing. Ideally, lay people would be able to remember with every breath that the ground of their being is walking the Eightfold Path. In reality, an infinite number of hooks draw our attention away from this awareness. A retreat is an opportunity to relieve ourselves of some of that distraction, and substitute, instead, a generous helping of reminders, held in a schedule of forms and practices and the collective intention of a group. In this way, a retreat offers the opportunity for us to form and strengthen those neural pathways that lead to wholesome states and mindful well-being, bringing balance into every aspect of our waking lives: walking, eating, working, conversing, even using the toilet.

In the Plum Village monastic tradition, the weekly schedule is a recognition of our striving for a balanced practice life, and it sets out a good example of how to do it. Along with the monastery or practice center—the physical setting of the retreat—the schedule is the muscles and bones of the sangha body. This is the template for retreats in general.

The week's activities fall into four categories, the four pillars of the Plum Village lineage: practice, study, work, and play/rest. Practice, study, and work are all (ideally) done in mindfulness—that is, a continuous practice of being mindful of the body in the body, the mind in the mind, woven into all that we do.[6] Out of seven days of the week, four days are a mix of formal and informal practice and monastery work. Two days are devoted primarily to formal study and practice called Days of Mindfulness. Those consist of formal practice, listening to teachings, sharing the teachings with others, and ceremony. Recognizing the need for balance, each of these days of mindfulness is followed by a period of laziness: the intensity of the training is followed by an equally intensive and essential period of rest and relaxation: no schedule, no pressure. It is a time to honor our individual needs as they arise. (See "Lazy Days" in Chapter 6 for a description of this important part of practice.) In the monastery, the collective nature of laziness allows a certain hush to permeate the air, supporting everyone in their intention to reset.

Retreats, like sanghas, come in all forms. Some are initiated and led by the monastic community, some by the lay community, and some by a collaboration of the two. They can last from an overnight to months, and they can be held anywhere: some are residential (everyone living together), and now, some have moved online, where your home is folded into a virtual outbuilding of a cyber center! Generally retreats have a theme, or a way to set a general intention. This could include studying a teaching; experimenting with stillness and silence; a special focus on healing; a practice through the lens of expressive arts; or being with the natural world. These are anchors for the common work of being present in the here and the now. No matter what the stated topic, our internal experience often surfaces as a surprise during a retreat, and our personal agenda unfolds alongside the set intention: we are reminded of family dynamics and cultural inequities and are reacquainted with small joys or forgotten ways of being.

In Chapter 8, we'll look at some specific ways we can plan and facilitate these kinds of experiences that integrate a neuro-informed sensibility into the offerings.

Collective Practices

As children, we probably didn't give a second thought to taking good care of our bodies—that is the job of a good parent. In fact, if a parent had never pointed out to us that it was important to eat certain foods to make sure we stay healthy, or that a bedtime routine and restorative sleep are necessary, we may not realize that bodies are something that need conscious care. Even as adults, if we are blessed with good-enough health, a body might seem like it is something that just maintains itself.

Similarly, it might not be immediately apparent that alongside our individual practice, collective practice is needed for the healthy maintenance of our sangha body. This involves experimenting with new ways of living: new ways of relating to ourselves, to other individuals, and to group interactions. Although we're focusing here on practices that support our spiritual lives, they are equally applicable to our lives in the outer world. They apply to rearing our children, relating to coworkers, handling our family dynamics, and processing everyday encounters. We can learn to drop the spiritual vocabulary without dropping the spirit these practices cultivate: openness to views, sensitivity to injustice, ways we are hijacked by inherited trauma, ways we treat our earth. The following sections give practical ways of entering into these explorations.

DHARMA SHARING: THE COLLECTIVE AS TEACHER

A collective opportunity for sharing is an essential practice in the Plum Village tradition. This is another powerful opportunity to experience the healing power of coregulation by the sangha, the aims and benefits of which are numerous. In Dharma Sharing, sangha members gather together and take turns sharing their thoughts, feelings, and truths with each other. These sharing sessions can be centered around a particular theme, such as sharing responses to a Dharma talk they just listened to or to a book they are reading together. But generally the sharings take on an aimless tone—simply, whatever is alive in each individual in the moment. This is a time for sharing both the challenges and joys of practice; it is an intimate, collective glimpse into practice life. Although there is no pressure to share, each person holds a wealth of experience from which others can benefit.

Dharma Sharing gives a person the opportunity to have whatever is in their heart witnessed. We can practice telling our story from well within the window of tolerance; we can learn to stretch it and recognize the growing of our own resilience. Dharma Sharing is also an opportunity for us to practice deep listening and loving speech, as outlined in the fourth of the Five Mindfulness Trainings. Here we listen to what is said and what is *not* said—a form of deep attunement. Listeners practice by noting what is arising, letting go of opinion and judgment.

In addition to the Five (and/or Fourteen) Mindfulness Trainings, each sangha adopts a clearly stated set of Dharma-Sharing guidelines that detail how to create a sensitive, safe space. The space is held by a member of the sangha who is a skilled facilitator, and anything shared in the group is received without judgment or comment. If those present in the sharing circle can follow the guidelines, they will be attentive and receptive to what is being shared.

Miraculously, our nervous system is capable of picking up not only what another person's body is doing, but also the intentions driving that state. In this way, the person sharing benefits simply from the *intention* of others being present. Some listeners may be holding the sharer with compassion, some with kindness, some with the joy of knowing that the person is being lovingly received, others with the even calm of equanimity. As a collective, then, the sangha can provide a healing experience, one of holding the nervous system within that window while being present with previously dysregulating feelings and images. There is a chant that addresses this directly: "The one who bows and the one who is bowed to are both by nature empty (not separate); therefore the communication between them is inexpressibly perfect."[7]

Dharma Sharing is about learning how to practice with difficulties, and it is not meant to be some sort of therapeutic catharsis—still, being witnessed, accepted, and held by fellow travelers can indeed be quite therapeutic. (Learning how to hold such space is a practice in itself, which we will see in the next chapter.) Although the sharer may feel somewhat rattled or dysregulated when they first begin to share, they slowly take on the stability surrounding them, held by this collective love and nourished by the calming vagal response it produces. In this way, the same event can now be experienced within the window of mindful opportunity and can be seen more clearly for what it is.

At times during Dharma Sharing the energy of a group is so extremely collected that it seems as if all of its members have just one heartbeat. It is as if they really are one organism, crying and laughing as one body. Should a thumb of the organism begin to throb with pain, the other hand will not hesitate to encircle it with care instantly.

It is important, as we will see in the next chapter, that sanghas clearly discuss how they view Dharma Sharing and adjust their guidelines to reflect the capacity of the group to hold individual suffering. Holding space means that both the facilitator and the sangha can remain within their window of opportunity as a person shares. This quality of holding space is what the sharer needs to benefit from the coregulation with group so they can stretch their own window. When difficulties arise in the presence of others who are not thrown out of their window, their compassionate presence can be healing, coaxing the nervous system into balance through mirror neuron mimicry.

Like all practices, the collective develops the healing capacity of Dharma Sharing over time. There is a learning curve; it is not necessarily something that happens consistently right away. At times a speaker may get carried out of their window or some of the listeners might not be able to maintain their own stability while listening. Depending on circumstances, this level of sharing may be beyond the group's capability to maintain its coregulating effects. At this point, the facilitator can sound a bell for a mindful pause, giving an opportunity for individuals, and hence the group, to reregulate with practices from Chapter 5. As a sangha becomes more and more skillful in holding space, the richness of Dharma Sharing becomes more available, and newcomers can more quickly experience the potential benefits.

BEGINNING ANEW

We may have the illusion that when we come together with kindred spirits, setting lofty intensions to live the mindful life, we'll be plopped down into a sort of heaven on earth. In fact, when we come together to form a community, we each bring in a lot of baggage along with those lofty intensions!

No matter how homogeneous you might think a group of people are, priorities and communication will not always be in harmony. Beginning Anew is a practice that helps groups raise and clarify such miscommunications, heading off potential problems. Being seen and heard allows us to let go of wrong thinking, making room for deeper understanding and harmony. Beginning Anew can be done in pairs, small groups, or large groups. It can be powerful, even vital, to the beneficial functioning of the group—so let's take our time here to really understand it.

Just as it sounds, Beginning Anew is a practice that creates the conditions for a fresh start. It follows, more or less, the same guidelines as Dharma Sharing, and like Dharma Sharing, it is *not* a simple back-and-forth discussion; it has a very specific form.[8] Although it may help resolve conflict, Beginning Anew is not in itself a conflict-resolution process. It is more like a reset of our nervous system so that we can maintain a harmonious default position. In fact, it is quite similar to many of the self-regulating tools we've already learned: it has elements of anchoring, making space to keep the body regulated, and drawing on resources. This sets the stage for increasing our own vulnerability within that safe container and ends with stretching the group's window of tolerance.

The practice starts out with the facilitator setting up a pleasant space, and inviting everyone to gather in a circle, placing something of beauty—a small bouquet of flowers, a candle, a simple drawing—in the center. After a brief period of sitting together and settling, the form unfolds. Each person who cares to speak begins their turn by getting up and mindfully walking to the center of the circle, picking up the object of beauty, and carefully taking it back to their seat. Right away, this practice is helping them regulate and remain within that window.

The form will vary from one group to another, but each session of Beginning Anew will have four key content areas: flower watering; beneficial regrets; naming a hurt; and asking for understanding and support.

1. Flower Watering

Flower watering is a practice in which the speaker talks about specific times when a person present made a positive contribution to someone in the group: a helping hand, an encouraging word, a show of kindness or compassion. In short, the speaker highlights that person's effort and how they contributed to the collective coregulating power of the others. (In the Plum Village way of thinking about it, their actions have watered wholesome seeds in our store consciousness.)

This first step in Beginning Anew can take up most of the group's time together. As you sit and listen, you may begin to remember, "Oh yes, I was uplifted by that, too," or even "Wow, I didn't realize that they could be like that." After 30 to 45 minutes of sincere flower watering in a group, the energy is amazingly transformed. You can feel, even in the tensest of times, the collective shoulders lowering.

Just like our nervous systems can discern between a real and fake smile (see the exercise "Smiling as a Resource" in Chapter 6), so too can we sense the difference between authentic and forced flower watering. Flower watering is a cultivated practice. Learning how to take judgment out of that water can be tricky, yet well worth our while, to learn. For example, being specific about how someone's action impacted another person can be more effective than just making a compliment that is still in the "judging" arena. When members know their sangha practices Beginning Anew happens on a regular (once a month or quarter, for example) basis, they are encouraged to develop habits of collecting these positive examples. This collecting alone is beneficial in creating a more harmonious group.

2. Beneficial Regrets

After a sufficient amount of time, when people are feeling settled and safe, there comes a natural opening into *beneficial regret*. Once we can feel seen and appreciated for the natural goodness we bring to the sangha, it becomes much easier to admit our shortcomings, or the unskillful moments when our habits may have had unwholesome impacts or consequences. Beneficial regret is *not* a time to berate oneself. It is a time to share that you see this in yourself and you intend to change. Feeling shame does not benefit anyone; that's why this step is called *beneficial* regret. It lets everyone know that *you* know, so they can relax, assured that your unskillfulness is being taken care of. Beneficial regret helps people become more patient the next time the issue arises because they will know that you're aware of it and are practicing to make a change.

Hearing the whole group offer their beneficial regrets creates a feeling of acceptance. When everyone acknowledges that we all do annoying and even hurtful stuff, it creates more breathing room in the group. The Dharma police can put down their flashlights and stop hunting in the corners for dust and grime. For many of us, we consider our own transgressions to be so much worse than everyone else's. It is a joyous discovery that owning up lightens everyone's load.

3. Naming a Hurt

Because Beginning Anew is a problem-naming rather than problem-solving process, the next parts may vary depending on the group. The third element of Beginning Anew is *naming a hurt,* in case one hasn't been brought to light already. Depending on the issue, this part can be done between individuals or in the larger group. It is a time to help others understand the impacts of their actions. It must be done in a way that expresses how the hurt landed without making judgments or assumptions about the intentions of the doer. After the Beginning Anew session has had its time to settle into the hearts of participants, perhaps hours or days later, there may still be a need for follow-up; anyone can make the request to get together to repair what is in need of further understanding and healing.

4. Asking for Understanding and Support

The last element of Beginning Anew is *asking for understanding and support.* Sometimes our troubles, even though they affect our sangha life, are not always apparent. Ill health, family or economic stresses, cultural inequities, and political or environmental devastations can take a hidden toll. Whatever is weighing you down, it is helpful for others just to know, regardless of whether anyone in the group is involved in the difficulty. This last section invites folks to be seen for these hidden burdens—and if others can be of support, that can be shared as well. Although the group may be unable to affect outer changes, they can help shoulder the burden and the support collectively.

A few fine points: You can do Beginning Anew solo, too, when you might be giving yourself a hard time. You might go stealth and do the first two parts while talking with a friend, when your energies are not as harmonious as you'd like them to be. They might spontaneously reciprocate, even if they don't realize what's going on! Doing Beginning Anew with the sangha monthly or every six weeks really helps keep things fresh.

In order to have examples for flower watering on hand when the time comes, you might even develop a lifestyle of deliberately collecting moments of goodness for each person in your group. (This is much like the practice of collecting resources in Chapter 5; see the "Resourcing Ourselves" exercise.) You needn't refrain from appreciating things as they are happening; they are welcome to be heard again in the future.

The Second-Body System for Lay Practitioners

The monastics in this tradition practice what is known as *a second-body system*: a support network to help each other maintain stability and provide mutual support when times are difficult. When they are in their monastery, monastics have a variety of mentor/mentee relationships that help buoy them through difficulties, in addition to other collective practices that help them through hard spots. When they go out into the world, they vow to continue to support each other, whether that is by accompanying each other on home visits or medical appointments, or by just lending a hand doing the shopping.

Lay people also, from time to time, institute a second-body system during sangha outings, celebrations, regular walks in the woods, or a silent day at the beach. Sometimes this is practiced like a telephone chain: one person calls the second in line to check in, and then the second person calls the third, and so on until the last calls the first. Potentially this can be both grounding and bonding, bringing a deep sense that you are a cell doing your particular job so that the larger organism can be healthy and well-functioning.

I was part of a second-body system during a ninety-day retreat in 2004. We created a chain of care by drawing names from a hat: in this way, each of us was gifted a person to care for, but the process also meant someone else had drawn our name and would care for us. Although "giving" and "receiving" may seem like separate activities, in this process our whole group became connected. I discussed with my "second body" just how he wanted to be cared for, and then followed three months of gift-giving: a rock, a smile, a "how ya doing?" and some deep discussion on issues as they arose over that time. Both he and his partner became sidekicks on this path. Today, eighteen years later, they live halfway round the world. We continue periodic check-ins, having followed each other's practice through the years; there is an ease, a continuity, and a continued sense of collaboration on the path.

THE SECOND BODY SYSTEM IN PRACTICE: A BROTHER'S JOURNEY THROUGH TRAGEDY

The following story of a Deer Park Monastery monk will help demonstrate how second-body system works in practice in support of a family tragedy. (As a caution, this story references suicide.)

> Two dozen tiny faces on a computer screen look at me expectantly. I take a breath and introduce myself to the others in this Survivors of Suicide Loss Zoom meeting: "I'm a monk. I recently lost my father, and then I lost my mother a few months later."
>
> The facilitator seeks clarification: "Did you say you lost both of your parents?"
>
> My parents were never very comfortable at the monastery, even when they were well. Though we'd always had a very loving relationship, when I told them I planned to become a Buddhist monk, they initially responded in anger. Family is always welcome at Deer Park Monastery, where I live, and my parents were only about a two-hour drive away, but the idea of staying here, even for one night, did not interest them. Nevertheless, during my first couple of years here, they would visit from time to time, and we'd spend a couple of hours chatting by the koi pond. I made the commitment to call weekly, and little by little, the relationship healed. By the time I was ordained in 2018, we had made peace, and they had come to accept my decision.
>
> However, following my mom's retirement, around the time of my ordination, both of my parents underwent bouts of severe anxiety and depression. When the pandemic began, short visits to the monastery became a logistical challenge, and longer visits were more or less out of the question. I watched on a screen, during our weekly calls, as they sank deeper and deeper into fear and despair, culminating in the loss of my father. Though everyone rallied in support of my mother, she had already been suicidal before my father's

death, and we were unable to prevent her further spiral downward.

Suicide loss has a way of coercing its survivors into comfort with paradox. Suicide is always shocking, but it's not always surprising. Although all of us—my sister, our family, my parents' friends, and doctors—will always wonder if we could have done more, we also know, somehow, that we did everything we could.

It has been my incredible good fortune to have gone through this ordeal while living in community. When my father died, a monastic brother came and stayed with me and my family for three weeks, knowing when to be by my side and when to recede. I was staying with my mother when she died five months later, and in fact I was the one who discovered her that terrible morning. Within hours, three monastic brothers arrived at the door. The next day, I shared with them, in detail, what I had seen and done. They listened generously and courageously. We proceeded to convert the house where I grew up into a monastery, practicing daily sitting and walking meditation, and even conducting a ceremony to honor my mother's life.

Some weeks later, a brother who had met my parents only briefly told me that when he heard the news that my mother had died, he lit a stick of incense, placed it on the altar, prostrated, and wept. He told me he had felt as if his own mother and father had died. His sharing was not particularly unique. Everyone in my community was and has been very supportive of me throughout this journey of loss, offering their deep listening, care, comfort, and encouragement, but more than that, they have been on the journey with me, every step of the way.

> I peer into the eyes of the faces on the screen. I don't pretend to have come through this unscathed. The last thing I want is to give the impression that my life as a monk affords me some superhuman power of invincibility. I have scars like everyone else on this call, but when I hear people talk about how alone they feel, I can only imagine how difficult that must be, and I do, and it's what keeps me coming back to these meetings. To the degree that I have been able to heal, it is thanks to the loving presence of the people around me. So building community is how I express gratitude and transform any insight I may have gained from tragedy into compassionate action.
>
> "I'm sorry you're here," says the facilitator, "but I'm glad you came."
>
> I am too.

Here is that same story from the perspective of a brother who accompanied this young monk through the entire journey and is continuing their support right up to today:

> My grandfather died when I was sixteen years old. When he was sick in the hospital, I didn't want to think about the possibility of his dying. When he died and I received the news, I tried to put it out of my mind, to pretend it hadn't happened, but I couldn't deny that sinking feeling. It felt like my heart had fallen into my stomach. I was deeply shocked. I had never lost someone before.
>
> When ten years later my monastic brother told me that he had just lost his father, I saw that same shock, that same sinking feeling, written on his face. It was anguish, disbelief, even desperation. There was nothing I could do to take

away that feeling, but I could at least be present for him and his pain. I could at least let him know that he wasn't alone.

But what else could I do? Before this tragedy, I had precious little experience with death. My own experience with my grandfather's passing was one of avoidance, denial, and even blaming. It was not a healthy expression of grief. To lose a grandparent to medical complications may be painful, but to lose a parent to suicide can be seriously traumatic. Even as I held my brother and felt the weight on my chest growing, I looked at him and could only imagine that he was a world away, trying to keep going but barely moving, sloshing knee-deep through a flood of emotions.

And yet, even as my brother's grief escaped my direct experience, I could still see when it was present in him and when it wasn't. Going to his family home with him, I tended to his pain and cultivated his healing. Supporting him during this difficult time taught me to be a gardener. I know now what to do to support someone in grief.

With the death of his mother, just a few months later, we came in force, three-strong. The four of us created sacred space in the house, transforming the living room in a way that was in keeping with family tradition but that was supported by adapted Buddhist elements of love and attention. We allowed it all to unfold from our direct experience and be grounded in our practices.

Grief needs to be able to run its course. We provided conditions for it to do so. We took care of practical things like cooking and cleaning so there was less thinking and more space in my brother's mind for that grief to come up and be seen. When it was present, we could be with our brother so that together we could bear witness to it and celebrate its truth.

> There are precious few opportunities for people to come together through the intimate knowledge of one person's pain. We are blessed in this aspect. When pain runs through one person it is tragic, but when it runs through a community it is not a great divider but a great unifier: a noble messenger of our shared humanity and individual fragility. We learned to celebrate and welcome this pain with open arms, and we are so much happier for it.

TOUCHING THE EARTH

Along with rituals of grief come rituals of holding pain and joy as one. The Touching the Earth practice, mentioned in Chapter 5 as a Plum Village practice for resourcing, is such a ritual. Originally offered by Thay as a way of touching the interbeing nature of all our life's experience, the practice has given fruit, like a pomegranate bursting forth its seeds, turning into an entire set of meditations that points us in the direction of seeing every situation for its joys and pains: our human inheritance, our ancestral inheritance, our cultural inheritance, our environmental inheritance. Each Touching the Earth practice invites us to celebrate inherited resources, while also acknowledging unskillfulness and collective traumas, and mourning their impacts—and, finally, it allows us to be inspired to take responsibility for healing what needs healing. Here the focus is on the collective nature of the suffering, and the collective nature of the vow to heal. This allows us to take our rightful place in that healing: not to be overwhelmed by it, yet clearly to be responsible.

The ritual is done by reading aloud a written text after a period of quiet sitting. Depending on your physical ability, you are invited to stand with palms joined to embody full sacred presence while part of the text is read. This part of the text connects us to the wholesome elements of the meditation. This is followed by lying down on the Earth, to hear, embody, and relinquish the pain and suffering contained in whatever difficulties we are facing. It is another way to roast the marshmallow—or maybe it's a bit like confession, confessing to Earth herself.

During the practice we do our best to stay present with the entirety of what is in the text being read. Although there is a rich body of such texts in Thich Nhat Hanh's book *Touching the Earth*, practitioners are encouraged to write their own specific texts to address issues relevant to their particular community, current concerns, places where response is falling short of their needs, or the suffering of specific communities or environments.[9]

Not really knowing my family's geographic origins, I spent years fruitlessly researching our family tree, looking for a sense of belonging. Then on one retreat, someone offered a Touching the Earth practice, which included just a single phrase about "Semitic people." In the moment of hearing those two words, something astounding happened inside me. I realized that this phrase touched my longing to be included; rather than the narrowness of my own personal family history, it bonded me with entire Middle Eastern cultures. Soon after that, I found myself working in Israel and the West Bank, with an ease and fervor I'd never felt before. It continues to this day, clearly stemming from those few minutes of Touching the Earth that lay dormant inside me my whole life, perhaps for generations before me. I was healing myself, my ancestors, and perhaps even my descendants.

8

Becoming Unshakeable

Managing Collective Dysregulation and Growing a Healthy Sangha Body

In the winter of 2003–2004, Thich Nhat Hanh came to Deer Park Monastery in Southern California for the grand opening of its big meditation hall, Ocean of Peace. I had come to Deer Park as well to help with preparations for the retreat, and I joined the garden and landscaping crew. That winter, we spent a lot of time setting up things so that they would be ecologically friendly. There was a vegetable garden with a drip irrigation system, a composting area, and a large worm bin. Those of us on the garden crew did our best to be in harmony with the environment—probably to the extent of becoming fairly proud of and attached to the job we were doing.

About a month into the retreat, both the worm bin and the compost area began cooking. We were very pleased; the strong smell emanating from them indicated compost was in the making! Then to our surprise, bright and early one morning, a grinning monk drove up in a front-loader tractor and made away with both the worms and the compost. Shocked and bereft, we asked Thay why such a thing had happened. We all knew that he was very ecofriendly; why the abrupt turnabout?

The answer was quick and short: The most important thing in the sangha is to cultivate *harmony*. Next question!

I grappled with that answer for months—well, in fact, years. Looking back, I see that the key to making mindful change is seeing both the narrow impact of decisions (in this case, on the environment) and also the impact on the overall harmony of the community. As it turned out, not everyone was enjoying the smell of the cooking compost! Solutions are only as good as the buy-in one has to keep it all going. The world already has lots of good plans to save this and that; what we sometimes neglect to bring along with these fine plans is the harmonious foundation to get everyone on board. In the case of the Deer Park compost project, it would take many years (and more high-tech methods of composting) before we successfully earned the respect and buy-in from the sangha, as they learned to enjoy seeing garbage turn into the fruits of practice.

"In order to save our planet Earth," says Thich Nhat Hanh, "we must have a collective awakening. Individual awakening is not enough. That is why one Buddha is not enough." Is Thich Nhat Hanh saying that the way to save the planet is for everyone to become Buddhist and belong to a sangha? Or is it possible to see the value in holding *all* groups that we belong to as if they were sangha organisms to be taken good care of?

In this chapter, we will look at what we can do to facilitate harmony and stability in our sanghas and communities by adopting the same neuro-informed practices we've been using to help ourselves regulate when things get rough. Although I'll mostly be talking about sanghas, keep in mind that these same practices can be extremely helpful in a wide range of contexts!

The Sangha Body: A Collective Nervous System?

The tenth of the Fourteen Mindfulness Trainings of the Tiep Hien Order, Protecting and Nourishing the Sangha, refers to the sangha as if it were a living being:

> [...] We are committed to learning to look with the eyes of interbeing and to see ourselves and others as cells in one Sangha body. As a true cell in the Sangha body, generating mindfulness, concentration, and insight to nourish ourselves and the whole community, each of us is at the same time a cell in the Buddha body.[1]

People are cells of a sangha body? Does that mean that a sangha is an organism rather than an organization?

Let's pick this apart a bit. An organism can be defined as a whole living being made up of interdependent parts. These parts each perform vital functions: ingesting and digesting nutrients, reproducing cells, breathing to move oxygen from the environment to our organs, and carrying waste out of the body—among many others. And, of course, in humans and other animals, a nervous system helps all the parts of the body communicate with each other.

In the last chapter, our focus was on how the individual practitioner benefits from being a part of a sangha: how one is nourished and kept healthy by spending time within this sangha body. Now, if we adopt the perspective of a cell in a larger body, the practitioner takes on the added challenge of keeping that collective body healthy. Some practitioners may bring nourishment to the organism in the form of understanding, compassion, connection. Others may assist with reproduction, helping to initiate and nurture newborn sanghas. Practitioners may have a variety of functions within the organism, but all of us have something to contribute to its overall health! Community dysregulation may surface when we get too caught up in focusing on being an *organization* rather than an *organism*—when we forget how truly vital we all are to each other.

No matter what the group is, if it is worth belonging to, it needs to be healthy: families, workplaces, social support services, classrooms—or thinking even more broadly, consider freeways, movie theaters, forests, even our own bodies. Can we learn to relate to all these systems as organisms we need to nourish and support?

We have explored our individual human existence through the lens of our nervous system's anatomy and functioning. We have seen how it can become unbalanced or dysregulated and what helps us rebalance so that we can fully enjoy and contribute to the well-being of all that exists. We know what it feels like to be in or out of our window of tolerance, and we have learned how we might stretch that window wider. How might we apply all of this to the sangha body, to the nervous system of our groups?

COLLECTIVE COREGULATION AND DYSREGULATION

To understand how the nervous system of our sangha body functions, let's return to the concept of coregulation. In Chapter 7, we explored how sanghas offer a powerful coregulating force to help us calm down when our nervous system starts to go haywire. We might think of our group nervous system as the sum total of the effects of coregulation on the individual nervous systems of the folks in the group.

Coregulation can be a powerful ally in helping us feel grounded and calm, both individually and collectively—but it can work the other way around as well. When those around us are distressed or unable to stay grounded, it can trigger the nervous systems of those around them to respond similarly. Here is an example of how that can happen, and how it can be remedied.

Into the second year of COVID-19, as the country began to tire of isolation, one particular sangha was itching to have a retreat. The planning team had met numerous times, trying to come to agreements about health and safety protocols. The meetings seemed a bit tense, but agreements were put into place. During the retreat, however, it became evident that not everyone was complying with the agreements, nor was anything being done to reinstate the guidelines that weren't being followed. As a result, tensions were high as the planning team worked together doing facility cleaning up at retreat's end.

In reflecting on the guideline setting process after the retreat, several dynamics came to light, along with a cascade of issues of coregulation. There seemed to be two sets of concerns: For some, needs for health and safety were primary, and these opinions were expressed quite openly. The other set of concerns had to do with inclusion and group harmony, as very little communication about alternatives to the proposals had occurred during the planning conversations out of fear of creating conflict with those expressing health concerns. During the planning, many people on the team had felt tense—perhaps very close to the edge of their windows—and everyone was unconsciously picking up on the tension, which only grew as the meeting went on. In order to sidestep these rising tensions and make them go away, guidelines were arrived at prematurely, without ever addressing the root of the tension. Because of this, the agreed upon guidelines lacked buy-in by some and follow-through by others. Those involved saw no way of addressing their concerns without creating conflict. Ultimately, this led to tension about the protocols in place when the retreat began, and as it went on, those "agreements" quickly broke down.

How could an awareness of neuro-informed practice and coregulation in that planning meeting have helped avoid the subsequent tensions during and following the retreat? From the outset, groups need to develop a baseline education of becoming neuro-informed, where individuals are accustomed to recognizing fight, flight, freeze, and fawn responses. This is a collective or institutional responsibility, not just one left to skilled facilitators during a time of concern or conflict.

Given this foundation, a neuro-informed group member could have suggested periodic pauses for the group to calm and settle. Grounding practices could have helped bring people back within their window of tolerance, and as some began to settle, the effects of positive coregulation might have helped others do so as well. Additionally, a skilled facilitator could have inquired about the underlying needs driving the various proposed strategies and articulated them to the group; this might have led to a greater number of options and more buy-in from the group. Perhaps this would have prevented the eventual polarization that occurred during the retreat and the erosion of trust that followed it.

SIGNS AND SYMPTOMS OF COLLECTIVE DYSREGULATION

This list spells out some common traits and behaviors that you might see in a dysregulated group—some of them may seem all too familiar. When you notice these signs and symptoms in a group, crucial factors may be lacking that can help regulate the group's collective nervous system, such as trust, leadership, clarity of communication, decision making, and accountability. For each of the following categories, we can see our individual survival instincts of fight, flight, freeze, and fawn manifesting in various ways. Recognizing the presence of these traits in a group (or an individual) is the first step to learning how to overcome them.

The behaviors can be categorized by the *lack* of conditions needed for well-being. A dysregulated group may have a lack of openness to views, a lack of connection, not enough leadership, insufficient deep listening and loving speech, a lack of accountability and commitment, and a weak ethical foundation. The particulars of any one category may very well also apply to another category. A predominance of individuals who themselves are dysregulated will greatly influence the health and well-being of the group.

LACK OF OPENNESS TO VIEWS

People do not take time to have deeper understanding;

Are not able to come to an enthusiastic consensus;

Do not acknowledge or recognize the cultural or power differences;

Do not express, do not recognize, or may gloss over implicit biases;

Disguise apathy or indifference as nonattachment to views;

Show lack of understanding of cultural or lived-experience differences;

Overprocess every micro-transgression and paralyze movement forward.

LACK OF CONNECTION

People do not build time to be together, only meeting for work or business;

Are not aware that the collective is dysregulated;

Lack group education as to nervous system regulation;

Lack transparency;

Fear being vulnerable or taken advantage of.

LACK OF LEADERSHIP/POWER IMBALANCE

People have poor boundaries;

Do not want to step into leadership role;

Lack clarity in decision-making;

Make decisions without group consent; take unilateral actions;

Micromanage;

Duplicate efforts due to lack of clearly defined roles;

Facilitate ineffectively;

Allow those who have the most power (social positioning or seniority) to be the primary voices;

Have institutionalized consequences for being different;

Come to a lukewarm consensus;

Are not able to grapple with unskillful behaviors;

Are not able to handle discomfort and being with suffering;

Avoid certain topics because they are complicated or tension producing;

Fear disharmony;

Lack skill-building as a group.

LACK OF DEEP LISTENING AND LOVING SPEECH

People gossip and triangulate (use go-betweens instead of being direct);

Take sides;

Feel an air of despair;

Avoid important issues;

Shun certain members, in the guise of accepting their difference;

Certain voices are habitually absent.

LACK OF ACCOUNTABILITY AND COMMITMENT

People do not follow through when decisions are made;

Do not support ways to follow through, in the guise of understanding and compassion;

Lack conflict resolution skills;

Do not follow the mindfulness trainings when making group decisions.

LACK OF AN ETHICAL FOUNDATION

People are seemingly driven by sensual pleasure, power, or economics rather than the foundational intention of the group;

Experience an unchecked imbalance between the realities of functioning in society and being caught up in societal drives for sensual pleasures.

Identifying and addressing the root causes of group dysregulation is a much bigger topic than the scope of this book. However, let's consider this: Since all groups are made of individual humans carrying with them their individual inheritances, group development is very complex. Sanghas are microcosms of the outer world, which all of their individual members come from, and as such, they also contain all of their healed and unhealed elements. It should come as no surprise that every group, spiritual or not, will encounter difficulties. Unless we are aware of our collective window of opportunity and train to stay in there as individuals and as a group, stuff will arise, for sure! This is especially true in times of collective stress: pandemics, the climate emergency, political divides, racial injustice, institutional and economic collapse. How do we stop the avalanche on the outside from invading on the inside?

The following story was told to me by a friend of mine, a seasoned mindfulness practitioner.

> A few years ago, I attended a retreat with an established Plum Village sangha in the United States. We had gathered along the shores of a mountain lake, a peaceful setting where we had held beautiful retreats for many years. Among the sixty-five retreatants and two senior Dharma teachers there were a dozen or so Order members and senior students. I'd become accustomed to these retreats running smoothly and feeling nourishing, and by the second day, as sense of ease was permeating the space. But that evening, the tone changed abruptly.
>
> During a panel presentation on the Five Mindfulness Trainings, a practitioner shared some very explicit personal incidents, along with troubling statistics, to bring home her concerns on the importance of trainings to prevent sexual misconduct. As a result of the explicit nature of the presentation, many women were very upset, and some were so disturbed that they didn't sleep that night. In later conversations, I learned that many of these women had been in or witnessed similar situations themselves.
>
> The next day, a few women brought the enormity and intensity of the situation to the visiting Dharma teacher. The

teacher suggested that they "just breathe" and sit with the difficult emotions—leaving the women feeling invalidated and without adequate guidance. During a question-and-answer session the following evening, I asked whether mindfulness was enough when it came to working with trauma, or if other practices and/or therapies were perhaps needed to heal. One Dharma teacher responded that just being mindful of the breath was enough to heal, while the other Dharma teacher responded that sometimes therapy was needed.

The final day was filled with chaotic attempts for the women to be heard; they even interrupted a ceremony with their concerns. There was no response other than a respectful pause. Despite the dozens and dozens of years of practice in our retreat space, no one seemed to have the skillful means for addressing the pain that was unleashed in the community.

On the one hand, I felt deeply for the women experiencing extreme distress, and I was angry that their voices were being silenced. But on the other hand, I felt a sense of relief that the issue was being made visible, and that the need to learn how to handle such a tender topic was being raised. Despite the prevalence of the Me Too movement around this time, it felt like there was some tacit agreement that we were not supposed to speak about these topics within our community: by trying to speak in keeping with Loving Speech, we were not able to find a way to be truthful at the same time. It felt cathartic to see the bubble burst. An opening had emerged, despite the clumsy and distressful way it landed in the space.

I continue to carry the question: How do we talk about systemic societal oppressions, a gargantuan part of human

> suffering, without injuring one another in our sangha communities? After that retreat, I began to take small steps to understand the importance of trauma-informed practices, both to support me in my own life and for me to be able to offer trauma-informed support as a sangha leader.

How will we not split apart with the deepening inquiries of social and environmental injustices as we discover their presence within every organization we care about? How do we balance our need to challenge these injustices with our deep vow to be good-hearted listeners, careful speakers, saying only what is true, and being kind and helpful from a place of balance and stability? Is it any wonder why it's so hard for us to have these difficult conversations?

During a period of time when I was diving deep into self-inquiry with a Jewish-Buddhist women's racial equity group, I was walking around more sensitive than ever to every inequity done to me and others. I was finding it hard to keep myself regulated in public discourse. At this time, I also found that just about everyone around me was bringing up similar fundamental issues. It felt understandable and validating; there was a lot to process in public discourse.

For every meeting I was in, I felt I needed to do these things: make sure I knew the various demographics (race, class, ethnicity, gender, age, power positions) of everyone in the room; give space to those less-represented voices and be aware of whether I was centering myself; decide whether to give my pronouns or not before speaking; agonize over how to make a land acknowledgment that was truly sincere; think about whether I should call someone out (or in), or if *not* doing so would appear to be colluding with them. Inevitably, someone would say something that triggered someone else, and we would need to process that thoroughly before moving on. By the time the meeting was over, everyone was a nervous wreck, angry or fearful, and nothing on the agenda had been covered. I began to dread meetings of endless processing and little outcome. Although this inquiry into the basic underpinnings of our society was necessary, the way we were doing it seemed to be effectively shutting down our organizational work while we became hyperfocused on dysfunction.

Think back to Chapter 4, when we talked about the problem of overtraining, and that hill-shaped curve. As we develop deeper awareness, we move to the right on that curve, heading up; but beyond a certain point, the benefits of those skills we've been developing start to drop off. The same is true for increasing the understanding we develop in our groups, like becoming aware of societal injustices and striving to do better. Or consider consensus practice, which is used in some sanghas and many social-justice groups: it can be a powerful force in bringing about collective wisdom, but it can also have a paralyzing effect of micromanagement, stifling creativity and timeliness. Similarly, a commitment to confidentiality within the group, or warnings against gossip or acting in anger, can go too far and create misunderstanding and mistrust due to a lack of communication and transparency. Developing strong traditions can be stabilizing and unifying, yet such traditions can also create rigidity and lose the spirit in which they were formed if they are adhered to too strongly.

To have healthy groups—to effectively address these issues without burning out—we must have ways to notice when we're out of balance, collect feedback, and take the opportunity to learn from experience. Here we are in search of a middle way: a way that can develop deep looking, understanding, and compassion and yet honor the need to get the food on the table and work toward a mission. We need to be able to name the predicament and consciously agree when and how to do both.

My dear friend and mentor Lyn Fine has a saying that helps me find my way through such challenges:

Have a big vision
Ground in our practice
Know just the next step.

Collective Practices for Regulation and Stability

We've all got our down days, and we're not always able to contain our own dysfunction. If we are participating in a well-functioning group, then individual dysregulation can be handled in a gentle, supportive way that both helps us rebalance and keeps our sangha body regulated as well. The Plum Village tradition has developed group practices that are intended to promote and reestablish harmony and point us in the direction of the collective awakening journey; we talked about some of them in the previous chapter. Now think back to the individual practices we learned in previous chapters: How might you apply them to a collective practice? This list includes some practices you've already read about, and a few other ideas to try:

TRACKING THE COLLECTIVE BODY

Daily or weekly group meditation practice

Weekly lazy day

Weekly Dharma Sharing

Beginning Anew

Second-body system practice

Day of Mindfulness

RESOURCING—CREATING RITUAL AND CEREMONY

Singing together

Walking together

Playing, exercising, and joining a sport

Cooking and eating together: regular and formal meals, picnics

Working together

Talent shows

Life cycle ceremonies: seasons, holidays, birth, commitment, sickness, death

Gestures (bowing, smiling, silent applause)

Affinity group or cultural-refuge gatherings (see Chapter 9)

Retreats and family camps

GROUNDING

Sitting posture

Touching the Earth practice

Deep relaxation

EMERGENCY RELIEF

Beginning Anew

Second-Body

Walking meditation

Working meditation

Contacting a trusted Sangha member

SENSE OF PURPOSE AND SHARED INTENTION

Sangha Service projects

Collective recitation of the Five and Fourteen Mindfulness Trainings and other meaningful ceremonies

Healing with Collective Grief Rituals

Just as the realization that you are going to die eventually can be softened a bit by knowing that all living beings do at some point die, grief can be softened when that grieving is done together/collectively. Thich Nhat Hanh demonstrated this power when he traveled to Vietnam in 2007 to perform three mass rituals mourning those who had died in the long, brutal struggles of ideology, poverty, famine, family division, and war. The streets were lined with thousands as practitioners packed temples to hear the Dharma talks and participate in ritual prayers to liberate the spirits of the wrongfully dead. This was a mass community grieving, each mourner lending permission to others to grieve, to let out the pent-up feelings that had, up to that point, been politically and culturally inexpressible.

In Chapter 1, I told the story of how Thich Nhat Hanh passed from this Earth, on January 22, 2022, and the immediate response in monasteries all over the world to mark this passing. We had been carefully preparing for this transition for several years, continuing to develop this beloved community in each of the several monasteries around the globe. So too, did we prepare for a massive communal way to grieve together.

In the following days, we watched as a united community, in large groups in the monasteries, and in small groups of lay sangha folk. We watched the procession of the body through the streets; the laying of the body and packing of the casket; the songs and chanting from senior students; the motorcade to the park, where a special cremation oven was set aflame; and the vigil into the wee hours of the night. We accompanied each other through it all, crying, breathing, feeling the resurgence of commitment to be diligent students. We held our own silent candlelit procession, had special meals in the meditation hall, and held large listening circles, hearing from elders of their decades-long experiences with the founder of this visionary path.

We had our individual relationships to Thich Nhat Hanh and we had our collective one. Going through the ceremonies together enveloped us with love and gratitude, which would accompany us through the difficult moments that were to follow as the community came to terms with a new beginning. There was an enormous, palpable surge of energy throughout the community in the days and weeks after his passing. The many different ceremonies and mourning practices of our sanghas focused and channeled that energy—it was a remarkable demonstration of collective mourning on a truly international level.

In the days and weeks following, there were ceremonies to receive ashes at each monastery and additional ceremonies on the forty-ninth and hundredth days after Thay's death. Each one was an opportunity to transition as a collective, hold grief as a collective, and renew vows as a collective. Were there rough spots? You bet! That's life. Did we lift up our spiritual bar in the process of collective awakening? No doubt about it.

Qualities of an Awakening Collective

Individual awakening is a person's ability to undo their conditioning, their innate neurological programming, to overcome dysfunctional avoidance of or aggression toward perceived threats and problematic grasping after desire; to enable suffering to cease and well-being to arise. What, then, does it mean for a sangha to become awake? How would we recognize it—what would it look and feel like? Further, how would the awakening of a collective body contribute to some of the biggest problems we face today?

Aspiring to be a truly awakened collective is both noble and daunting. We all can come with our good intentions, yet throwing ourselves in that rock tumbler that is the sangha is going to be, well, bumpy. Like any group, a sangha will go through cycles as it develops. In the mid-1960s, Bruce Tuckman identified four key stages of development that groups go through: forming, storming, norming and performing.[2] As we work to become an organism contributing to collective goodness, let's consider each of these stages.

Forming: We come to our sangha full of hope and noble intentions and we do our best to be the best selves we can be as we get to know each other. During this time it is really helpful to share life stories so you can understand the contexts that have impacted your fellow seekers. Make time to develop individual friendships, and have fun together. Doing so builds a solid ground of understanding and goodwill to draw on when things get messy. During this time, we do our best to expand those areas we already know to be in need of stretching, we try to resist old habits, and we breathe into it when things become challenging. Although each of us can probably pull all this off to some degree in the short run, let's face it, all honeymoons do usually come to an end, and when that happens, it can be sorely disappointing. Take heart; this is normal, this is messy, and hopefully you've got a bag of tricks and practices, as a group and as individuals, to stay in the stretch zone as the group slips into the next phase: storming.

Storming: As the ride begins to get bumpy, we can celebrate—we're moving into intimacy. If we expect this and have ways to help each other stay regulated, this can be a rich and broadening time. Know that conflict generally arises from misperception and unskillful ways of communicating; think of conflict resolution as being an invitation to deepen our knowing of each other. Plan to spend more time than you expect gathering courage, acknowledging what is coming up, bringing curiosity to conflict, and being willing, eager even, to change your internal narratives. When members of the sangha see that the dynamics in their group may mirror past dynamics in each person's history, they can see the conflicts as opportunities to heal past wounds and establish different strategies for similar issues. Storming is the stage where power dynamics of every kind come into full view. If we can get beyond guilt, shame, blame, and placating to see that we are all victims of an accumulation of unskillfulnesses, we can hold these conflicts with understanding and compassion, thus bring us out of the storm to create our own group culture in the next phase: norming.

Norming: When the group has journeyed through enough of the storm to begin to ride in the direction that brought them together, it's another moment for celebration. In this phase a group moves more smoothly through its journey, putting into practice what the members learned in the storm while they were creating new habits and a new history together. Each step toward the goal is similar to what is achieved by a clever rider who dangles a carrot on a string in front of the donkey to get it moving in the right direction. So too this phase urges the group into new levels of trust and appreciation. It is important that the group acknowledge each person for the unique contributions they make in the group. As folks take on tasks that may need support, this is a time when mentoring can happen showing each person how they can become a resource for others less skilled in their particular talent. This is a time when the magic of conflict resolution can really come into play. Often, conflict can arise from the inadequate handling of different levels of skill. Think of this as being the difference between being a supervisor or a mentor. If someone with more skill or seniority can inhabit a mentorship attitude, and the one learning can be both enthusiastic and respectful, what might have been a point of conflict can transform into a dynamic partnership. Each member of a sangha can potentially inhabit both the mentor and the mentee position around some element of the group journey. This optimal working relationship between group members brings about the final phase: performing.

Performing: This phase is when the group begins to realize some successes and senses accomplishment in the journey. Both the group as a whole and the individuals are feeling a sense of growth, and the organism is gathering energy. Individuals have stretched their sense of self so they each identify as a vital cell of a living, growing body. At this point, a group can feel the emergent quality of their functioning; they are able to extend their journey to fit the inevitable changes in circumstances, gathering strength and determination to take on new challenges. At this point, a group may find themselves beginning the next level of forming, and so the cycle continues.

It is also important to realize that during this process members may come and go; the various stages may apply to different people in the same moment. Realizing this and finding skillful ways to integrate others helps maintain understanding and harmony in the sangha.

Seven Practical Qualities for the Process of Collective Awakening

The four phases of group development are a description of what tends to naturally occur in groups. Knowing what stage we are in is a bit like monitoring the ways our nervous system can get activated. When we know which state we are in—fight, flight, freeze, or fawn—we are more likely to find skillful ways to self-regulate. Likewise, knowing a group's developmental stage can help us manage problems that arise. In addition let's consider the Seven Factors of Conscientious Action identified by Bikkhu Bodhi, a venerable Theravadan monk of New York Jewish roots who was a student of Thich Nhat Hanh in the early 1960s. These factors include faith, compassion, justice, worldly wisdom, self-care, respect, and grace. These qualities sustain us and encourage us to actively engage with compassion, or what Bikkhu Bodhi termed *conscientious compassion*. Although these qualities usually develop in individuals, we can apply them to groups as well.

Faith: Faith, in this sense, has a broad, secular meaning. It is the conviction that altruism, working for the greater good, is supported somehow by whatever forces are at play in our world. This is a faith in the power of goodness. So, when we commit ourselves as a group to follow this path of wholesome intention, unexpected support will cross our collective path—support that we could never have imagined, nor could we have made it happen directly. We can reinforce this kind of faith by making sure the group practices coregulation when doubt or difficulty arises. This way the group practices seeing the self and the collective as an integral part of the whole. The notion of "self-sacrifice" takes on a new meaning as one realizes that the greater good benefits all the individuals that make up the whole. When the group recognizes and celebrates this faith, they will find that it intensifies as they cultivate it, much like a resource.

Compassion: Developing compassion in the group can be part of the forming and storming phases of development as members become more understanding of what they initially perceived as shortcomings in others. Another way of increasing compassion in the group is by committing to take active care of each other; for example, the group can set the expectation each group member should extend help (in the form of presence and of service) to other group members when they need it. Another way to cultivate compassion is for the group to become more deeply intimate with the suffering of their particular focus of service. Some examples might be a group who adopts a refugee family or a group who does prison work, where the daily trials and tribulations are held in common. It takes courage to look deeply and hold the pain, but this can be fortified by the group itself—no one person should carry the burden of exploration alone. Rather, each person helps bring a new perspective to whatever the group's focus is.

Justice: Here we look at justice from a very generic standpoint: the group must agree that all beings should have ways to meet their basic needs, both physical and social. This can include having access to food, shelter, clothing, and health, as well as less concrete things such as experiencing a sense of connection and belonging, feeling respected, having the ability to further their education or develop their intellect, being able to express creativity, having a sense of purpose, and having a way to contribute.

Worldly Wisdom: This refers to a having a clear vision and skillful way to offer service toward a common good. It is the group's ability to look deeply at all the current conditions to find direction. If the group forms to walk together toward a vision, then it behooves them to study carefully the best route for getting there, considering both the inner conditions of the group and the outer conditions in the world.

Self-Care: In order for a group to maintain its spirit and physical energy to do inner and outer work, each individual must know how to take good care of their energies. They must understand that by taking care of themselves they are actually taking care of the group. They are like a well that must be able to continually replenish itself from a source of clean water. The group must really support individuals in learning how to care for themselves and making space for this self-care. It important that the group as a whole find ways to refresh their energy through careful pacing of group work, through mind-strengthening contemplative practice, and through patience, rest, play, and celebration. A careful balance is required; this is the middle way between burnout and indulgence. Often groups run into bottlenecks when a project requires more energy than they have available; this can pressure members to go beyond their limits. Instead, the group should ask what they can do while still practicing enough self-care. They should craft the project to fit the energy available.

Respect: This sixth factor for collective awakening is a personal lesson that was taught to Bikkhu Bodhi by Thich Nhat Hanh: developing the ability to constantly ask yourself, *Am I sure?* There is a humility in recognizing our own attachment to views. Such attachment can make us narrow-minded, keeping us in the limbic network's fight mode instead of allowing us to adopt a respectful and curious approach to others' views. Groups, as well as individuals, can hold tight to their views, and these tendencies toward narrow-mindedness must be recognized and guarded against. In approaching right view, as many perspectives as possible should be considered. Everyone and every group has some sort of wisdom to contribute. Creative and effective action comes as a direct result of this kind of open investigation and embracing of all perspectives.

Grace: This last factor of collective awakening is not one that the group cultivates directly; it is more about tapping into an aspect of that first factor, faith. Faith and grace go together. What seems to happen with regularity is that when individuals become part of a group and let go of their individual aspirations to contribute to the group, they are able to become more healed, whole, content, and free than through any manner of individual striving. Even micromoments of individual and collective awakening can add up, growing like a snowball.

Lending a Hand to Others: Facilitating Collective Stability from a Neuro-Informed Lens

With our deepening understanding of neuroscience and trauma healing and the connection to Buddhist psychology, we now can look at the ways that the Plum Village practices might reflect this sensibility more explicitly. The practices remain solid; the ways we approach practice can be clarified and expanded.

This section is intended for those who guide sanghas or other intentional groups, but it can also be useful for the recipients of that guidance. You can help cocreate a wholesome experience for yourselves and your fellow travelers. As a work in progress, these practices are a place to begin.

Make neuro-sensitivity concepts available right from the start. It is helpful if everyone enters into the practice knowing what they're getting into. Many sanghas have a way of introducing the practice to new folks, either through a website or personal contact in the form of emails, orientation sessions, or telephone calls. This also allows the sangha to assess their capacity to support individuals who join them. In a time of such turmoil and disconnection, having reasonable expectations is important for finding a good match between a sangha and its members. This is a path toward peace, not a therapeutic community: There is a difference, and that needs to be clear to us all.

Given all the ways people experience suffering, there are always going to be occasions in which practitioners get a button pushed or encounter something that takes them outside of their window of opportunity. Being sensitive to trauma does *not* mean trying to avoid all triggers. No mud, no lotus. We do want people to know that mud exists and how to deal with it, of course; we all need to understand that dysregulations happen and what to do in the event they arise.

Have a clear list of sangha agreements. Sanghas can nurture safer space by clarifying expected behaviors of their members as well as clarifying what commitments or responsibility look like in that particular group. It helps to state clearly what the sangha can and cannot provide. Make clear it is not a place for finding partners, nor is it something an individual can use for personal profit. Clarify how decisions are made and who to go to for guidance if difficulties arise. Here are some suggestions for creating safe space:

- Describe a typical sangha meeting agenda and process.
- Describe the physical meeting space before people arrive; when they first attend, show them around and point out where the restroom is, as well as emergency exits and any other important spaces.
- Clarify what, if anything, they will be expected to contribute financially to the group.
- Indicate if the space is open to all or dedicated to a particular group (as we recognize the need at times for cultural refuge or safety).
- Explain the practice and traditions you follow and their origins, and offer suggestions for where they can find more information.
- Explain the guiding principles, values, and behaviors of your sangha, making reference to the Five Mindfulness Trainings; acknowledge that although there is no pressure to commit to those trainings, behaviors within the sangha should be in keeping with the foundations of this lineage.
- Ask new practitioners if it would be okay to follow up with them after their first time attending to find out how their experience was. This gives the message of caring and respect for boundaries and makes it easier for you to check in with them later (either immediately after their first practice, or via a phone call some days later).

In addition to these guidelines for preparing the space before a meeting, there are many ways to help make a sangha and practice space more inviting and inclusive while in the flow of the meeting itself. Needless to say, these suggestions are helpful for facilitating meetings of any kind, not only in spiritual contexts.

Use invitational language and establish the notion of choice. Sangha facilitators learn to speak in such a way that practitioners know that they are in choice: remind them that they are free to adapt practices in ways that will give them support—physically, emotionally, or spiritually—as long as these alternatives do not intrude on others' choices. This applies to posture; to following specific instructions; to the length of time they practice; to whether they keep their eyes open or shut; or any other aspect of practice.

Offer time for people to orient themselves before beginning practice. When offering practices, give an overview of what is to unfold in your time together so people know what to expect and how to take good care of themselves within that context. Begin practice by making space to orient and settle before inviting the bell. This may be guided or just suggested: for example, "Please allow yourself to settle in in whatever way allows you support and brings you a feeling of safety. This may involve looking around or taking time to get comfortable."

Offer practices with open-ended outcomes. I have heard Thay say that practice should be enjoyable and offer relief; otherwise, it is not real practice. This can be true—but it might take a while to get there. In our wish to be inclusive, we may want to encourage people to recognize that there are no right or wrong ways to experience a practice and not assume a particular experience is common to everyone. For example: "This practice has the potential to bring relief right away, or it may take some time. You may like to notice if you experience any elements of relief, either right now or over a bit of time." This is not a promise; it is an invitation to be curious and present with the actual experience rather than jumping into evaluation right away.

Have a comprehensive list of Dharma Sharing agreements. It can be helpful to remind the group of these agreements before each sharing opportunity as well as invite them to add any other agreements that seem important for creating safe space. This is not an invitation for a lengthy discussion about the value of the agreements, rather it is to set a tone of openness and care. If new people take issue with any of the agreements, they can talk to the facilitator afterward. This avoids taking up time that might otherwise be available for the Dharma Sharing session. As mentioned earlier, sharing these kinds of agreements as part of an orientation for new practitioners ahead of time can help avoid confusion and make your group feel more inclusive.

Helping Others Who Are Outside Their Window

Despite our best efforts, sometimes a practitioner will not be able to stay within the window of mindful opportunity and may need guidance to help reorient themselves. If a practitioner is being carried away by strong emotions, you might suggest one of the regulating practices from Chapter 5. Invite the practitioner to reflect on their own previous experiences to identify what has felt stabilizing for them in the past. In addition to these grounding practices, practitioners might try switching to walking meditation instead of sitting; you might find it useful to have someone accompany them during this time. At other moments, you may find that just lending an ear is the best thing you can offer.

Here are some common signs that may indicate that a participant needs assistance:

- Fidgeting, being visibly upset, or having a hard time settling
- Leaving the gathering abruptly, without speaking to anyone
- Being very slow to respond in interactions or appearing confused
- Consistently sleeping through practices
- Having trouble staying within the guidelines of Dharma Sharing
- Hanging around after the gathering, yet not appearing to make connections with others
- Mentioning a lack of support (inner or outer) during their sharing.

The sangha is just one healing element along each person's journey. The practice is not a panacea, even though it has tremendous healing potential. Sometimes, the needs of the practitioner may exceed the capacity of the sangha or may not be within the scope of our practice. In these cases, additional support is important to best serve that individual and also to maintain the stability of the sangha. Every sangha should have a list of support services (including licensed clinicians and alternative healers, both physical and emotional) to refer to when the sangha alone cannot provide the support a practitioner needs. The facilitator may want to look for the following indicators that outside help may be needed for a particular practitioner:

- Has frequent or dramatic changes in mood, or is unable to contain their emotions: for example, they can't stop crying, they exhibit strained speech, they are overly cheery or speak very quickly without pauses, or they are prone to outbursts
- Discloses a history of mental illness or substance abuse, along with present stressors that are exacerbating that history
- Reports having nightmares, flashbacks, significant difficulties with attention, or reports that they are significantly over- or under-sleeping
- Discloses a history of trauma or reports unrelenting stress that is causing difficulties currently
- Is under the care of a mental health professional who does not know that they are involved in mindfulness practice
- Uses psychiatric medications or drugs for mental/emotional support (whether prescribed or not), or is in the process of stopping taking them
- Has a recent history of violence or self-harm or talks about hurting themselves or others
- Appears to be neglecting personal self-care and hygiene
- Misses many practices or sleeps through practices, days of mindfulness, or retreats

It is important to note that if a practitioner is on medication or has a history of mental illness or substance abuse, this does not mean they can't be a wonderful benefit to the sangha, and the sangha a benefit to them! Some folks will benefit from both sangha and a support person. However, it is really important to make the overall stability and harmony of the sangha a clear priority. It is never easy to say to someone that the sangha does not have the capacity to meet their needs, and a sangha should never send someone away lightly, but the sangha may simply not be able to embrace someone's behaviors in a clear and loving way; it's just not a match at that time. Sending someone away can be painful, and might be a point of reflection for the sangha as they move forward. It is especially helpful to have some alternate resources readily at hand.

LENDING AN EAR

The Plum Village lineage places a very high value on being a good listener. Learning to listen without judgment can be a lifelong process—I know it has been for me. Good listening is about being compassionate while also staying stable ourselves. Every time we listen to another, we have the capacity to be a coregulator: our own internal state can be quite contagious to someone being witnessed. Because of this, every listener has the responsibility to know how to self-regulate, so what they bring to the conversation is immediately beneficial. Here's where self-care practices really are for the benefit of others. Do what you need to ground yourself before jumping into the conversation. Invite the other person to do it with you, if they care to. This also models good practice.

How might we deepen our skills to provide a strong and gentle presence for others? What follows is a step-by-step exercise in how to bring your neuro-informed awareness into your listening practice. You can do it with a friend, or even better, include it as a focus for your sangha. (Consider having a really good listener available at a Day of Mindfulness or in a retreat setting and announcing who they are and how to connect with them.)

EXERCISE 8.1: Lending an Ear

DURATION: 20–40 minutes
FREQUENCY: At your discretion and interest
PURPOSE: Practice in neuro-informed listening

For this exercise you will need a partner who understands that you want to practice being a listener. The exercise can be one-way, or your partner can also take a turn at being the listener.

Before the person begins speaking, ask if it is okay to interrupt them from time to time—as if you were sounding a tiny bell of mindfulness—so they can keep themselves stable. You may also ask them what it is they might need to be comfortable to talk. Agree on an amount of time that you can happily offer. This sets the boundary so there is no awkwardness or assumption of unending availability.

You can ask what it is that they hope will unfold from the conversation: do they just want you to witness, or do they need help settling or functioning in the setting or guidance in practice?

Your job here is to help your person stay within their window of opportunity. This can be done by suggesting or inviting them into the various stabilizing practices.

Your partner may launch right into the story of what is happening. You might take a mindful pause at a convenient moment to reflect to them something like: this really does sound difficult; what is getting you through this, how have you been getting through this, or how have you gotten through something similar in the past? If they share something that sounds like a resource (see Chapter 5), encourage them, before they continue sharing, to really get in touch with the elements of that resource, either internally or aloud with you. Don't rush, this can be the most important moment of the conversation—when they realize that they *do* have an internal resource and that they can use it in that moment effectively.

While they are telling you their situation, if you sense they seem upset, or if you are feeling their upset, you can interrupt gently by asking, "What are you noticing inside right now? If what you are noticing is unpleasant, is there anywhere else that might be more neutral or pleasant to focus on for a few breaths?" This may help bring them back into their body with less focus on difficulty.

At times it may be a helpful to suggest that they keep their eyes open while sharing, that they take breaks to look around and reorient to this present moment, that they feel the support of gravity where the ground, chair, or their skeleton is supporting them.

Do your best not to insert your own agenda, how they should feel, what actions they should take; try not to lead them to the silver linings or embedded lessons that you may think helpful. Just listen. This is a practice as much for you as for them if done well.

If you notice that the person seems lighter, more grounded or at ease, you can draw them again to look inside and to what they notice. Do not guess out loud as to how this is for them, rather ask if this is beneficial. If they say it is beneficial, allow a moment or three to just savor that space. You can ask them, if they are comfortable doing so, to share what that is for them. Is there some aha or message they are getting? If so, savor it along with them. Celebrate. This is a good use of coregulation—supporting the sustaining of well-being, for yourself and them.

Here are some phrases that can help draw them back into resourcefulness, depending on the particular situation:

Who has been a support for you in this?

What have you found helpful in keeping you afloat?

When did you realize that you were safe?

How have you found the strength to . . .?

What have you drawn on in the past to support you through difficulties?

FACILITATING THE FACILITATOR

Once you've got the ability to stay within the window of mindful opportunity, you won't trigger others like you might have before, and folks will probably be more open to what you have to offer. As you begin to benefit from these neuro-informed practices, you may begin to see the potential for integrating them into all manner of situations. Even if you are not a formal leader in a group, you might find ways to gently facilitate the leader or facilitator by "wondering aloud":

Do you think it might be helpful if . . .?

I'm wondering if folks might be supported by considering . . .?

I've been in a group that tried this solution—do you think it might be helpful here?

I notice we haven't heard from everyone yet, and I'm curious as to how this is all landing on others.

Is it OK if we just observe . . .?

Is it OK to modify that suggestion?

What other options might there be if we find that this doesn't work for us?

A well-placed phrase or inquiry can really save the day—even after the fact, it can correct an unskillfulness before it snowballs into something destructive.

Offering Retreats and Days of Mindfulness

To provide a safe and caring atmosphere when people will be in an extended period of practice together, one that encompasses basic physical needs of food, shelter, and extended social contacts, you'll need to make careful plans in advance.

RETREAT STAFFING

No amount of advanced preparation will substitute for having a harmonious and collaborative team. We need many eyes: those that focus on the program, those that focus on the community energy, and those that shoulder the practicalities. Just as mindfulness is the optimal balance between attention and awareness, good leadership has to strike an optimal balance between guiding and being receptive. A small organizing and staffing team can more fully hold this balance than any one individual. Not only is such a team able to lend a broader perspective to all that is offered, it helps plan and tend to how we do each task. In such groups we learn to step back if we tend to offer easily, and to step forward if we tend to shy away—in both cases, supported by the team. We learn to let go of what we think of as good ideas, recognize assumptions we've made, see our habit energies surface. We learn to support others by "calling in" rather than "calling out" their shortcomings.

ORIENTATION TO A DAY OF MINDFULNESS OR RETREAT

If you are an organizer of a Day of Mindfulness or a multiday retreat, you are probably already familiar with how to craft a full program: not too much, and not too little. Giving participants a brief overview of what to expect is also a good idea. For example, some people registering for a "retreat" may assume that it will all be in complete silence, perhaps even with an injunction on eye contact. Letting people know in advance when practices are silent and when they are not can help those not familiar with your traditions adjust. This may also help people unaccustomed to silence understand the beneficial effects of periods of silence. Consider writing such things in an introductory handout or briefly acknowledge them when appropriate.

Similarly, organizing teams are now more likely to ask retreatants about their own background, sense of stability, and needs through a questionnaire. This is not to stigmatize or label; rather, it is to prevent harm and provide deep hospitality. (For a sample questionnaire, please see Appendix C.)

For each retreat, staff must assess their own capacity to accommodate special needs and communicate clearly to retreatants what they are able and unable to provide. One such special need may be food, if it will be provided. Make sure to clarify for both participants and staff the general dietary regimen (vegan, vegetarian, etc.) the retreat adheres to and provide participants with a way to safely store a small amount of their own personal food if their dietary restrictions cannot be met.

ECONOMICS

I cannot go into this topic adequately here, but be aware that economics is a big divider for many retreats. Retreat attendance often reflects the greater context in which we live; it is often reserved de facto for those with cultural privilege. We have numerous strategies that attempt to address the painful economic realities of our cultural institutions—how bound we are by them in this historical dimension, and how we can possibly navigate them with the least amount of harm to those most vulnerable. Generally scholarships, work trades, sliding scales, and gift economics all are all intended to take the burden off of those with less economic privilege, but be aware that practices such as work trades can in fact create different classes of retreatants, and even if you waive fees, some potential participants find simply taking time off work financially daunting. No matter how good our intentions are, we cannot fully mitigate the impacts of cultural inequities until the underlying structures are changed. However, exploring this issue is a necessary practice, and at the very least, doing so can fortify our intention to continue working for a more equitable society.

9

Designing Mass Transit

Moving toward Collective Awakening

Thich Nhat Hanh once said that the next incarnation of the Buddha might not be an individual, but a sangha.

> The Buddha, Shakyamuni, our teacher, predicted that the next Buddha would be Maitreya, the Buddha of love. We desperately need love. And in the Buddha's teaching we learn that love is born from understanding. The willingness to love is not enough. If you do not understand, you cannot love. The capacity to understand the other person will bring about acceptance and loving kindness.
>
> It is possible the next Buddha will not take the form of an individual. The next Buddha may take the form of a community, a community practicing understanding and

> lovingkindness, a community practicing mindful living. And the practice can be carried out as a group, as a city, as a nation.[1]

What did Thay mean by this? Think of it this way: our individual inner journeys allow us the freedom and power to operate harmoniously in a collective, maximizing its creativity and collaborative productiveness. In turn, participants in such a group experience individual healing as they engage in collective work with others. This is because they continue to practice in the midst of the suffering they are working to alleviate; collective work offers up the grist that helps mill the suffering into nutritious flour, making bread for the journey. Being part of such a group is a reciprocal relationship. Our work together gives us direct experience of interbeing, a nutritious cycle that goes round and round healing and strengthening the outer while also healing and strengthening within. Such a sangha body *generates* energy rather than consuming it. This is how the Buddha can incarnate in the form of a sangha.

In the last chapter, we touched on how social oppressions and the stresses of the world can contribute to the dysregulation of our sangha body. Now, let's dig deeper into how unpacking these seemingly external stresses affecting our communities is an essential part of our path toward individual and collective awakening. Through a committed engagement with the problems facing us collectively, and through the wise action of our communities and sangha bodies, we can gain transformative power in the world.

Cultural Toxins and Implicit Bias

I was probably about four when we first got a TV. One of the first shows I remember watching was *Howdy Doody*, a seemingly benign program featuring white men, white puppets, a white clown, and a "peanut gallery" of up to fifty little white children. Of course, people of color showed up in other TV programs I watched: there was *Beulah,* a comedy series, that introduced me to African Americans as domestic workers (and which was later condemned by the NAACP for its stereotyping); there was *The New Adventures of Charlie Chan,* featuring an Irish-American actor in "yellowface" makeup; and let's not forget all those shows about cowboys and Indians . . . well, need I go on? I was a child, and this was my window into the world.

These were only the first of many toxins that nourished my assumptions, where I focused my attention, and my actions. Remember the saying, "what fires together, wires together"? The applies just as well to our ability to make sense of the world around us as it does to our nervous system. All of these cultural toxins we take in result in what's called *implicit bias,* the unconscious, unrecognized prejudices that reinforce the strength of the dominant cultural group (which, in the United States, has been embodied in white Christian men).

Let's consider the "Four Nutriments" discussed in Chapter 3: edible foods, sense impressions, volition, and consciousness. We know we need to be mindful of what we consume in these four categories, and we know that with understanding, careful guidance, awareness, and diligent practice, we can take charge of what we feed ourselves. But when it comes to the culture we're raised in, we have been practically force-fed a diet of fear, hatred, and delusion since childhood, long before we grasped the concept of conscious consumption. We believe that cultural "food" to be nourishment, and we even come to depend on it for stability, even if it is actually toxic.

Those toxic, biased messages penetrate our consciousness, no matter what group is the target—even if the group is one we ourselves belong to. I grew up Jewish in the late 1940s and 50s. It was not unusual for me as a child to hear about the Ku Klux Klan and cross burnings on the lawns of Jews; the terrifying significance of these acts were beyond my comprehension. My parents' relentless mentioning of who was Jewish and who was not also made me self-conscious about being different from most people on the street, of not belonging. It wasn't until college, when I realized how guarded I was about saying I was Jewish, that I recognized how much I had internalized a fear of being Jewish, and a fear of my embodying stereotypes that might be held against me.

I had failed to see just how saturated I'd become over the years with implicit biases, how they affected both my view of myself and my relationships with others who were different from me. Of course, I found "big R" Racists to be reprehensible, and I sure didn't want to be seen as one of them! But I didn't need to be an overt racist to be someone who perpetuated racism; as someone with still unrecognized implicit biases, I was—and still am, at times—inadvertently wounding many people I have sought to befriend. Holding these biases limited my world view, deprived me of the richness that diversity brings, and deprived me of right view, upon which everything else on the Eightfold Path is based.

It was through this process of examining my implicit biases that I first began to see myself as white. I grew up not thinking of myself as white—"white," to me, was synonymous with blue-eyed, blond-haired Christians. What I didn't realize was that I nevertheless *did* grow up with white privilege, because in many ways I was seen as white and had a lived experience of being white. This was a struggle for me because I worried that seeing myself as white would mean giving up, in part, my (non-white) Jewish identity—an identity of belonging, comfort, and self-esteem.

Being able to accept a white identity was major emotional labor. I learned that it was emotional labor that many didn't want to do, emotional labor that had been exhausting my friends of color for their whole lives. Doing this work involves a process of identity-shifting that is too uncomfortable or threatening for many white people. This work is not for the faint of heart! Well, that is what this practice is all about: finding enough comfort with discomfort to not be carried away by it—and to know that, once again, the only way out of this stuff is through. With curiosity, we can see deeply how racism, sexism, classism, or any "ism" is made and know how to begin to unmake it.

As a result of my labor, I had a sense of personal expansion. It was a bit like traveling to a culture foreign to me. Once I started truly seeing and appreciating the range of perspectives in more diverse groups, I noticed a number of dynamics I'd never considered before. I encountered dimensions of human thought and experience that I hadn't know existed, not just the sufferings and inhumane soup, but joys and perspectives that illuminated a much bigger territory than I'd visited before. Although it was scary to realize how skewed and narrow the views I'd held fast had been, I also encountered an aliveness I had not anticipated; or rather, my labor highlighted for me a dullness that I'd been living.

Developing cultural humility like this is a prelude to cultural competency. *Humility* in this context means that we admit that unseen, unacknowledged dynamic are playing out and that we need to dive deeper to explore and understand these to find harmony. Every one of our various identities has a list of values and priorities. We've all got jargon, rituals, norms, and customs whether we recognize them or not! The following are some basic categories of cultural difference we should consider.

In taking into account how a group of diverse folks can come together to live or work harmoniously in community, it helps to see that each of the following categories is a continuum, and each carries its own benefits and challenges.

Power: How is power distributed and how accepted or challenged are social inequities?

Uncertainty Avoidance: How comfortable are people with uncertainty and ambiguity? Do they try to control the future or just let it happen? Are codes of behavior and belief rigid and fixed, or flexible and tolerant of unconventional behavior or ideas?

Individual vs. Collective: Is the basis of identity "I" or "we"? Who is expected to take care of whom?

Tough vs. Tender: Does the culture value achievement, heroism, assertiveness, success, and material rewards? Or does it allow cooperation, consensus, modesty, caring for the vulnerable, and quality of life?

Tradition vs. Innovation: What is more valued: traditional links with the past or innovation to prepare for the future?

Indulgence vs. Restraint: Does the group allows relatively free gratification of basic and natural human drives, or does it value restraint (which may require regulation and suppression of needs)?

A cautionary note here about the idea of cultural competence being reduced to this list. People are so much more than their culture and myriad intersectionalities (class, gender, and health to name a few). Keep an open mind. Might such a list leave us vulnerable to jumping to conclusions, stereotyping, or othering? Might even the term *competence* make us blind to the wisdom that deepening personal relationship and dialog might afford us? Might the "don't know" beginner's mind and curiosity be just as valuable as developing cultural competencies?

Until I started thinking seriously about cultural difference and bias, I wasn't aware of how my own set of intersecting cultural identities have conditioned much of my world view. It has given me pause, helped me drop some of my tendency to judge, and caused me to realize the value of a wider spectrum of positions. As we practice stretching the window of opportunity, we become more and more aware of a formidable set of objects of mind. At this point we have an opportunity to be at ease with what is and, from that base, we can act for the benefit of all life.

When we choose to explore our own internalized biases (no matter what our identity or lived experience is) and the biases that exist in our families, communities, and institutions, we come face to face with the foundational problems of being human—and these insights teach us how we might overcome them. I am now going to highlight some key concepts that, I propose, lay and monastic members alike need to become more aware of in order to fully understand how our actions play out in a society in which we are all steeped in implicit bias. Deepening our understanding of these processes helps undo the knots that can prevent our awakening together.

Privilege: Being part of a culturally dominant group comes with certain unearned advantages. Although we may feel entitled to (or oblivious of) the privileges we have grown up with, or transitioned into, we enjoy them at the expense of other groups with equally unearned disadvantages. Much of our "privilege" may actually be experienced as a feeling of comfort or security. For example, someone who has grown up wealthy might feel completely at ease walking through an upscale neighborhood where they do not reside full of fancy houses, yet in my experience as a working-class person, the same stroll might cause me to tense up and become hypervigilant of my appearance. But even in my discomfort I must remember that my own privilege as a white person allows me to not experience the fear, as a black person might, that I will appear *so* out of place as to trigger a call to the police.

Intersectionality: Each of us embodies a mixture of different character traits, identities, and lived experiences: in the previous example, my position as a white person situated me differently in an affluent neighborhood than it would if I was a black person, and my position as a working-class person situated me differently than it would if I was a wealthy person. We are all a mixture of positionalities. *Intersectionality* is a term coined by the sociologist Kimberlé Crenshaw to describe how these different kinds of inequalities or oppressions intersect and influence each other. I find this concept helpful when I'm asking myself where my reactions are coming from: for instance, am I exercising my white privilege to speak up first, or am I overcoming sexist or heterosexist marginalization in doing so? I must look inside to see the intention, and look outside at the social context to understand the potential impact. Then I can choose wisely.

Othering: Far back in our ancestry, we developed a tendency to view groups of people who are strangers or in some way different from us as fundamentally Other. This was a survival mechanism, allowing us to quickly identify those who would be either sources of positive coregulation or potential threats. In our modern culture, *othering* is not just about distinguishing one group from another; it is entangled with a set of stereotypes that the dominant culture holds about various groups, and it is inseparable from a hierarchy of privilege. Seeing this dynamic from an evolutionary perspective, I know I do not have to hold my implicit biases with shame and guilt. I do, however, have a responsibility to learn how to not cause harm and to undo the personal and structural harm that othering causes. Once we see this tendency in action, we can see how to go about undoing it and preventing harm.

Microaggressions: Sometimes, a person might make what seems to them like a casual comment, but it lands like a crushing sack of cement on the person they're addressing. Such situations arise when we are unaware of how our implicit bias is expressing itself and impacting those around us. For example, a white person might exclaim to her black friend, "Oh, your hair is so beautiful!" while reaching out to touch her hair without even asking for permission. A person of color might experience the question, "Where do you come from?" differently than a white person would, because when posed to them, the question implies that they look "different" from what the speaker thinks is the norm, and that they therefore belong elsewhere.

Although the conscious intent of the speaker may be to connect, such microaggressions may significantly compromise whatever sense of safety the recipient of the microaggression had beforehand. What may seem like a casual comment to the speaker, may have a significantly different impact on the person hearing it. When a microaggression happens, it can take the participants quite by surprise or at least send them close to or over the line in their window of mindful opportunity: the speaker, aware only of their intent; the receiver, aware only of the impact and implications. In these situations it is vital that we accept that intentions and impact can be very different, so acknowledging the impact first and foremost helps soothe the uncomfortable response. Without this acknowledgment, we can easily slide into defensiveness and self-absorption rather than empathic connection.

It's not easy to stay in a curious mode and skillfully unpack our own intentions in such a situation; it's not easy to look deeply to see whether implicit bias is present. With practice, we can calm our nervous system, name and accept what has happened, express compassion, and come to understanding. It isn't easy, but it is essential because of the interbeing nature of our reality. Each person in communication carries this responsibility to look deeper—a responsibility to our ancestors, our descendants, and to all of life. Each deeper look takes us closer to a concept found in a multitude of paths for a truly healthy human society: the promised land, heaven on earth, the awakened sangha, Beloved Community.

Beloved Community

I have been a sangha organizer for many years—a sangha primarily composed of older, white, professional members, mostly reflecting my own demographic. I have long yearned for the richness and aliveness of a more diverse sangha. This is a common theme in many of the Buddhist-convert, English-speaking sanghas in our tradition.[2] But what was for me a lack of diversity was for many others (especially my friends of color), a lack of *inclusivity*: the absence of spaces that were accessible, physically or economically; the inattentiveness of sangha organizers to how livelihood and family obligations might impact members' ability to join in activities; and the simple lack of spaces that reflected their physical presence, where they might see others like themselves. These sanghas weren't structured to meet the needs of a diverse community.

Dr. Martin Luther King Jr. frequently spoke of building *beloved community*, meaning a society where all can live harmoniously and equitably. Thich Nhat Hanh adopted these words as well to refer to a harmonious or awakened sangha body. I saw this as highlighting his connection with Dr. King and using it as a bridge to bring about harmony among diverse peoples and all of life.

Let's for a moment step into the truly inclusive meditation hall we hope to see. The people are of all ages, colors, and creeds—a cross section of the outer world. There are folks who have spent years in transit from some place of devastation—whether it was caused by a natural or political disaster—who have lost a language, culture, family. There are those who have suffered some sort of life-threatening discrimination and those who have secretly suffered from or witnessed abuse as children. There are some who grew up in great poverty and others who grew up with wealth; some who grew up physically healthy, and others whose experiences of health have been significantly compromised. With every one of those categories comes implicit bias, which will get expressed as we grope along, trying to get to know each other. Creating beloved community requires our ability to understand and unpack the system we live in that offers unearned privilege to some, undeserved separation for others, and deep, traumatizing suffering for all of humanity.

Safe Space

We know now that in order to really be present, to be able to settle into a place of *home* and experience the present moment, it is necessary to feel safe enough to calmly watch what is unfolding, moment by moment. But some people who have been longing for safe space may have very different needs than those yearning for diversity. How do we find ways to bow to both of these valid needs: for a sense of *home* and to deepen the connections between communities?

Plum Village began as Thay's hope of offering a refuge to Vietnamese refugees, where they could ease their sufferings through their renewed Buddhist tradition, as well as simply be around other Vietnamese people, relaxing into familiar spaces of culture: language, song, food, ritual. It was a way to access their ancestors and bring their children up with a sense of rootedness, resilience, and belonging. When it was clear that this lineage had something profound to offer Westerners and it was brought to the US, two quite separate communities developed in each of the emerging centers of the Plum Village lineage. The two groups had different lived experiences and needs. In the beginning, the Vietnamese Plum Village community was made up of refugees and immigrants who had left behind everything in the traumatic aftermath of the war. They were retaining their connection to their culture as vital while reestablishing the basics of daily life. For many, sangha was a life raft. Some sangha founders were avid students of Thay's renewed lineage, while others came from more conventional backgrounds; in either case, they brought their lived experience of practice from Vietnam.

At the same time, many people in North America, Australia, and Europe were finding themselves drawn to Thich Nhat Hanh, his teachings, and community. Many of these tended to be privileged, white-identified, and well-educated. Some had a strong interest in meditation, perhaps fueled by the Western penchant for psychology and self-help.

In bringing these two communities together, Thay was encouraging them both to see what each could learn from the other. The two communities have, over the decades, each grown toward incorporating the other into their wholeness, and many personal cross-cultural friendships have blossomed along the way.

Yet in the US, Vietnamese-language-based sanghas and English-speaking sanghas have remained fairly separate. Deepening connection between communities can be a complex challenge, requiring both a strong intention to do so as well as an ability to self-regulate and an understanding of issues of implicit cultural bias. It's perhaps no wonder, then, that sometimes communities may find that they require some degree of separateness in order to function harmoniously together: this is what is called *cultural refuge*.

CULTURAL REFUGE

For about two years, a dozen of us—sangha members from different racial, ethnic, and cultural backgrounds who practiced in the Plum Village lineage—had met on the phone to explore ways in which our sanghas and our Plum Village community could better meet the needs of practitioners from many heritages and could be more aligned with our community's deep aspiration for inclusivity. Then we decided to gather together in person for a few days. Although we had connected with each other by telephone for some time, we had never met in person as a group. It was time for the next step, to get to know one another, build our understanding, and see what could emerge that we could propose to the Plum Village community as a whole.

After just one day, I realized I felt very tense: I was preoccupied with trying not to say the wrong thing and was having lots of judgments about how it was all unfolding. I sensed these feelings and judgements arising but lacked the vocabulary to put them into words and the stamina for that sustained kind of tension. By the second day, the BIPOC folks had gotten together and decided that we should no longer meet as a whole group. They proposed we meet in smaller caucuses, with BIPOC practitioners and white allies meeting in separate groups, and this is what we did.

In my caucus of white people, I realized I felt relief: my white self could take a deep breath and speak without fear that I would say something inadvertently offensive. Many white practitioners—including me—had never before done this kind of race-awareness work, and it wasn't until we white folks were meeting in a separate caucus that I felt able to let down my guard and feel just how unaccustomed I was to it. I also came to learn that for our friends in the BIPOC group, "race work" was not new. Simply by being in the world as who they were, living in the US society they were in, they had been compelled to do race work, whether they'd wanted to or not. After our first, tension-filled day, they knew how to pace themselves, protect themselves from getting bone-weary. For them, being in a separate caucus meant a bit of refuge from the white folks in the group. This was a learning they had already experienced from a lifetime of living with racism.

At this point, you might be thinking, Aren't we all one? Why do we need to divide ourselves up into these artificial groups? If we separate into groups based not on language or shared experience (e.g., the loss of a loved one) but on "identity," doesn't that reify and solidify the very concept of "self" that we are aspiring to see through?

Well, in fact, we do need places of refuge because for many of us, our lived experience is one of being devalued and attacked. In that kind of atmosphere, our nervous systems don't yet recognize this oneness. As we've talked about many times in this book already, being curious first requires the perception of being safe. Without any sense of safe space, we are always on defense; we cannot recuperate and regain the strength and curiosity to look deep inside.

Until we have developed close-enough relationships with those we have come to view as Other (through a lifetime of toxic cultural messages and internalized bias), we're just not going to feel as safe in mixed groups. Of course, all groups are going to be a mix of diverse and intersecting identities and opinions, but when I sit in a room where I am already aware of my commonalities with the other folks there, the nervous system reads that as a time to rest and digest—*phew!*

Slowly, over the last many years, monastic-led retreats have begun to offer Dharma-Sharing spaces focused on particular affinity groups: BIPOC, LGBTQIA+, language-based, and so on. Some question whether that it is just a way for people to avoid their discomforts and say that it leads to more division in the community. Others say it is the only way they can feel safe enough to be vulnerable and be open with their issues, or to feel they can truly be themselves without worrying that anything they express could be taken as reinforcing a stereotype of their group identity. How can participants tell which it is?

One suggestion from Kazu Haga, a trainer in nonviolence and restorative justice, is to ask whether or not participants feel more at ease in mixed spaces after participating and processing in such a cultural refuge group.[3] This is a noble guideline if we are aiming for the ideal of the beloved community. Through our neuroscientific lens, subgroup members might reframe the question: Can we stretch our window of mindful opportunity wide enough to include more and more people, people who each may be at different levels of understanding and skillfulness? How long we need to be in a cultural refuge to know whether the feelings of safety it provides are helping us stretch or are shrinking that window—this is a question that can only be answered by each of us individually.

At the same time, *too* much of an emphasis on individual responsibility can inadvertently shift the focus away from the institutions that have contributed to the need for cultural refuges in the first place. In some ways, individual responsibility may siphon off the energy necessary for a collective effort to make significant change to the great ills of our world today: environmental devastation, racism, wealth inequities, weapons manufacturing, prisons—an exhausting list. We must take individual responsibility, but we must also not lose sight of how we can have great impact as a collective on the institutions and structures around us. One outcome of these kinds of inquiries into inclusivity has inspired a series of powerful contemplations on the Five Mindfulness Trainings by Black Dharma teachers Valerie Brown and Marisela Gomez to specifically address this aspiration. Their "Contemplations on the Five Mindfulness Trainings, a New Paradigm for Racial Justice and the Global Pandemic" is shared on the ARISE (Awakening through Race, Intersectionality, and Social Equity) sangha website, *https://arisesangha.org*. Indigenous people and people of color who face poverty, sickness, displacement, and death are not alone. Our lives and livelihoods are interconnected. We are called forward.[4]

The Way In Is Out: Engaged Buddhism

The Plum Village lineage is the first of several modern "engaged" lineages of the Buddha, meaning Buddhism applied to and engaged with social life in order to support healthy social change.[5] Engaged Buddhism proposes that the gift of monasticism to our world is to deeply understand, cultivate, embody, and offer Buddhist wisdom to all in human form; the gift of the lay community is to put those teachings to practice on the ground. This could mean bringing these wisdom practices into your organization's meetings to quell division, or using them to keep your spirits up while volunteering at a shelter. It could mean being able to listen more deeply to someone's suffering, to speak out or stand up when encountering intolerance and bigotry, or to set aside your pride and listen to a family member with a more open heart. It means being married to the path in all we do.

Sensei Kazuaki Tanahashi—renowned Zen artist, writer, and peace and environmental worker—offers four principles, or as he says, Commonplace Truths, to embrace as we march out into the world:

1. No situation is impossible to change.
2. A communal vision, outstanding strategy, and sustained effort can bring forth positive changes.
3. Everyone can help make a difference.
4. No one is free of responsibility.[6]

No one is free of responsibility? What about single-parent families scraping just to get by, or the ill or physically challenged who use all their energies just to survive, or seniors who may not be able to get out and about? Does this call to engagement really apply to everyone? Well, yes! Unless we are literally fighting for physical or emotional survival, we all need to at least be able to lend a hand, or a smile, or a hug. Keep in mind that there is no formula to determine how much action is "enough." We simply continue practicing our intention setting, and continue our active engagement, no matter how much or how little we have to give.

When we engage in the world in integrity with these Buddhist teachings, all manner of gifts come back to us as a result. The gifts that the work gives to us are embedded in the work itself. It calls us, from our caring, to stretch more, see more, care more, connect more with others and with life in all its forms. Chewing on that grist catalyzes our own awakening, individually and collectively.

Armed with our stability and these principles, how do we go about making the biggest difference we can possibly make while leading a full and sustaining life? When I look at the individual prescriptions for transforming suffering we have, from the Four Noble Truths and the Full Awareness of Breathing (Anapanasati Sutra), through the psychotherapeutic, trauma-oriented modalities, and all the other tools we've explored in this book, I see the following commonalities.

- Begin by grounding in a sense of well-being.
- Learn how to respect and be in the presence of pain without being carried away.
- Know how to see deeper and with a broader perspective, letting go of preconceptions.
- Be so intimately involved in life that caring rather than fear guides your actions.
- Persist in your caring whether or not you can experience its impacts.
- Use the insight gained in this process to keep going.
- Reground in a sense of well-being.

Buddhist teacher and scholar Joanna Macy argues that engagement is the antidote to despair; she calls it "the work that reconnects." Macy's work, while applicable to individuals, really focuses on how this process can be transformative for collaborations, groups, and whole communities. She envisions an engaged Buddhist practice on a community level that "maps ways into our innate vitality and determination to take part in the healing of the world."[7] In her invaluable, practical guide to transforming social consciousness, *Coming Back to Life*, Macy and her coauthor Molly Brown explore how we can open the collective heart with gratitude for the gifts of the world, feeling a oneness with the earth in our bones. The book is filled with finely detailed group experiences, exercises that build skills in gratitude, hold pain, broaden perspectives, and promote wise action on both individual and group levels. With this practice to shelter and buoy us through the storm, we can become intimate with the pain that the world suffers—and to know it as our own pain, both personally and collectively, by creatively reaching back into our ancestry, across time and all species of living things. These group processes are aimed at bringing us a clarity of calling and action and offering us support while we plan, support that can hold our groups together in action.

In this way we find the courage to look at the narratives we have swallowed from the past, from unwholesome institutions to our own wounded selves. We must allow ourselves to hold a bigger truth than what we have previously been able to see, to hold it without crumbling, because we have the strength and compassion and stability to do this all at once. We must be multitaskers in the best sense of the word, developing our capacity to hold joy and suffering at once, developing our balance between self-care and staying in our window, so that we can find that space where fear falls away and is replaced by the energy to heal.

The stability that you are learning here, and the healing you may experience, is not just good for yourself. Once you've got these teachings under your belt, whether you are thinking of them as Buddhist practices or just psychological well-being methods, you will be able to apply them in other situations you find yourself in. You may find yourself picking up on more interpersonal cues. You may be more aware of what might be helpful in a staff discussion, or what might make a difference around the dinner table when a comment causes tension, or what might shift the energy on the bus when an awkward situation arises. Do you just think, "It's not my place to intervene," or do you begin to take wise risks? This could mean pointing out small injustices on the street corner in a way that moves others to step up as well; or saying something to the boss at work from a place of caring rather than criticism; or calling in someone, without shaming them, when you see a microaggression happening.[8]

No matter who we are, whether we see ourselves as leaders or not, we generally exist in relation to others. And when others are in trouble, that trouble is part of the environment, affecting all of us in it, whether we are conscious of it or not. Could we see everyone we encounter as if they were sangha members?

Spiritual Trauma: Is There Such a Thing? Could It Be a Collective Trauma?

For some years, the Plum Village community offered retreats and retreat space specifically for US veterans of the war in Vietnam. At one of them one veteran attendee shared his remorse and despair about an ugly retaliation he had made against a village where most of his unit was killed, in which he laid explosives that killed children. It was a gruesome story that had haunted him for many years, immobilizing him emotionally. Having never shared his story outside his family, it took him several days of being on retreat in a safe space before he was able to even begin to open up.

Later, after a private consultation with the veteran, Thich Nhat Hanh related what he'd said:

> Now look, you killed five children, yes. And that is not a good thing to do, yes. But don't you know that many children are dying in this very moment, everywhere, even in America, because of lack of medicine, of food? Do you know that 40,000 children die every day in the world, just because of the lack of medicine and food? And you are alive, you are solid physically. Why don't you use your life to help the children who are dying in this moment? Why get caught in the five children who have died in the past? There are many ways . . . if you want, I will tell you how to save five children today. There are children who need only one tablet of medicine to be saved, and you can be the one who brings that tablet of medicine to him or to her. If you practice like that every day, the children who died because of the explosives [you laid] will smile in you, because these five children have participated in your work of saving many children who are dying in this very moment.[9]

The door was opened so that the man was no longer eternally trapped in his guilt, shame, and feeling of culpability. That is the *amrita*, the ambrosia of compassion, of wisdom, offered by the Buddha: there is always a way out. That particular war veteran practiced and was able to help many other children in the world. He has gone back to Vietnam, he has done the work of reconciliation, and the five children who died have begun to smile in him and become one with him. In the beginning his memory was purely distressing, but now the five children have become alive in him and have become the energy helping him to live with compassion, with understanding. The garbage can be transformed into flowers if we know how to compost our trauma and transform it into compassion for ourselves and others.

This story highlights what can happen when we get stuck in remorse and are prevented from seeing ways out of that suffering. In the recent past, it has come to public attention that many people who have served in the armed forces have suffered greatly from doing their "jobs." In fact, post-traumatic stress disorder (PTSD) was initially created as a diagnosis for veterans—a product of those jobs of war being done, and done well. That was the "discovery" laid bare from the victims of our involvement in the devastation of Vietnam. What is now coming to light is a more subtle fallout from operators of remote drone strikes in Afghanistan and Iraq, in what is now called *moral injury*. According to the US Department of Veterans Affairs, National Center for Post Traumatic Stress Disorders,

> In traumatic or unusually stressful circumstances, people may perpetrate, fail to prevent, or witness events that contradict deeply held moral beliefs and expectations. . . . Moral injury is the distressing psychological, behavioral, social, and sometimes spiritual aftermath of exposure to such events.[10]

Although the research is not yet definitive, investigation is being done by neuroscientists to determine how moral injury impacts our nervous system. It is thought that the default mode network is majorly impacted, as well as the amygdala and parts of the prefrontal cortex. Moral injury involves feelings of guilt, remorse, and unworthiness; the inability to self-forgive; and subsequent self-sabotaging behaviors. Although symptoms of moral injury may not include the hypervigilance of PTSD, many of the other symptoms apply. (In order for a moral injury to occur, the person must feel like they have been complicit in some way, which is not necessarily the case for PTSD.) All of this takes a toll physically, emotionally, and spiritually, as faith-based beliefs come severely into question following moral injury.

There are countless other sufferers of moral injury beyond veterans. Healthcare workers, for example, may find themselves in the position of having to deny care or support to a gravely ill person, may risk serious malpractice due to extreme fatigue while on long shifts, or may put their loved ones at risk of infectious diseases. Or consider teachers, social workers, police, and anyone else who must witness a myriad of social ills in the course of their daily work, finding themselves at a loss for how to respond. These workers suffer individual trauma, yet it is the institutions that put them in these untenable situations. Our culture's highly individualized focus on treating trauma can be a distraction from the underlying moral failings of our institutions. Seen in this larger context, there are ways of healing these moral injuries that go beyond just individual healing—leaving the individual even more empowered in the process. When healing a moral injury is done in a way that undoes the causes of that inner conflict on a structural or institutional level, it is a contribution not only to healing the individual, but also the collective, the culture, the entire web of life.

As we begin to look deeper and deeper into the interbeing nature of human existence and begin to identify and address the cultural toxins we've all taken in, we might wonder whether *all* of us are suffering some kind of moral injury simply by complying with social norms. Just as we are all suffering from one type of trauma or another, is our culture actually suffering a collective moral injury?

Because the causes and impacts of these moral injuries have so many parallels to other kinds of trauma, we can take heart in assuming that the way through, the way out, is similar as well. Because the nature of these injuries is a collective one, the way out must also have a substantial collective component. Without this collective action, the individual toll continues to mask the underlying culprits.

How do we cure moral injury?

How do we prevent moral injury?

How do we grow resilient in the face of moral injury?

How do we change dysfunctional institutions?

How do we prevent dysfunctional institutions?

How do we grow resilient institutions?

Oh, such a big list! And oh, what a relief to find out that all these questions have one common answer: by following an ethical, body-based system such as the path we have begun to explore over the course of this book. Consider Thich Nhat Hanh's compelling statement: "Meditation is to get insight, to get understanding and compassion, and when you have them, you are compelled to act."

That's easy to say—so how do we do it?

We start with the basic self-regulation practices the book begins with and follow that with some sort of collective deep looking (whether in a sangha or whatever group is grappling with these fundamental social change issues). We develop and embrace nonjudgmental safe spaces to find our common humanity and deepen our understanding of our present condition. Following the insights we gain from such a process, we must take action. This is the collective follow-through to address what has been missing, or what was taken away by moral injury. It is through our practice that we gain, regain, or strengthen the ability to act with integrity on behalf of our most basic values. This is reparative and potentially transformational for ourselves, our communities, and the world.

The Four Questions

A seder is a Jewish ritual meal celebrating freedom from slavery, both literal and figurative. We begin this evening with ritual foods that are symbolic of enslavement: for example, bitter herbs to remind us of the harsh reality of slavery, or the matzo as a symbol of relentless rushing and stress. Then we tell the story of the way out—how the Jews were liberated from enslavement—and often follow it with other, more recent stories of oppression and liberation. For example, when my clan gathered for our seder in 2022, we decided to drop the telling of the story. The story always seems to have the same basic plot: we were slaves, we found a way to escape, we wandered a long time and finally attempted to create a new, just world. But we did want to retain the part of the telling that involves asking four questions—about why this night is different from other nights—to prompt reflection on the path to liberation. This year, we focused our thoughts on the people of Ukraine, which had recently been invaded by Russia—many of us had roots in Ukraine, and one of us was a Ukrainian immigrant. We decided that this year, the questions should take on a different tone. What followed was an invitation to touch the source of our strength, the manner of our enslavement, and the path to our strength, courage, and liberation through engagement.

I invite you to do the same, as an exercise by yourself, or in the company of close friends or your beloved community as part of a gathering.

EXERCISE 9.1:
The Four Questions

DURATION: 20 minutes
FREQUENCY: Open; as you are moved
PURPOSE: To inspire you to put your caring into action

Settle into relaxed attention, allowing the body to recognize the safety of this moment. Take your time, attending to the neutral and pleasant sensations of your immediate experience. When you feel ready, entertain each of the following questions, allowing whatever comes up to surface, just noticing your response in body and mind. Allow yourself to marinate in that awareness, whether it is pleasant, unpleasant, or neutral. Allow it to speak to you. Each question will be the foundation for the next.

What do you care about so much that you are (or were) willing to suffer the pain of vulnerability with it? Pause; savor.

Thinking of a difficulty you've been through in the past, how are you now more resilient as a result? Pause; savor.

Where do you find your strength and support?

How do you find your way through despair?

L'Chaim to Life!

Epilogue

A Love Letter to Our Worldwide Community

During Thich Nhat Hanh's cremation ceremony, a monk who had been his attendant for fifteen years said, "I remember having this conversation with you, Thay, when you said to me that you wanted all of us, your students, to continue to renew Buddhism. And that you, Thay, have been able to do 60 percent of the work, and there is still more for us to do. It is up to us, your monastic and lay descendants around the world, to keep the Dharma wheel going, to translate the practice and teachings into the language of our times, to make them accessible and practical for us in our world today."

Within the Plum Village lineage, ordained members of the core Plum Village community have begun to offer regular opportunities to skillfully explore Thay's legacy aspiring to renew Buddhist practice that strives for a truly inclusive, beloved community. For example, the ARISE sangha (Awakening through Race, Intersectionality, and Social Equity), led by Dharma teachers of color and white teachers, now offers retreats and support groups in racial and social justice, with a foundation in Plum Village practices. Still, it must also be noted that although Buddhism has had 2,600 years to develop—hundreds of years or more in each of its various cultural incarnations—Buddhism in the West is still a child, and the Plum Village lineage merely a toddler, precocious as it may be! Because of this, we can't expect all sangha members and leaders to pick up our neuro-informed knowledge right away, or be on top of cultural and political shifts that impact our groups. What's more, there may actually be resistance to changes required because of fear of losing the essence of the lineage.

However, awakening to the oppressions of our dominant culture, and acknowledging the diversity of traumas and hardships we all bring with us to the practice, is necessary to find a way through these personal and collective wounds to harmony. This awakening is vital if Plum Village is to survive as a community, to wake up as a community, and to have some wisdom to offer the larger world from our real experience as a community. Although we know that many people are benefitting from the practices, we also know that others have, inadvertently, been pushed out of their window of tolerance, retraumatized, or alienated from their practice communities because of institutionalized racism and other internal biases. Some flee the sangha without our ever knowing what happened. It is our task, now, to learn how to minimize these risks to ourselves and others.

> *Dear Sanghas and Sangha Facilitators,*
>
> *This letter is meant to inspire you, to renew your energy and remind you that our hope is to make our path available to all who care to join us. In the revolutionary spirit of our beloved teacher Thich Nhat Hanh, our dear Thay, we know that the times compel us to keep our practice both fresh and relevant to the needs of the people. In this commodified world, where mindfulness practice is supposed to give us a "competitive edge" in securing material goods, power, and prestige, we*

need to keep our practice safe for the vulnerable and in integrity with our guiding vows of the Five and Fourteen Mindfulness Trainings.

We know that right mindfulness, concentration, and insight are central to our collective awakening, and we want to make the teachings available in a way that causes no harm. We know that we must train in order to use powerful tools in a way that is safe and helpful, and it is our responsibility when offering those power tools to others to so it responsibly.

As practitioners, we must be skilled in discerning which practices are appropriate for us in any given moment, knowing what kind of nourishment is needed in each moment of our practice lives. Sometimes, we may need to focus on stopping and resting, or on cultivating joy and happiness. At other times, we may need to focus on difficult states of being. Knowing our own capacity for practice in each moment is vital—vital for a successful experience in transforming our suffering, and vital for helping us to guide others as well. Jumping into difficulties when we don't have the capacity to remain calm and stable risks us drawing further into our suffering. Likewise, avoiding these difficulties simply because we are unfamiliar with discomfort, or because we've found ways to avoid them, only fools us into thinking that they aren't there, prolonging our suffering. Jumping into the ultimate dimension—thinking, "We are all one," or, "A cloud never dies," before acknowledging the lived historical dimension may actually be skirting vital inquiry by avoiding difficulties prematurely.

Therefore, getting familiar with our nervous system, and learning how to use the practice to ready ourselves for transforming our suffering and that of others, is our job. We must learn true resilience: the ability to identify our strengths and put them into action, to meet challenges in a way that promotes understanding and harmony. Resilience is a healing presence that maintains all of us within a window of mindful opportunity, able to hold compassion, clarity, and a sense of the greater good. It is by learning to sit with and be curious about discomfort that we stretch that window open ever wider and get a better view of reality.

These are the steps to freedom, one step at a time on our long journey home to our true self, becoming unshakeable like a mighty oak in a meadow.

Thank you for sharing the journey,
Jo-ann

Appendix

A

The Anapanasati Sutra

Here are the Sixteen Exercises of Mindful Breathing from the Anapanasati Sutra translated by Thich Nhat Hanh, collected together with notes for ease of practice.

> *"Breathing in a long breath, I know I am breathing in a long breath.*
> *Breathing out a long breath, I know I am breathing out a long breath.*
> *"Breathing in a short breath, I know I am breathing in a short breath.*
> *Breathing out a short breath, I know I am breathing out a short breath.*
> *"Breathing in, I am aware of my whole body.*
> *Breathing out, I am aware of my whole body."*
> *The practitioner practices like this.*

Here, the focus is centered on the body. Beginning with a long breath, the practitioner engages the vagal nerve in a rhythm that calms the nervous system. First, bring your attention to your breath and then expand your attention to encompass the entire body, which develops self-regulation.

> *"Breathing in, I calm my whole body.*
> *Breathing out, I calm my whole body."*

The practitioner practices like this.
"Breathing in, I feel joyful.
Breathing out, I feel joyful."
The practitioner practices like this.
"Breathing in, I feel happy.
Breathing out, I feel happy."
The practitioner practices like this.

In these next three exercises, you are encouraged to see the nature of the sensations and become aware that you are able to find pleasant-enough sensation to be considered joyful and happy in your ability to be aware and relaxed.

"Breathing in, I am aware of my mental formations.
Breathing out, I am aware of my mental formations."
The practitioner practices like this.
"Breathing in, I calm my mental formations.
Breathing out, I calm my mental formations."
The practitioner practices like this.
"Breathing in, I am aware of my mind.
Breathing out, I am aware of my mind."
The practitioner practices like this.

The focus switches to the mental faculties; again this allows us to understand that we can effect those formations (emotions and thoughts) in a way that maintains relaxation; we have agency.

"Breathing in, I make my mind happy.
Breathing out, I make my mind happy."
He or she practices like this.
"Breathing in, I concentrate my mind.

Breathing out, I concentrate my mind."
He or she practices like this.
"Breathing in, I liberate my mind.
Breathing out, I liberate my mind."
He or she practices like this.
"Breathing in, I observe the impermanent nature of all dharmas.
Breathing out, I observe the impermanent nature of all dharmas."
He or she practices like this.
"Breathing in, I observe the disappearance of desire.
Breathing out, I observe the disappearance of desire."
He or she practices like this.
"Breathing in, I observe the no-birth, no-death nature of all phenomena.
Breathing out, I observe the no-birth, no-death nature of all phenomena."
He or she practices like this.
"Breathing in, I observe letting go.
Breathing out, I observe letting go."
He or she practices like this.

Appendix

B

Dharma Sharing Guidelines

A variety of guidelines promote a smooth road when we are participating in a conversation in a group. Some are standard, fostering communication in any situation, whereas others are especially suggested for neuro-informed practice.

1. Indicate when you wish to speak and when you are finished, knowing that you will not be interrupted except for occasional mindful pauses.
2. Speak from your heart and your own experience.
3. Honor confidentiality within the group.
4. Practice compassionate speaking and listening. Address everyone present in an inclusive manner.
5. You are invited to move up if you rarely talk and to move back if you tend to talk a lot. Try to be concise.
6. In a diverse community, we remember the difference between intention and impact; we try to remember that

what we intend to say and how it is received (the impact) may differ.

7. Support the facilitators in nurturing a welcoming and safe space for all.
8. Stay within the window of tolerance in both speaking and listening.
9. Feel free to ask for acknowledgment at the end of your sharing.
10. Refrain from advice-giving even when it is requested.
11. Speak with courageous authenticity and listen with curiosity and care.
12. Everyone has the right to pass. Let everyone know so that it is clear it's OK not to speak, and it's also OK to change your mind.

Appendix

C

Well-Being Questionnaire

This letter to potential retreat participants is something your sangha may find helpful.

> *Dear Practitioner,*
>
> *If you are requesting to join our retreat, we kindly ask you to fill out this questionnaire. Your answers to the questions will help us to better understand your situation, allowing us to support your overall experience in the most appropriate and skillful ways during your stay with us. These questions help us make sure everyone attending the retreat is safe and nourished.*
>
> *Confidentiality: This information will only be shared with our teacher, the registration team, the medical team and your Dharma Sharing leader. The information will only be shared if needed.*
>
> *If you need more space than this form allows, please use a separate sheet of paper and the number of the question it pertains to.*
>
> *Thank you in advance for this collaboration.*

PERSONAL INFORMATION

1. Name:

2. Date of birth

3. Home address

4. Current occupation and how you spend your time

MINDFULNESS PRACTICE EXPERIENCE

1. Have you practiced mindfulness before? Please list dates and length of any prior experiences, as well as the traditions. If you have attended many retreats, just give us a good sample.

2. What was your first experience with the Plum Village tradition?

3. What brings you to us at this very time?

4. What is your aspiration in attending the retreat?

PHYSICAL HEALTH INFORMATION

1. What physical ailments, pains, or chronic conditions do you deal with? For each, please let us know your approach to treatment and whether or not you take medication, need equipment, or have physical support needs.

2. If you are under a doctor's care, do you have regular contact with them? Have you needed to be hospitalized for this ailment? If so, please include dates.

SOCIAL/EMOTIONAL HEALTH INFORMATION

1. Describe your living situation and social/emotional support people.

2. Do these folks know you plan to attend, and are they supportive of your attending?

3. What current stressors are you facing?

4. Are there experiences you've had in the past that are still causing you stress?

5. Do you have a history of trauma, or extreme or unrelenting stress, and if so, are you actively experiencing symptoms that feel connected to this? (e.g., flashbacks, nightmares, difficulties with attention, etc.)

6. Are you currently working with someone for treatment, and if so, are they aware and supportive of your decision to retreat with us?

7. Have you ever attempted to hurt yourself or take your life, and if so, would you be willing to tell us more about this?

8. Are you currently taking medications or any kind of supplement for psychological support? If so, please share

what they are. The expectation is that you not change your medication regime while you are on retreat without consulting with us ahead of time.

9. Are there any other health considerations that you think we should be aware of?

10. Is there anything else you would like us to know at this time?

Appendix

D

A Sample Pre-Retreat Statement

Before holding a retreat, it is helpful to share guidelines that set up and hold the space to be as safe and neuro-informed as possible. The following is courtesy of Magnolia Grove Monastery, the mindfulness practice center in Batesville, Tennessee, in the Plum Village tradition.

> Here at Magnolia Grove, we have been doing our best to prepare for a retreat that we hope will be beneficial for you—a calming, peaceful, and healing environment, and a schedule of activities that we hope will support your practice of mindfulness and healing. Although we are doing our best to try to meet the needs of everyone, we are aware that this is impossible.
>
> That is why we would like to encourage you to take responsibility for yourself during your stay and be aware of your own needs. Give yourself permission to do what you need to. This may mean missing some activities if you feel the

schedule is too full. Or it may mean reaching out to someone else for support.

We hope you will be able to stay within your window of tolerance (opportunity) by practicing

- self awareness,
- self-care,
- self-soothing, and
- getting help from others if you need it.

The practice of mindfulness helps us be aware of our body, thoughts, and feelings, and the environment here is very calming, nurturing, and soothing. We know that much healing and transformation is possible during our retreats. We certainly hope this is true for you, too.

With a lotus for you,

a Buddha to be

GLOSSARY

amygdala A pair of small, almond-shaped regions deep in the brain that help regulate emotion and encode memories—especially when it comes to more emotional remembrances.

attention Being able to direct focus on an object with the mind, located in the cerebral cortex.

awareness Peripheral perception of what is going on in the surroundings.

bodhisattva A Sanskrit word meaning a person who dedicates their life to the well-being of others as their path to awakening.

cerebral cortex The outer layer of the cerebrum composed of folded gray matter that plays an important role in executive functioning, learning, language, problem solving and experiencing the senses.

coregulation How human bodies attune to others' emotional states.

default mode network (DMN) A network of interacting brain regions that is more active when a person is not focused on the outside world.

Dharma Sanskrit word for teachings of the Buddha.

dharma Sanskrit word (in Buddhism) for an aspect of truth or reality; basic principles of existence.

explicit memory Memories of experience that are within conscious awareness.

gatha Small poem that aids mindfulness in daily life activities.

hippocampus A complex brain structure embedded deep in the temporal lobe. It has a major role in learning and memory.

implicit bias Opinion held out of conscious awareness.

implicit memory Those memories stored as unconscious and automatic responses.

limbic system A group of structures (the hypothalamus, the hippocampus, and the amygdala) deep inside the brain that are concerned especially with emotion and motivation.

meditation Mental exercise of sustained and relaxed attention, contemplation, or reflection in a particular way.

mindfulness An optimum balance in any given moment between attention and awareness in order to have the fullest experience possible of the object of focus.

monastic A religious follower who takes vows to live a lifestyle of complete dedication and simplicity.

neuro-informed Incorporating the understandings of neuroscience.

parasympathetic nervous system Controls the relaxation of the body for rest and digestion.

retreat An event that one can participate in alone or with others that removes the participant from daily life in order to focus completely on their spiritual practices.

sangha Sanskrit word for community of practice.

stress Something internal or external that activates the nervous system to a higher activity level.

sutra Sanskrit word referred to in this book as a Buddhist discourse generally attributed to the Buddha.

sympathetic nervous system Controls the activation level of the body for heightened physical activity including responses to a perceived threat in a fight-or-flight response.

trauma An automatic nervous system response to overwhelming conditions where the body reacts to protect when no immediate threat is present.

vagus nerve Also known as the vagal nerves, the main network of nerves of your parasympathetic nervous system that controls specific body functions such as your digestion, heart rate, and immune system.

window of tolerance The range of nervous system activation within which the person has agency over their responses.

NOTES

Introduction

1 Some important figures in this field include Francine Shapiro (the founder of EMDR, or Eye Movement, Desensitization and Reprocessing) and Gary Craig (EFT, or Emotional Freedom Technique; also called "Tapping"), Bessel van der Kolk (author of *The Body Keeps the Score*, 2014), and Peter Levine (founder of Somatic Experiencing therapy). I was also inspired by the neuroscientists surrounding the Dalai Lama, including Daniel Goleman, Paul Ekman, Matthieu Ricard, Richard Davidson, and those affiliated with the Mind & Life Institute, as well as psychiatrist Daniel Siegel (whose important concept of the window of tolerance we'll explore in Chapter 2), neuroscientist Stephen Porges, and therapist Deb Dana (Polyvagal Theory).

Chapter 1

1 One of the gathas, or practice poems, in Thich Nhat Hanh's collection of gathas for daily life, *Present Moment, Wonderful Moment*.
2 Plum Village, "Thich Nhat Hanh: Extended Biography."
3 Nhat Hanh, *Fragrant Palm Leaves*, 50–51.
4 Nhat Hanh, *Call Me by My True Names*, 32.
5 Khong, *Learning True Love*, 67–68.
6 Khong, *Learning True Love*, 76.
7 Nhat Hahn, *Guide to Walking Meditation*.
8 Chan Khong, *Learning True Love, Chapter 11, "In the War Zone."*

Chapter 2

1 One of the core principles of Buddhist thought is that the mind and the body are not distinct entities—and many scientists are

now coming to the same conclusion. The inner world that is to be discovered and contemplated is both the physical and the psychological. The body is keeping track of it all; what we know about that inner world is due to physical experiences that we interpret through thoughts and emotions.

2 Stephen W. Porges, *The Polyvagal Theory*.

3 Was this right action? Does it perhaps seem not very Buddhist? This story is also a lesson that every moment has a myriad of conditions to be considered, and only the doer can know for themselves what was skillful.

4 In the West we have made a big distinction between issues of the physical body and the less concrete concept of mind. As we have deepened our understanding of the functioning of both, we have learned that the distinction becomes more and more unclear. *Body/mind* is a term for the blend of the two into one integrated whole, which more accurately describes how our system works!

5 Of course, trauma is not the only thing passed down to us by history or by our ancestors. When we look deeply into our past, we may find that it also reveals many strengths and talents that have been nurtured by those who came before us. Just as trauma can be passed on outside of awareness, so too can resilience.

Chapter 3

1 These four elements together comprise the *brahmaviharas*, the four heavenly abodes.

2 In the Plum Village community, those who commit themselves to these five precepts, referred to as the Five Mindfulness Trainings, are considered part of the extended community. Later, when we talk about sangha life (see Chapter 7), we will explore a next level of commitment practitioners can make by committing to Fourteen Mindfulness Trainings, becoming part of the core community. This includes both deepening their practices and taking on responsibilities in the community itself.

3 The Plum Village approach to the five mindfulness trainings expands the definition of each one to reflect the various facets

of each training as it applies to modern daily life. Each training emphasizes both the individual and collective impacts of careful cultivation. For more information, visit *https://plumvillage.org/mindfulness/the-5-mindfulness-trainings*.

Chapter 4

1 Treleaven, *Trauma-Sensitive Mindfulness*.

2 This is meant as a guide for individual practitioners, but these principles are even more important for sangha leaders and meditation teachers!

3 Baer, Crane, Miller, et al., "Doing No Harm in Mindfulness-Based Programs,"101–14; Baer, Crane, Montero-Marin, et al., "Frequency of Self-Reported Unpleasant Events," 763–74; Britton, "Can Mindfulness Be Too Much of a Good Thing?," 159–65; Britton, et al., "Polysomnographic and Subjective Profiles,"539–48; Lindahl, et al., "The Varieties of Contemplative Experience," e0176239.

4 Hua, *Surangama Sutra: New Translation*.

5 Ekaku, *Wild Ivy*.

6 Hua, *Surangama Sutra: New Translation*.

7 The Vipassana tradition, made popular in the West through both the Goenka lineage and the Insight Meditation Society, puts no emphasis on the potential for sickness. However, today, trauma sensitivity has been incorporated into many Vipassana teacher trainings.

8 Gilsinan, "The Buddhist and the Neuroscientist"; Goleman and Davidson, "Lion's Roar, How Meditation Changes Your Brain"; Walton, "7 Ways Meditation Can Actually Change the Brain."

9 Shantideva, *The Way of the Bodhisattva*, 63.

Chapter 5

1 Song by Betsy Rose, written in 1988. Visit *https://www.betsyrosemusic.org/*.

2 Nhat Hanh, *Blooming of a Lotus*.

3 Nhat Hanh, *Blooming of a Lotus*.

4 Napier, *Getting through the Day*.

Chapter 6

1 After so many years of oral tradition, you might imagine that the resulting texts that were written down in different locations varied some. From forty years' worth of teaching, we only have some two hundred remembered talks that have been passed down to the present day. It is conjectured that most of those talks were lost, so we are really practicing with the tip of the iceberg. Hopefully these teachings are the highest ones—the ones that have remained visible, above the surface, after all this time.

2 Nhat Hanh, *Breathe, You Are Alive* and *Transformation and Healing*.

3 For the full text of this sutra, see Nhat Hanh, *Breathe, You Are Alive.*

4 For the full text of the Satipatthana Sutra, see Nhat Hanh, *Breathe, You Are Alive?*

5 Nhat Hanh, *Our Appointment with Life*, 1.

6 I recommend Nhat Hanh, *Reconciliation: Healing the Inner Child,* in which students in the Plum Village tradition compile Thich Nhat Hanh's teachings about "healing the inner child," and share how they have benefitted from those teachings to heal their childhood wounds.

7 Nhat Hanh, *Heart of the Buddha's Teaching*, 135.

8 Nhat Hanh, *The Long Road Turns to Joy*, 10 photo.

9 Nhat Hanh, *Present Moment, Wonderful Moment*, 15.

10 For a bit of coregulating and inspiration, you might enjoy watching this 1-minute clip on YouTube of Thay playing with a lotus petal, savoring his joy and the joy of those around him: *https://www.google.com/search?client=firefox-b-1-d&q=thich+nhat+hanh+lotus+petal%27#fpstate=ive&vld=cid:de044b64,vid:jSkR4TjvJnY.*

11 Forest, *Eyes of Compassion*, 21.

12 Thich Nhat Hanh, *Call Me by My True Names*, 200.

13 Jim Forest, *Eyes of Compassion*, 35.

14 Nhat Hanh, *Call Me by My True Names*, 126.

Chapter 7

1 Nhat Hanh, Stepping into Freedom.

2 After more than forty years of retreats given by Thich Nhat Hanh and his disciples, many hundreds of small groups around the US, and groups throughout every populated continent in the world, are doing their best to support each other in practice. To find a Plum Village sangha near you, or online, visit *https://plumvillage.org/community/international-sangha-directory*.

3 As mentioned earlier, the Plum Village tradition highly emphasizes sangha as a vehicle for awakening, both individual and collective. The interbeing nature of the individual and collective awakening means they are not the same and they are not different, they co-arise and are interdependent.

4 To study these mindfulness trainings, you can visit *https://plumvillage.org/mindfulness/the-5-mindfulness-trainings*.

5 For more detailed descriptions, see *https://plumvillage.org/mindfulness/the-14-mindfulness-trainings*.

6 "The body in the body" and "the mind in the mind" refers to the embodiment of the Four Foundations of Mindfulness (Satipatthana Sutra): we learn about the body and mind from our direct experience of them. See Chapter 6, page 169.

7 Nhat Hanh, *Chanting from the Heart*, 398.

8 Each lay sangha is invited to adapt this form, originally developed in Plum Village, in its own unique style. The point is to create forms that speak to the spirit wanting to be cultivated; the repetition of the form creates a neural pathway to support the spirit of the moment. The form itself is not sacred. The intention is key.

9 Nhat Hanh, *Touching the Earth*.

Chapter 8

1 Plum Village, "The Fourteen Mindfulness Trainings, accessed June 18, 2023, *https://plumvillage.org/mindfulness/the-14-mindfulness-trainings*.

2 Tuckman, "Developmental Sequence in Small Groups," 384–99.

Chapter 9

1 Nhat Hanh, "The Next Buddha May Be a Sangha."

2 *Convert* refers to a practicing Buddhist who was not born into a Buddhist home.

3 The founder of the East Point Peace Academy, Kazu Haga has written two books on the subjects of nonviolence, direct action, and social change: *Healing Resistance* and *Fierce Vulnerability*.

4 See ARISE Sangha https://arisesangha.org/ and Valerie Brown, Marisela Gomez, and Kaira Jewel Lingo, *Healing Our Way Home*.

5 Noteworthy here are other Buddhist lineages in the US that have taken up this deep work of social engagement and social change: The Buddhist Peace Fellowship, The Zen Peacemaker Order, The East Point Peace Academy, and The East Bay Meditation Center, to name a few. There seems to be a thirst for engagement!

6 Tanahashi, *Painting Peace*.

7 Macy and Brown, *Coming Back to Life*, 3.

8 *Calling in* is a way to name a possibly unwholesome exchange or communication without blame or shame in a way that invites deeper exploration. For a list of tips to calling in, see *https://edib.harvard.edu/files/dib/files/calling_in_and_calling_out_guide_v4.pdf*.

9 Dharma talk, May 10, 1998, Plum Village, France.

10 Norman, "Moral Injury."

BIBLIOGRAPHY

Agsar, Wendy Biddlecombe. "Frequency: When You Seek Direction." *Tricycle*. Winter 2021. *https://tricycle.org/magazine/meditation-sickness/*.

Andrus, Marc. *Brothers in the Beloved Community: The Friendship of Thich Nhat Hanh and Martin Luther King Jr.* Berkeley: Parallax Press, 2021.

Baer, Ruth, Catherine Crane, Edward Miller, and Willem Kuyken, "Doing No Harm in Mindfulness-Based Programs: Conceptual Issues and Empirical Findings. *Clinical Psychology Review* 71 (2019): 101–14, *https://doi.org/10.1016/j.cpr.2019.01.001*.

Baer, Ruth, Catherine Crane, Jesus Montero-Marin, Alice Phillips, Laura Taylor, Alice Tickell, and Willem Kuyken, "Frequency of Self-Reported Unpleasant Events and Harm in a Mindfulness-Based Program in Two General Population Samples," *Mindfulness*, December 2, 2020, *https://doi.org/10.1007/s12671-020-01547-8*.

Barger, Nicole, Kari L. Hanson, Kate Teffer, Natalie M. Schenker-Ahmed, and Katerina Semendeferi. "Evidence for Evolutionary Specialization in Human Limbic Structures." *Frontiers in Human Neuroscience* 8, no. 277 (May 20, 2014). *https://doi.org/10.3389/fnhum.2014.00277*.

Bodhi, Bikkhu. *The Buddha's Teachings on Social and Communal Harmony: An Anthology of Discourses from the Pali Canon*. Somerville, MA: Wisdom Publications, 2016.

Britton, Willoughby B. "Can Mindfulness Be Too Much of a Good Thing? The Value of a Middle Way," *Current Opinion in Psychology* 28 (August 2019): 159–65, *https://doi.org/10.1016/j.copsyc.2018.12.011*.

Britton, Willoughby B., Patricia L. Haynes, Keith W. Fridel, and Richard R Bootzin, "Polysomnographic and Subjective Profiles of Sleep

Continuity Before and After Mindfulness-Based Cognitive Therapy in Partially Remitted Depression." *Psychosomatic Medicine* 72, no. 6 (July 2010): 539–48, *https://doi.org/10.1097/PSY.0b013e3181dc1bad.*

Brown, Valerie, Marisela Gomez, and Kaira Jewel Lingo. *Healing Our Way Home: Black Buddhist Teachings on Ancestors, Joy, and Liberation.* Berkeley, CA: Parallax Press, 2024.

Cheetah House, *cheetahhouse.org*.

Church, Dawson, Peta Stapleton, Phil Mollon, David Feinstein, Elizabeth Boath, David Mackay, and Rebecca Sims. "Guidelines for the Treatment of PTSD Using Clinical EFT (Emotional Freedom Techniques). *Healthcare* 6, no. 4 (December 12, 2018) 146. *https://doi.org/10.3390/healthcare6040146*.

Dana, Deborah. *Anchored: How to Befriend Your Nervous System Using Polyvagal Theory*. Boulder, CO: Sounds True, 2021.

Eisenstein, Charles. *Sacred Economics: Money, Gift, and Society in the Age of Transition*. Berkeley: North Atlantic Books, 2011.

Faircloth, Amelia. "Meditation Sickness: Bridging a Gap between Medicine and Buddhism." UC Santa Barbara: Humanities and Fine Arts. October 25, 2021. *https://www.hfa.ucsb.edu/news-entries/2021/10/25/meditation-sickness-bridging-the-gap-between-medicine-and-buddhism*.

Flynn, James. "Buddha and Mind: How a Religious Practice Came to Fascinate Neuroscientists and Gave Birth to the Mindfulness Movement." *Humanities* (a publication of the National Endowment for the Humanities). Summer 2021. *https://www.neh.gov/article/buddha-and-mind*.

Forest, James. *Eyes of Compassion: Living with Thich Nhat Hanh*. Maryknoll, NY: Orbis Books, 2021.

Gilsinan, Kathy. "The Buddhist and the Neuroscientist: What Compassion Does to the Brain," *The Atlantic*, July 4, 2015.

Goleman, Daniel, and Richard Davidson, "Lion's Roar, How Meditation Changes Your Brain—And Your Life," *Lion's Roar*, May 7, 2018.

Haga, Kazu. *Fierce Vulnerability: Direct Action That Heals and Transforms*. Berkeley: Parallax Press, 2024.

———. *Healing Resistance: A Radically Different Response to Harm*. Berkeley: Parallax Press, 2020.

Hai, Brother Phap. *The Eight Realizations of Great Beings: Essential Buddhist Wisdom for Waking Up to Who You Are*. Berkeley: Parallax Press, 2021.

Hakuin, Ekaku, *Wild Ivy: The Spiritual Autobiography of Zen Master Hakuin*, trans. Norman Waddell (Boulder, CO: Shambhala, 2010).

———. "Zen Sickness, by Zen Master Hakuin." *Buddhism Now*. September 12, 2015. *https://buddhismnow.com/2015/09/12/zen-sickness-by-zen-master-hakuin/*.

Helderman, Ira. "Meditation Sickness: Everyone Is Talking about How Nobody Is Talking about the Risks of Meditation." *Religion Dispatches*. July 10, 2022. *https://religiondispatches.org/meditation-sickness-everyone-is-talking-about-how-nobody-is-talking-about-the-risks-of-meditation/*.

Hofstede Insights. *https://www.hofstede-insights.com/*.

Hua, Hsuan. *The Surangama (Shurangama) Sutra: A New Translation with Excerpts from the Commentary by the Venerable Master Hsuan Hua*. Ukiah, CA: Buddhist Text Translation Society, 2009.

———. "The Shurangama Sutra: The Fifty Skandha-Demon States." Dharmasite.net. Accessed June 22, 2023. *https://www.dharmasite.net/bdh60/thefiftyskandhademonstates.html#top*.

Khong, Sister Chang. *Learning True Love: Practicing Buddhism in a Time of War*. Berkeley: Parallax Press, 1993, 2007.

King, Ruth. *Mindful of Race: Transforming Racism from the Inside Out*. Boulder, CO: Sounds True, 2018.

Levine, Peter. *Waking the Tiger: Healing Trauma—The Innate Capacity to Transform Overwhelming Experiences*. Berkeley: North Atlantic Books, 1997.

Lindahl, Jared R. Nathan E. Fisher, David J. Cooper, Rochelle K. Rosen, and Willoughby B. Britton, "The Varieties of Contemplative Experience: A Mixed-Methods Study of Meditation-Related Challenges in Western Buddhists," *PLoS One* 12, no. 5 (May 24, 2017), e0176239. *https://doi.org/10.1371/journal.pone.0176239*.

Lingo, Kaira Jewel. *We Were Made for These Times: Ten Lessons for Moving Through Change, Loss, and Disruption*. Berkeley: Parallax Press, 2021.

Macy, Joanna. *World as Lover, World as Self: Courage for Global Justice and Ecological Renewal*. Berkeley: Parallax Press, 2007.

Macy, Joanna, and Molly Young Brown. *Coming Back to Life: The Updated Guide to the Work That Reconnects*. Gabriola Island, BC: New Society Publishers, 2014.

Macy, Joanna, ad Chris Johnstone. *Active Hope: How to Face the Mess We're in without Going Crazy*. Novato, CA: New World Library, 2012.

Manuel, Zenjy Earthlyn. *The Way of Tenderness: Awakening through Race, Sexuality, and Gender*. Somerville, MA: Wisdom Publications, 2015.

Maté, Gabor. *The Myth of Normal: Trauma, Illness, and Healing in a Toxic Culture*. New York: Avery, 2022.

Menakem, Resmaa. *My Grandmother's Hands: Racialized Trauma and the Pathway to Mending Our Hearts and Bodies*. Las Vegas: Central Recovery Press, 2017.

Miller-Karas, Elaine. *Building Resilience to Trauma: The Trauma and Community Resiliency Models*. New York: Routledge, 2015).

Mind and Life [Podcast]. *https://podcast.mindandlife.org/*.

Moore, Christopher. *The Gandhian Iceberg: A Nonviolence Manifesto for the Age of the Great Turning*. Reno, NV: Be the Change Project, 2016.

Murphy, Sean. "Get Out of Your Head." *Tricycle: The Buddhist Review*. Spring 2019. *https://tricycle.org/magazine/five-aggregates/*.

Napier, Nancy J. *Getting through the Day: Strategies for Adults Hurt as Children*. New York: W. W. Norton and Company, 1993.

Nhat Hanh, Thich. *Anger: Wisdom for Cooling the Flames*. New York: Riverhead Books, 2001.

———. *Being Peace*. Berkeley: Parallax Press, 2005.

———. *The Blooming of a Lotus: The Essential Guided Meditations for Mindfulness, Healing, and Transformation*. Trans. Annabel Laity. Boston: Beacon Press, 2009.

———. *Breathe, You Are Alive: The Sutra on the Full Awareness of Breathing*. Berkeley: Parallax Press, 2008.

———. *Call Me by My True Names: The Collected Poems of Thich Nhat Hanh*. Berkeley, CA: Parallax Press, 1999.

———. *Chanting from the Heart: Buddhist Ceremonies, Verses, and Daily Practices from Plum Village*. Berkeley, CA: Parallax Press, 2007.

———. *Cultivating the Mind of Love: The Practice of Looking Deeply in the Mahayana Buddhist Tradition*. Berkeley: Parallax Press, 1996.

———. *Fear: Essential Wisdom for Getting Through the Storm*. New York: Harper One, 2012.

———. *Fragrant Palm Leaves: Journals, 1962–1966*. Berkeley: Parallax Press, 2020.

———. *The Heart of the Buddha's Teaching: Transforming Suffering into Peace*. New York: Broadway Books, 1998.

———. *Interbeing: Fourteen Guidelines for Engaged Buddhism*. Berkeley: Parallax Press, 1987.

———. *Joyfully Together: The Art of Building a Harmonious Community*. Berkeley: Parallax Press, 2005.

———. *The Long Road Turns to Joy: A Guide to Walking Meditation*. Berkeley: Parallax Press, 2011.

———. *Love in Action: Writings on Nonviolent Social Change*. Berkeley: Parallax Press, 1993.

———. *The Miracle of Mindfulness: An Introduction to the Practice of Meditation*. Trans. Mobi Ho. Boston: Beacon Press 1975, 1976.

———. "The Next Buddha May Be a Sangha," *Inquiring Mind* 10, no. 2 (Spring 1994), *https://www.inquiringmind.com/article/1002_41_thich-nhat_hanh*.

———. *No Mud, No Lotus: The Art of Transforming Suffering*. Berkeley: Parallax Press, 2014.

———. *The Other Shore: A New Translation of the Heart Sutra with Commentaries*. Berkeley: Parallax Press, 2017.

———.*Our Appointment with Life*. Berkeley, CA: Parallax Press, 2010.

———. *Peace Is Every Step: The Path of Mindfulness in Everyday Life*. New York: Random House, 1992.

———. *Plum Village Chanting Book*. Berkeley: Parallax Press, 1991.

———. *Present Moment, Wonderful Moment: Verses for Daily Living*. Berkeley, CA: Parallax Press, 2022.

———. *Reconciliation: Healing the Inner Child*. Berkeley: Parallax Press, 2006.

———. *A Rose for Your Pocket: An Appreciation of Motherhood*. Berkeley: Parallax Press, 2008.

———. *Stepping into Freedom: An Introduction to Buddhist Monastic Training*. Berkeley: Parallax Press, 1997.

———. *The Sun My Heart: Reflections on Mindfulness, Concentration, and Insight*, rev. ed. Berkeley: Parallax Press, 2010.

———. *Touching the Earth: The Five Prostrations and Deep Relaxation.* Louisville, CO: Sounds True, 2004.

———. *Transformation at the Base. Fifty Verses on the Nature of Consciousness*. Berkeley: Parallax Press, 2001.

———. *Transformation and Healing: Sutra on the Four Establishments of Mindfulness*. Berkeley: Parallax Press, 2002.

———.*Vietnam: Lotus in a Sea of Fire*. New York: Hill and Wang, 1967.

Norman, Sonya B. "Moral Injury." PTSD: National Center for PTSD, US Department of Veterans Affairs. Accessed August 15, 2023. *https://www.ptsd.va.gov/professional/treat/cooccurring/moral_injury.asp.*

Plum Village, "Thich Nhat Hanh: Extended Biography," accessed June 4, 2023, *https://plumvillage.org/thich-nhat-hanh/biography/thich-nhat-hanh-full-biography/#earlylife.*

Plum Village. *The Way Out Is In.* [podcast]. *https://plumvillage.org/podcasts/the-way-out-is-in.*

Porges, Stephen. *The Polyvagal Theory: Neurophysiological Foundations of Emotions, Attachment, Communication, and Self-Regulation.* New York: W. W. Norton, 2011.

Ricard, Matthieu, and Wolf Singer. *Beyond the Self: Conversations between Buddhism and Neuroscience.* Cambridge, MA: MIT Press, 2017.

Shantideva and the Padmakara Translation Group. *The Way of the Bodhisattva (Bodhicaryavatara).* Boston, MA: Shambhala, 2006.

Shapiro, Francine. *Eye Movement Desensitization and Reprocessing (EMDR) Therapy: Basic Principles, Protocols, and Procedures*, 3rd. ed. New York: Guilford Press, 2018.

Siegel, Daniel. *Brainstorm: The Power and Purpose of the Teenage Brain.* New York: Jeremy P. Tarcher/Penguin, 2013.

———. *Mindsight: The New Science of Personal Transformation.* New York: Bantam Books, 2011.

Stephenson, Bryan. *Just Mercy: A Story of Justice and Redemption.* New York: One World, 2015.

Sue, Derald Wing. *Race Talk and the Conspiracy of Silence*. Hoboken, NJ: Wiley, 2015.

Tanahashi, Kazuaki. *Painting Peace: Art in a Time of Global Crisis*. Boulder, CO: Shambhala Publications, 2018.

Treleaven, David. *Trauma-Sensitive Mindfulness: Practices for Safe and Transformative Healing*. New York: W. W. Norton, 2018.

Tuckman, Bruce W. "Developmental Sequence in Small Groups." *Psychological Bulletin* 63, no. 6 (1965): 384–99.

van der Kolk, Bessel. *The Body Keeps Score: Brain, Mind, and Body in the Healing of Trauma*. New York: Penguin Books, 2014.

Walton, Alice G. "7 Ways Meditation Can Actually Change the Brain," *Forbes*, February 9, 2015.

Wilkerson, Isabel. *Caste: The Origins of Our Discontents*. New York: Random House, 2020.

Yang, Larry. *Awakening Together: The Spiritual Practice of Inclusivity and Community*. Somerville, MA: Wisdom Publications, 2017.

INDEX OF EXERCISES IN *UNSHAKEABLE*

ACKNOWLEDGMENTS

Much of the research and writing for this book was done at Deer Park Monastery, the largest of the US Plum Village monasteries, in the shadow of Thay's passing. Reviewing Thay's life and writings in a very condensed period of time was like a near-death experience, the scenes of a long and amazing life passing before my eyes in a flash. The practices began to take on added meaning: rather than just being techniques to further my path, or the collective path, each and every aspect became a testimony to an amazing manifestation of human potential. Were Thich Nhat Hanh just to have lived a life of risky and compassionate acts in a time of great turmoil and danger, or had he solely been an international peace activist, or a trainer of monks, or a teacher of countless numbers of lay practitioners, or a developer of the rebirth of engaged Buddhist practice, or a scholar, a poet, a master calligrapher—any one of these would have been enough to feel that this was a life well lived, a noble contribution to the stream of life. The fact that his life manifested in *all* these ways simultaneously is a wonder. To practice any one of his wisdom teachings is to take the opportunity to slip into his shoes and perhaps, even if only for discrete moments, to taste the wonders of the life he savored, to breathe a breath that allows for freedom, and to contribute your moments of peace in every step.

On a very practical level, I was really just the point person for the coming together of this book, but hardly the sole author of the ideas or their articulation. When I pick it all apart there is no beginning or end to what was supportive. That is the insight of interbeing.

Short of that, there were my cheerleaders ready with pom-poms of encouraging words. Katie Eberle, you kicked it off with endless late-night talks and coaxing Hisae Matsuda to enjoy a weekend of practice at the monastery. Hisae, your warmth, enthusiasm, calm knowhow, and practical advice have bolstered me in every way through this foreign land of publishing. Erin Wiegand, you helped me whittle the book down to a manageable size and shape. Apologies for shouldering the brunt of my lack of experience as a writer of books. Thanks also to Rebecca Rider and Maureen Forys for your work producing the book.

To the initial readers, your kindness and helpful hints kept me going through endless periods of nervous system release: Karen Hilsberg, Marty Behrends, Cathy Schaef, Melanie Gin, Kim Deckman, AJ Johnston, Dylan Tweney, Armand Brint, and all the EMBRACE sangha who test-drove some of the chapters. Thanks to Lyn Fine and Anne Woods for being my second bodies in the eleventh hour to meet deadlines, drinking up your steady energy as well as feedback catapulted me over what seemed like a final hurdle, wow! Lyn, my dear friend and mentor for decades now, thanks for the endless hours of conversation and for finding the road by walking it together.

Thanks to the many monastics who helped me parse out the muddled fine points in my mind: Venerable Thay Phoc Thien, Thay Phap Dung, Thay Phap Luu, Sister Than Nghiem, Sister Tri Nghiem, Thay Phap Vu, and Brothers Minh An and Minh Luong.

I am indebted to Elaine Miller-Karas and David Treleaven who were formative in both my understanding and the practicalities of my neuro-informed work.

Thanks to my inner circle of support, my chosen family who supported me through the extraneous crises that threatened to derail me along the way, especially to those of you who suffered through my less *unshakeable* moments, especially Sage, who suffers the brunt of my human inheritance.

And finally to my EMBRACE cofounders, Kim Nguyen, Eric Guico, Socorro Maldonado, and Anne Woods, and the growing EMBRACE sangha facilitators, continuing gratitude and awe. While we have been learning to be a neuro-informed organism together, my faith in what this work can nurture has grown. Our sangha has helped us as individuals transcend bumps and ruts into knowing the joys of being a cell in a healthy, growing, and thriving organism. May neuro-informed mindfulness be a contribution for a wholesome future to be possible.

ABOUT THE AUTHOR

Jo-ann Rosen is a licensed psychotherapist who has worked for the last thirty-plus years with individuals, families, and groups, and in workplace settings with a special focus on individual, group, and institutional trauma.

Applying this work with a neuro-informed lens, she has offered workshops and trainings in elementary school classrooms, among school faculty members and social service workers, and with underserved communities in the US, Mexico, Israel, and the West Bank.

Having received the Lamp of Wisdom and the encouragement to teach the Dharma from her teacher the Venerable Thich Nhat Hanh in 2012, she cofounded the international EMBRACE sangha, which integrates a neuro-informed lens into Buddhist psychology. She lives in rural northern California with her partner of forty years.

Monastics and visitors practice the art of mindful living in the tradition of Thich Nhat Hanh at our mindfulness practice centers around the world. To reach any of these communities, or for information about how individuals, couples, and families can join in a retreat, please contact:

PLUM VILLAGE
33580 Dieulivol, France
plumvillage.org

LA MAISON DE L'INSPIR
77510 Villeneuve-sur-Bellot, France
maisondelinspir.org

HEALING SPRING MONASTERY
77510 Verdelot, France
healingspringmonastery.org

MAGNOLIA GROVE MONASTERY
Batesville, MS 38606, USA
magnoliagrovemonastery.org

BLUE CLIFF MONASTERY
Pine Bush, NY 12566, USA
bluecliffmonastery.org

DEER PARK MONASTERY
Escondido, CA 92026, USA
deerparkmonastery.org

EUROPEAN INSTITUTE OF APPLIED BUDDHISM
D-51545 Waldbröl, Germany
eiab.eu

THAILAND PLUM VILLAGE
Nakhon Ratchasima
30130 Thailand
thaiplumvillage.org

ASIAN INSTITUTE OF APPLIED BUDDHISM
Lantau Island, Hong Kong
pvfhk.org

STREAM ENTERING MONASTERY
Beaufort, Victoria 3373
Australia
nhapluu.org

MOUNTAIN SPRING MONASTERY
Bilpin, NSW 2758, Australia
mountainspringmonastery.org

For more information visit: *plumvillage.org*
To find an online sangha visit: *plumline.org*
For more resources, try the Plum Village app: *plumvillage.app*
Social media: *@thichnhathanh @plumvillagefrance*

THICH NHAT HANH FOUNDATION

planting seeds of Compassion

The Thich Nhat Hanh Foundation works to continue the mindful teachings and practice of Zen Master Thich Nhat Hanh, in order to foster peace and transform suffering in all people, animals, plants, and our planet. Through donations to the Foundation, thousands of generous supporters ensure the continuation of Plum Village practice centers and monastics around the world, bring transformative practices to those who otherwise would not be able to access them, support local mindfulness initiatives, and bring humanitarian relief to communities in crisis in Vietnam.

By becoming a supporter, you join many others who want to learn and share these life-changing practices of mindfulness, loving speech, deep listening, and compassion for oneself, each other, and the planet.

For more information on how you can help support mindfulness around the world, or to subscribe to the Foundation's monthly newsletter with teachings, news, and global retreats, visit tnhf.org.

PARALLAX PRESS, a nonprofit publisher founded by Zen Master Thich Nhat Hanh, publishes books and media on the art of mindful living and Engaged Buddhism. We are committed to offering teachings that help transform suffering and injustice. Our aspiration is to contribute to collective insight and awakening, bringing about a more joyful, healthy, and compassionate society.

View our entire library at parallax.org.

THE MINDFULNESS BELL is a journal of the art of mindful living in the Plum Village tradition of Thich Nhat Hanh. To subscribe or to see the worldwide directory of Sanghas (local mindfulness groups), visit mindfulnessbell.org.